Electives

D1513688

Electives and international midwifery consultancy

A resource for students, midwives and other health professionals

Tiger stripes and tears

Dr Gaynor D Maclean

QUAY BOOKS
A division of MA Healthcare Ltd

About the author

Dr Gaynor D Maclean is an international consultant (maternal and newborn health) contributing to global efforts to promote safer childbirth. With more than 20 years' international experience and a background in midwifery practice, education and research she is an honorary fellow of Swansea University and has been awarded an MBE for her contribution to midwifery overseas.

Note
Healthcare practice and knowledge are constantly changing and developing as new research and treatments, changes in procedures, drugs and equipment become available.

The author and publishers have, as far as is possible, taken care to confirm that the information complies with the latest standards of practice and legislation.

1007525449
Quay Books Division, MA Healthcare Ltd,
St Jude's Church, Dulwich Road, London SE24 0PB

British Library Cataloguing-in-Publication Data
A catalogue record is available for this book

© MA Healthcare Limited 2013.
ISBN-13: 978-1-85642-502-5

Copyedited by Jessica Anderson
Designed by Alison Cutler, Fonthill Creative, Jesses Barn, Snow Hill, Dinton, Salisbury, Wiltshire, SP3 5HN

Printed by Mimeo

Contents

Preface

Nothing ever becomes real till it is experienced.

(Keats)

Our 21st century world has become a place where global travel is increasingly widespread. In a matter of hours a person can be transported into a totally different climate, culture and time zone. Various experts with diverse professional backgrounds are in escalating demand worldwide and students are facing unique opportunities to receive some of their education and experience in a totally different environment through an elective period overseas. The fact that I have travelled extensively during a great deal of my professional life predisposes me, even if it does not qualify me, to write on the subject. In an academic and professional world where evidence is extolled, experience is sometimes under-rated. However, I would venture to claim that experience is valuable if we are resolved to learn through it. I would like to think that I am akin to that hypothetical type of person who can claim 20 years' experience rather than the one who has one year's experience 20 times over. I have therefore chosen to use my experience as a starting point in sharing some of the insights that I have gained through the years. Some experiences are shared within the country or regional context of the chapter. However, due to the nature of the event or the need to respect confidentiality, some experiences are shared in the first or last chapter in a more general context. I have then examined the available evidence on some of the topics relevant to cross-cultural experience, whether this is in the form of consultancy practice or student elective opportunity. The principles are very similar even though the practice will obviously differ.

It was my experience of following on after consultants who had seemingly caused more problems than they had solved that prompted me to focus on such issues in my doctoral research. I sought to examine the matters of acceptability and unacceptability in these cross-cultural contexts. Using a microscope or fine tooth comb is not inevitably a comfortable experience, but in countries that are always being examined, assessed, evaluated or rated, I found it a salutary exercise to turn the tables and examine instead how we are perceived. I received copious answers to my enquiries, as respondents seemed to find it especially cathartic to convey their experiences of unacceptable consultants. Unfortunately there seemed to be no shortage of this species, whom I dubbed 'nightmare consultants' in my original thesis. It is my hope that, in some small way, this book will help raise awareness of some of the critical issues that are best heeded in cross-cultural encounters and provide a resource for those who aspire to excel at it.

A book of this size could in no way share all the experiences of a professional lifetime, nor could it offer an in-depth resource of evidence that relates to the subject matter addressed. However, the reader is alerted to some of the issues that could impact his or her practice or study, in order to stimulate consideration of some of the critical issues that may take a lifetime to examine thoroughly. At the end of each chapter I share my own reflections on some of my experiences. Then I offer for your consideration some of the lessons I have learned, on the premise that you will make your own mistakes as I have, but maybe you will not need to make the same ones as me! The reflective exercises offer opportunities for you to consider some issues in preparation for the task that you are considering or may have recently completed. I offer them hoping that they may provide some signposts in an area that may well be for you a strange land. No one can walk your path, but someone has walked a similar path – and survived! References, resources and websites are also provided.

The focus is on countries where I have worked. This does not discount the importance or relevance of other parts of the world of course, but serves to provide a selection of examples and illustrate the situations with which the reader is likely to be confronted in cross-cultural exchange. *Chapters 2–9* contain background information on the country or countries considered therein. Such data are inevitably subject to change, but serve to paint the backcloth to the scene set within the ensuing text. As the book's subtitle conveys, each chapter contains a 'tiger stripe' and a 'tear'. The tiger stripes reflect the individuality of clients, consultants and students as well as well as the countries they represent. Examples of the diversities we meet are entwined in each tiger stripe. We are aware too that while some solutions have been developed from time-honoured experience or convincing evidence, just as the pattern of tiger stripes is unique to each animal, so individual situations demand unique attention. One size does not fit all. The tears share insights into what experience and evidence have demonstrated. Cross-cultural assignments offer a medley of joys and sorrows. The tears may be of joy, sadness or sheer exasperation, but the text is rooted in reality and is offered to fellow travellers along this road of mutual development.

Ralph Waldo Emerson urges:

Be an opener of doors for such as come after thee.

I trust that in some way this book opens a door for you.

Gaynor D Maclean

Acknowledgements

I am grateful for the assistance and inspiration of numerous colleagues throughout the world and especially for feedback on specific chapters from the following on the regions with which they are most familiar: Theary Chan, Cleide Correia, Aggie Horne, Uzo Iwobi, Keumhee Kim, Jaesub Lim, Dr Christina Mudokwenyu-Rawdon, Enid Mwebaza, Dr Rosabind Nyar, Dr Shershah Syed, and Annie Wang-Evans. I am also grateful to Dr Julia Magill-Cuerden for her initial review of the book. I have appreciated learning and sharing with a number of consultant colleagues with whom I have worked over the years and especially Valerie Tickner, Betty Clement (nee Sweet) and Dr Barbara Kwast. I also acknowledge the skilled assistance of Clare Boucher (Subject Librarian: Health Sciences and Medicine, Swansea University) in carrying out my research in writing this book.

Technical art: Sheila D Maclean

Foreword

Globalisation has generated a culture whereby sharing of midwifery education, practice and research is strongly encouraged. However, few health professionals and academics from high income countries have the opportunity to gain first-hand understanding of the varying contexts of maternity care. This is a fascinating book that describes the author's journey as she navigates continents, countries and cultures, providing insight into midwifery challenges across the globe. Each chapter provides the reader with unique information on the multiplicity of factors that hinder or facilitate successful maternity outcomes. However, this book is not merely a narrative diary of events experienced by the author; it offers practical and emotional advice to assist others who may be embarking on similar work.

This book raises awareness of the unpredictable nature of working in different settings and provides many interesting examples that illustrate the diversity within and between nations. It encourages readers to suspend their own beliefs and be open to different perspectives. Uniquely, it provides readers with an opportunity to not only 'observe' the practice of others but also to reflect on their own practice; viewing oneself as others may do so is advised. This book has clearly been written from the heart and the author's passion shines through every chapter. However, what makes this book special is the way it has been written. The author draws on evidence where appropriate; she uses the words of those she has met to powerfully illustrate points; and describes not only her successes but also her failures. This latter point reflects the humility of the author, but also provides valuable information which may prevent others from repeating similar mistakes.

At the end of each chapter there are sections on the author's personal reflections on practice, lessons learned and shared, and reflective exercises. These sections make a valuable contribution to the book and could be used individually or in group training. The reflective exercises are likely to take readers out of their 'comfort zone' but they will certainly emerge as more enlightened practitioners.

I have no doubt that this book will provide a valuable resource for many, including midwives, obstetricians, community workers, sociologists, anthropologists, students and volunteers. Anybody who reads this book should view it as a real privilege to share the lifetime experiences of such a compassionate and altruistic midwife.

Professor Dame Tina Lavender
University of Manchester

Dedication

For my twin sister Sheila, my constant friend, support and inspiration, especially when I return from numerous sojourns across the world; and for young Erin and Seren Lim who call me 'Nana' and have that inimitable capacity of turning raindrops into rainbows.

Chapter 1

Global dynamics in 21st century development

When a needle falls into a deep well, many people will look into the well, but few will be ready to go down after it.

(African Proverb)

Before criticising the differences in the way that 'they' practice, try managing with (or without) the equipment with which 'they' wrestle day by day

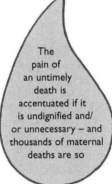

The pain of an untimely death is accentuated if it is undignified and/ or unnecessary – and thousands of maternal deaths are so

Subject strands introduced

- Global health issues
- Maternal mortality
- The Safe Motherhood Initiative
- Skilled attendance during childbirth
- The 5th Millennium Development Goal

- Traditional healers and birth attendants
- Ethical dilemmas
- Elective issues
- Roles and responsibilities of the international consultant
- Policy makers, politics and political commitment

Practice points

- Essential preparatory actions
- Personal clinical skills
- Identifying the scope and limitations of practice

- Establishing reflective practice

Table 1.1. Background and international data

A tale of two worlds

Globally, it was estimated that 287000 women died from pregnancy-related causes in 2010, representing an MMR of 210; of these deaths 245000 (85%) occurred in two regions, sub-Saharan Africa (56%) and South Asia (29%). This represents a 47% decrease since 1990. At the same time, 40 countries were rated as having a high MMR (≥ 300); Chad and Somalia were rated as very high (>1000). Four countries in sub-Saharan Africa were rated as having a low MMR (< 99) – Mauritius, Sao Tome, Principe, and Cape Verde. Ten countries achieved MDG 5 by 2010 and nine more were considered to be on track at this time demonstrating the expected annual decline of 5.5% in the MMR during the preceding 20 years. Whilst 50 countries were considered to be making progress, 14 countries had made insufficient progress and 11 had made no progress. Most maternal deaths occurred during birth or immediately afterwards. The proportion of births attended by skilled health personnel in the developing world rose from 55% to 65% between 1990 and 2009. Globally more than 7.5 million children die before they reach their fifth birthday with 40% of deaths occurring within the first month of life. The majority of maternal and child deaths occur in the developing world and most could be prevented.

Developing countries	More developed/industrialised countries
In around 35% of cases of child death, malnutrition is an underlying cause. Around half of these children experience this deprivation in utero as their mothers are undernourished. The anaemia which can occur as a result is the most widespread nutritional problem affecting women and girls in developing countries. It is a significant predisposing cause of maternal death and is associated with premature and low birth weight. In the developing world exclusively breastfed babies are at least six times more likely to survive.	In these countries, malnutrition is rare, but infants are more likely to be exposed to the risk of obesity. Exclusive breastfeeding for the first six months is only 1% in the UK and Belgium, whilst Australia, Canada, the USA and several European countries achieve this in just 15%. It is estimated that in the USA low breast feeding rates add $13 billion dollars to medical costs and cause more than 900 deaths per year. In Britain it is estimated that a 10% increase in breastfeeding could prevent almost 3900 cases of gastroenteritis and a saving of £2.6 million.

Data indicating average figures in contrasting regions of the world

Developing countries	More developed/industrialised countries
• MMR: 240 (2010) – the highest is in Sub-Saharan Africa (average 500), the lowest is in East Asia (average 37) • MMR: proportion related to HIV/AIDS = 91% of the global total occurred in Sub-Saharan Africa, 5% in S Asia • Lifetime risk of maternal death*: 1 in 150, least developed: 1 in 52 (Sub-Saharan Africa: 1 in 39). • Mothers index ranking**: Niger, Afghanistan, Yemen, Guinea Bissau and Mali rate lowest. • Births attended by skilled personnel: Figures vary from 99% in Sri Lanka to 6% in Ethiopia	• MMR: average 16 (2010) – the lowest is in Europe • MMR: proportion related to HIV/AIDS = 4% of the global total. • Lifetime risk of maternal death*: 1 in 3800, (Europe: 1 in 4200; N America: 1 in 2600). • Mothers index ranking**: European countries including UK, Australia and New Zealand rank within the top 10. Norway, Iceland and Sweden rate highest. • Births attended by skilled personnel: 99-100%

MMR = estimated maternal mortality ratio per 100,000 live births; MDG 5 = Fifth Millennium Development Goal
*Assessed according to life expectancy, educational and economic factors
**Ranked globally (within three tiers: I = more developed, II = less developed, III = least developed) according to health, education, economic and political status of women

Sources: Black et al, 2008; Department of Health, 1995; Save the Children, 2012; United Nations, 2010; UNICEF, 2012; WHO, 2012a

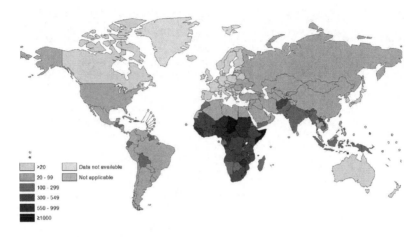

Figure 1.1. Maternal mortality ratio (per 100 000 live births) 2010 (Reproduced with permission from the World Health Organization).

Exploring experience

Birth of a new era

At the birth of the new millennium the world was in an expectant state; hopes and fears, aspirations and dreads confronted many on the brink of a new era. I was, at that time, totally immersed in a literature search, seeking evidence that skilled attendance during delivery could be instrumental in promoting safer childbirth across the world. Warnings about millennium bugs and other sinister cybernetic threats were offered by the computer buffs. Vigilance bordering on paranoia could have described my frantic activities to protect precious data. Of course, for many, a new year, leave alone a new century or millennium, would go unnoticed. For some cultures marked by other timelines it had little relevance; for others, life's local or personal struggles superseded global issues.

My work during the latter part of the 20th century had taken me to many parts of the world where maternal, perinatal and child mortality rates remained unacceptably high. Responding to an unexpected need for a facilitator at an international workshop had led me back into a different world. The workshop was for midwives from developing countries and was held in Japan. I had had experience of working in India as a young woman and more recently in Botswana; this served to provide me with some insight into the situations with which my colleagues now wrestled. Together we worked on an educational framework considering prevention and management of the main obstetric causes of maternal death. At the end of the workshop I was invited to take the framework and from it prepare a global template for safe motherhood modules containing resources that would assist midwifery teachers in their task (WHO, 1996, 2006).

Leaving my job as a midwifery teacher in the UK and taking a post as a consultant with the World Health Organization (WHO) in order to write the modules, I have subsequently continued in consultancy work. I have travelled to many parts of the world, mainly across Africa and Asia, and my experiences have included teaching, examining, assisting with curriculum reviews, evaluating programmes, and other advisory roles concerned with midwifery education and practice. My doctoral studies had caused me to reflect on what I was doing in this context and to evaluate it. It seemed to me that there was much to learn and hopefully much to share in this process of offering consultancy or technical assistance across cultural divides.

The way we do it

Professional practice in a totally different environment brings its own challenges. Having become accustomed once again to working in the National Health Service in a British hospital, returning to countries with low resources tests one's flexibility and fortitude, and most certainly calls for a sense of humour. Equipment can be faulty, flimsy or simply unavailable. While working in an antenatal clinic as part of a teaching programme in one country, I had to wrestle with an ill-functioning sphygmomanometer; it would not support a column of mercury beyond a certain level. The hospital matron, who was working alongside me as another 'trainer', offered her advice: 'Just add 20 and it will be about right' she instructed, adding, 'That's what I do!' Any hope of gaining accurate readings and acting on them diminished dramatically. Working with non-functional or faulty equipment hampers efforts by professionals in many situations.

In another country I was confronted with the dying form of a young teenager, tied to a metal stretcher with a spoon strapped into her mouth. The doctors accompanying me on a tour of the hospital wanted to show the disastrous lack of equipment that led to such levels of care. Seized with eclamptic fits the desolate and diminutive figure has remained etched in my memory as her life was snatched away, in a manner undeserved, undignified and untimely.

In most countries where I have worked, accessing a fetal stethoscope in the labour ward borders on the luxurious; learning to use it and interpret the findings, a distant aspiration for many who struggle to provide care. Evaluating one programme, I discovered that every fetal heart rate recorded on the immaculately completed partographs indicated total unison in their unrelenting 120 beats per minute. It was indeed not a national average but the only reading that I could find across several centres. In a different setting the teaching of an obstetric life-saving skills programme had been designated to a dentist and a public health inspector. These men were literate and educated sufficiently to warrant their appointments for the job, and since the course was totally theoretical it proved difficult at first to convince the authorities of this unsatisfactory state of affairs. In some countries there is no organised system of recruiting, training, assigning and retaining adequate numbers of professional nurses, midwives or paramedics who usually form the backbone of a health service. In other countries, efforts to produce the required numbers of skilled staff become self-defeating where there is inadequate supervised clinical experience for large cohorts, or very short programmes that stand no chance of preparing skilled health professionals. I learned early on that where there is no political commitment to safe motherhood, there is no real progress. The lives of many of the most unfortunate in such societies hang in the balance and women continue to die or suffer disabilities that could have been prevented.

One must learn to expect the unexpected; in a labour ward preparing for the night shift, motorcycles were parked beside the beds. During the hours of darkness they were deposited there, apparently in the only secure place, their owners at least assured that they would have transport to travel home in the morning. In the same room, frogs hopped among the limited available equipment in the humid tropical climate.

Degrees of dexterity

In a desert environment in another continent, in a labour ward where equipment posed no problem, it was acquiring skilled medical assistance that proved challenging. A woman continued to bleed after giving birth and it became apparent that she had a cervical tear. However, the process of getting it repaired proved lengthy and the situation was further complicated by the fact that when the doctor eventually arrived, it was evident that he was not skilled in obstetrics. My colleague and I had not only to advise and instruct but also to assist him in the necessary interventions. Fortunately, the outcome in this case was good, but undoubtedly some women are lost in such circumstances.

I was reminded of a story which I included in the Safe Motherhood Foundation Module (WHO, 2006: 94–100) that questioned why a woman (Mrs Y) had died while giving birth to her fifth child. As a result of delay in finding transport, the lengthy admission process, delays in calling the midwife and arrival of the doctor, and lack of necessary equipment and suitable blood donor, Mrs Y died. This type of problem can confront students undertaking electives and can be particularly distressing when insufficient skilled help is available. University authorities make every effort to ensure adequate supervision of elective students, but in reality, some situations may be encountered that sorely test the skills and the staying power of both visiting students and experienced professionals.

These incidents illustrate the real issues that confront those exposed to the sharp edge of practice in low resource settings. The issue of delay is explored further in *Chapter 9*. Education or training programmes led by those without the essential clinical skills themselves predispose to producing another generation handicapped by the same inabilities. On one occasion, evaluating the skills of midwives who had completed a national life-saving skills programme, I was encouraged to find a midwife who correctly identified a urinary tract infection in a pregnant woman. Having confirmed the diagnosis I then asked the midwife what she was going to do about it. 'I will tell her to come back after one month,' she replied. We were in an antenatal clinic attached to a large hospital and immediate referral and treatment posed no problem, yet there was clearly no understanding of the situation or any linking of the diagnosis to the need for treatment. Notwithstanding, the woman was clearly in considerable pain.

Evaluating programmes I have repeatedly encountered those who have completed a life-saving skills programme but cannot interpret a partograph. To the initiated, the chart provides a simple but comprehensive record of the maternal and fetal condition and the progress of labour. Discovering incomplete labour records in ill-equipped and grossly understaffed labour wards comes as no surprise, but at times I have discovered that it is associated not with lack of equipment or opportunity to examine a woman and assess progress but rather a total lack of clinical skills. Completing such a record, leave alone interpreting and co-ordinating the readings, calls for numerous clinical skills, an understanding of the physiology of labour and insights into the pathology so that there may be appreciation of the significance of deviations from normal with appropriate and timely action. Instruction provided by the unskilled, and theory without application in practice are therefore incompatible with the preparation of a skilled birth attendant. Certainly there are degrees of dexterity, but skill needs to be underpinned by a knowledge that can be applied and adapted to meet each demand.

Cost-effectiveness

In one country it was common practice for midwives in rural areas to demand payment before intervention when dealing with a retained placenta. Women often gave birth with the local traditional birth attendant, a member of the family or even alone. However, if the placenta was retained a midwife would sometimes be called. In a poor community, having a qualified health professional to attend the birth was often not considered affordable, but some perceived it necessary and indeed possible when there were complications.

To many Western Europeans, the demand for payment upfront in such a life-threatening situation is a case of 'your money or your life'. However, it should be understood that the midwives themselves were also poor and that they, sometimes, along with medical colleagues, would have to wait many months before the government paid them. Given such a situation and the fact that these midwives also had families to feed, it can be appreciated why this happened, even if the ethics of the approach seemed unacceptable.

My longest wait for a pay cheque during many years of consultancy experience was nine months. This was difficult for me at the time, but nothing compared to these midwives, who literally did not know where the next meal was coming from. Poverty can be perceived as relative, but for many in the developing world it can threaten survival, particularly among the most vulnerable, i.e. women and children and the elderly.

What is affordable and what is justifiable can vary according to the cultural setting. In some situations, even life itself seems to be of very little worth where women are considered as commodities rather than being valued and cherished. I recall a young woman dying of puerperal sepsis. She had been brought to the referral hospital from a village in an advanced state of septicaemia. The medical staff had fought in vain to counteract the infection caused or at least exacerbated by the interference of traditional healers. A midwife explained the prognosis to the husband and uncle who waited at the bedside. Expressing her sorrow and regret that nothing more could be done to save this woman's life, she was met with the response, 'Don't worry sister, we can get another one.' The midwife was more distressed than the relatives who seemed to view the replacement of a woman in the family as a mere procedure. This issue is considered later in this book, notably in *Chapter 9*.

Mind what you say

Having an understanding of the working language of the country of assignment is, of course, critical. Universities will ensure that students are placed where they can communicate sufficiently, and consultants normally do not accept assignments outside of their linguistic scope or at least where there is no adequate arrangement for interpretation.

Learning to use basic greetings and terms in the local vernacular can be advantageous but fluency is hardly a realistic aspiration for the short-term visitor. However, skilled use of both spoken and written English is essential and cannot be assumed. I have on occasions been asked to interpret the meaning of an English colleague's report where local staff have struggled to discover form and meaning. It is important to remember that English is usually a second or subsequent language for local staff and ambiguity places them at an unfair and unnecessary disadvantage. Holding a higher degree does not always provide immunity from this embarrassing and inconvenient affliction, but it needs to be addressed in those aspiring to serve overseas. Regional dialects can also pose problems and for those whose vernacular poses particular difficulties it is worth considering how one's spoken language can be simplified. Providing they are not too complicated, differing accents can usually be understood if speech is slowed and understanding periodically checked, but the use of idiom should be reserved for those with an advanced ability in the language.

In the past, I have helped those preparing formal presentations. On one occasion I was asked to write a speech for an overseas Government minister. I had to ensure that a significant message was delivered, getting it right for the country, and also presenting it in a culturally acceptable way. Not many countries would entrust a foreigner with putting words into the mouth of one of its politicians, but international travel and cross-cultural assignments are filled with surprises, challenges and opportunities.

Examining the evidence

Women's struggle for survival: The global situation

Worldwide, during the first decade of the 21st century, at least 1000 women died every day from pregnancy-related causes. For women of childbearing age this death toll lies second only to that related to HIV/AIDS. More than 80% of these women lived in sub-Saharan Africa or South Asia, the larger number in the former region (*Figure 1.1*). The lifetime risk of maternal death varies greatly across the world (*Table 1.1*), the toll on the health of survivors is also enormous and morbidities include anaemia, fever, fistulae, incontinence, infertility and depression. Four of the five main causes of maternal mortality account for 70% of these deaths (*Box 1.1*) and most such fatalities are deemed preventable (WHO, 2010).

In addition to the four major obstetric causes of maternal mortality, obstructed labour is responsible for the deaths of up to five women in every 1000 live births, mostly occurring in the developing world. Obstructed labour is also associated with a higher incidence of fetal death and is the cause of numerous maternal morbidities. These include obstetric fistulae,

---

Box 1.1. Four major obstetric causes of maternal death

- Haemorrhage
- Infection
- Hypertensive disorders
- Unsafe abortion

Source: WHO, 2010

---

estimated to affect between 50000 and 100000 women and girls each year (WHO, 2012b). About 16 million girls between the ages of 15 and 19 years give birth each year, representing 10% of total births. In many countries the overall risk of death from pregnancy-related causes is doubled in adolescent mothers by comparison with others (WHO, 2010).

The International Federation of Gynaecology and Obstetrics (FIGO) launched an initiative in 2011 focusing on the prevention and treatment of obstetric fistulae in one Asian and 11 African countries. The intention is to ensure high quality clinical training for the comprehensive care of women and the management of fistulae, implementing a structured surgical programme with a standardised training curriculum (FIGO, 2012). For this purpose FIGO has produced a training manual to enable physicians to acquire the knowledge, skills and professionalism needed both to prevent and surgically repair obstetric fistulae (FIGO, 2011). This issue is further discussed in *Chapter 9*. The drive across the world to train midwives who are able to provide skilled care during labour is a key initiative in preventing prolonged and obstructed labour, the precursors of obstetric fistulae. Those who can identify, prevent and manage complications in pregnancy, labour and the postnatal and neonatal periods are in considerable demand at the beginning of the 21st century. However, at the end of the first decade, still less than 17% of the world's midwives were available to care for women in the countries carrying the heaviest burdens of maternal and perinatal mortality and morbidity, and it is in these 58 countries that 91% of maternal deaths, 80% of stillbirths and 82% of neonatal deaths occur (UNFPA, 2011).

Global initiatives

It is no surprise, therefore, that excellent clinical skills have been regarded as a priority in addressing the unacceptably high incidence of death and injuries that persist in these vulnerable groups across the globe. The slow progress in reducing the maternal mortality ratios has been attributed to a lack of skilled health professionals and in the five years preceding 2015 it was estimated that 330000 more midwives needed to be trained if every woman was to be able to acquire the help of a skilled attendant during childbirth (WHO, 2010). The Safe Motherhood Initiative was launched 13 years prior to the drive to promote skilled attendance and the issues addressed in these global enterprises are summarised in *Boxes 1.2 and 1.3*.

The proportion of women who are attended by skilled health personnel is one of the indicators used to determine progress towards the fifth Millennium Development Goal (MDG 5) that aims to improve maternal health and enable universal access to reproductive healthcare (UN, 2011). Whilst the incidence of skilled attendance has increased from 55% to 65%

Box 1.2. The Safe Motherhood Initiative

The Safe Motherhood Initiative (SMI) launched in 1987 represents a global effort to reduce maternal mortality and morbidity. It has become a unique partnership of governments, non-government organisations, technical agencies, women's health advocates and donors cooperating to raise awareness, set priorities, stimulate research, mobilise resources, provide technical assistance, and provide and share information. Such co-operation and commitment has enabled governments and non-governmental partners from more than 100 countries to take actions at national level aiming to make motherhood safer. The SMI aspires to enhance the quality of the lives of girls and women through numerous strategies. It highlights the need for better and more widely available maternal health services including the extension of family planning education and services, as well as effective measures aimed at improving the status of women.

Sources: SMI, 1987; Family Care International, 1998

Box 1.3. The skilled attendant and skilled attendance

A skilled attendant is an accredited health professional, such as a midwife, doctor or nurse, who has been educated and trained to proficiency in the skills needed to manage normal (uncomplicated) pregnancies, childbirth and the immediate postnatal period, and in the identification, management and referral of complications in women and newborns.

Skilled attendance implies care provided within an 'enabling environment' which includes:

- a functioning health system
- appropriate training and support for skilled attendants
- evidence-based policies, standards and protocols
- essential supplies and equipment
- ample numbers of staff and the right professional mix
- adequate buildings
- satisfactory terms of employment
- supportive supervision
- effective monitoring and evaluation
- a functioning referral system

Sources: WHO, 1999, 2004

---

in the decade preceding 2009 in developing countries, inequalities remain (UN, 2011). Socio-economic inequity and women's education were among the factors highlighted in a study in Bangladesh influencing whether women seek skilled care (Anwar et al, 2008). Even in a country such as Namibia that made marked progress in increasing the numbers of women attended by skilled healthcare professionals, inequality has been implicated. Zere et al (2011) identify socio-economic disparity, residential location and differences in levels of education as determinants influencing the uptake of skilled care in that country. These issues have repeatedly been associated with health disadvantages (Houweling et al, 2007; Starfield and Birn, 2007; Marmot et al, 2008; Ahmed et al, 2010) and it is evident that any approaches to make childbirth safer must therefore incorporate a multitude of factors that go beyond the preparation of skilled healthcare professionals.

Traditional healers and birth attendants

The acceptability of traditional birth attendants has been debated with increasing ardour since the advent of promoting skilled attendance for all (Bergström and Goodburn, 2001). For decades the issue as to whether traditional birth attendants can contribute to reducing maternal and perinatal mortality has remained controversial. The consensus has surrounded the need to integrate them into healthcare systems, to gradually replace them with skilled attendants and to ensure the existence of an effective referral system to access quality essential obstetric services (Yadav, 1987; Wollast et al, 1993; Fleming, 1994; Alisjahbana, 1995; Kwast, 1995, 1996; Koblinsky et al, 1999; Jokhio et al, 2005).

There is evidence that traditional birth attendants have been receiving some training since the end of the 19th century although this increased during the latter part of the 20th century only to decline later (Sibley and Sipe, 2006). Whereas in 1972 only 20 countries had any form of traditional birth attendant training programme, 20 years later this had increased to include 85% of developing countries (Fleming, 1994). When the Alma-Ata Declaration was made in 1978 (WHO, 1978), WHO was fully supportive of traditional birth attendant training, but by 1997 the focus had moved from training traditional birth attendants to an emphasis on training skilled attendants.

In an analysis of studies including more than 2000 traditional birth attendants and 27 000 women, Sibley et al (2009) conclude that when combined with improved health services, traditional birth attendant training offers promising potential for reducing perinatal mortality. However, they concede that lack of evidence ensures that the effectiveness of the actual traditional birth attendant training cannot be verified. Evidence from Guatemala suggests that staff attitudes towards traditional birth attendants can be more influential in facilitating referral than whether or not the latter have received training. In that country, the referral rate increased by more than 200% through incorporating two basic strategies. These involved training hospital staff in improving standards of obstetric and neonatal care, along with stressing the importance of being understanding and supportive towards women and traditional birth attendants (O'Rourke, 1995). In a rural district in East Java, a government scheme providing financial incentives to traditional birth attendants for referring women to skilled attendants succeeded in promoting cooperation between midwives and traditional birth attendants. It also dramatically reduced the numbers of women giving birth with traditional birth attendants from 86% to 1% between 1984 and 2007 (Analen, 2007).

Attitudes towards traditional practitioners vary with time and between different people and professional groups. Traditional birth attendants tend to be the preferred choice in rural communities and some poor urban districts. However, choice may not feature in the available assistance for women in many communities where traditional practitioners are the only resource.

Following an extensive review of the evidence, Bergström and Goodburn (2001) acknowledge the psychosocial and cultural support that traditional birth attendants provide for women during childbirth. They stress that the cultural competence and empathic skills of traditional birth attendants make an important contribution to the care of women and their newborns. Attitudes toward traditional healers and traditional medicine have experienced turning points at the beginning of the 21st century. The Beijing Declaration (WHO, 2008) recognised and promoted several issues concerning traditional practice. These include the injunction that the knowledge of traditional medicine and practices be preserved, respected, promoted and widely communicated and that governments should regulate practice to promote safety and effectiveness. Furthermore, it is urged that traditional practice should be researched in order to develop further, and be integrated into national health systems. Qualification, accreditation and licensing of practitioners were also recommended. Collaboration between conventional and traditional practitioners and between governments, international organisations and stakeholders was encouraged.

There is some evidence of efforts to establish recognition and approval. For example, during July 2012, Angola recognised 54 000 traditional healers in an attempt to integrate their knowledge into the national health system. In that country traditional medicine is believed to be the sum of all practices, treatments and methods incorporating the experience and spiritual dimensions of generations and of particular importance to rural populations (Annual Action Programme, 2012). This topic is pursued further in *Chapter 3*.

It would seem that where skilled attendants are able to embrace the cultural competence and sensitivity evident in the best examples of traditional practitioners, there might be a greater meeting of minds and actions for the ultimate good of the childbearing woman and her offspring. The visiting student or professional is likely to encounter these polarised approaches to care during childbirth and witness the evolution or revolution that ensues.

Ethical dilemmas

Not only in respect of traditional practitioners, but short-term visitors to another country may well experience a very different value system in operation throughout a national health system. It is not difficult to appreciate therefore that in a contrasting culture their pre-existing ethical codes of practice may be challenged. Benatar et al (2003) maintain that discourse on formal ethics remained in the realm of philosophical and theological studies until the 1960s. Until that time professional groups and individuals held their own personal ethical views, but these were not generally discussed. Increasing concern about individual freedom and human rights along with advances in medicine and technology brought biomedical ethics into the public domain as issues such as the doctor–patient relationship and withholding or withdrawing treatment became matters of general concern. The writers conclude:

Education and the development of such human values as empathy, generosity, solidarity, civic responsibility, humility and self-effacement require an interdisciplinary space to thrive...

and they propose that

...global health ethics offers such a space, and that it can help to catalyse crucial improvements in global health.
(Benatar et al, 2003: 138)

Global health may be easy to define in idealistic terms, but not so easy to achieve in vastly different settings. Global ethics is by no means a homogenous concept and the science may not be transferable across cultures. The challenge arises for short-term visitors in the professional context when they encounter a totally different cultural environment enshrined in a set of values that seem alien to the outsider. In addition, the institution in which they work may not have adopted an institutional code of ethics that is compatible with previous experience and the code of national and public health ethics may also appear alien to the outsider. Issues surrounding personal choice, informed consent, the rights of the individual, dignity, privacy and prohibitive costs that prevent life-saving interventions are but a few of the challenges that may be handled very differently in other countries, especially those at a different stage of modernisation and development.

In an extensive consideration of medical ethics from a cross-cultural perspective, Veatch (2000) points out that anyone faced with an ethical dilemma is working, at least implicitly, from within a certain framework. He goes on to explain that pre-existing frameworks have been designed to deal with normative questions that seek to clarify, for example, what principles and norms are in use and 'whether morality can be reduced to rules' (Veatch, 2000: xvii). Health professionals in many countries work from within a framework that may be derived from the Declaration of Geneva (World Medical Association, 2006). This declaration or one of a similar genre is affirmed by emerging professionals on graduating from many of the world's schools in medicine, nursing, midwifery and other health sciences. In making such a declaration, the graduate avows, for instance, to practice the profession with conscience and dignity, regard the health of the patient as the first consideration and treat teachers with due respect and gratitude.

The British General Medical Council (GMC), in its responsibilities for medical practice, adopts the approach based on the ancient Hippocratic Oath from which many doctors through the ages have derived their ethical stance. The GMC expects doctors to treat patients as individuals, be honest and open and work in partnership with them (GMC, 2006). The Nursing and Midwifery Council (NMC) declares the similar shared values of all the UK healthcare regulatory bodies in expecting the practitioner to abide by principles that respect and protect patients or clients as individuals (NMC, 2010). International consultants and elective students are likely to be confronted by issues that demand ethical judgements. The WMA has produced a manual of medical ethics that has been translated into numerous languages and distributed throughout the world (WMA, 2009). The volume contains case studies which the student could find useful to discuss with supervisors before leaving for an elective. Obviously, there are no easy or standard answers to the ethical dilemmas of practice, but reflecting on some cases with the help of an experienced and trusted teacher or supervisor can only be advantageous in preparation. The WMA (2006:11) maintains

The study of ethics prepares medical students to recognize difficult situations and deal with them in a rational and principled manner.

It is in this spirit that preparation is encouraged not only for clinical practice, but also for the ethical conflicts that may arise in cross-cultural encounters.

Perkins et al (1998) urge all health professionals to show sensitivity and respect towards the values expressed by colleagues from other cultures in matters affecting patient care. In an attempt to bridge the gap between Western and Chinese systems of medical ethics, Nie (2011) offers an ethical paradigm designed to traverse different cultures. The theory purports to uphold the primacy of morality and resist the temptation of stereotyping cultural norms while appreciating the dynamism, richness and internal plurality that can be evident in different systems of medical ethics. The matter of conflicting ethical standpoints has been raised repeatedly as a matter of concern in connection with student electives and evidence is considered in this context below.

Elective issues

Confrontation by clinical dilemmas in unfamiliar and ill-equipped settings can be a particular issue for elective students as the instances related above have illustrated. Unless addressed adequately, such concerns may penetrate beyond initial culture shock into an area involving ethical conflict as well as very real risks to personal safety and health.

Elit et al (2011) carried out a study designed to explore the ethical issues that confront medical students undertaking electives in low resource settings. They report that five main themes emerged and these include uncertainty about how best to help and the issue of moving beyond one's scope of practice. They conclude that students would benefit from some formal preparation before departure and that this should embrace an evaluation of their expectations and motivation as well as exploring and discussing professional and ethical issues. They advise that preparation should also include learning about the local context of their placement which needs to be carefully selected. An onsite supervisor or colleague is considered advantageous and maintaining contact with the home institution is also recommended along with a formal debriefing on completion of the assignment. Hanson et al (2011), drawing from a critical analysis of relevant literature, also express concerns about ethical issues as well as the content of the curriculum and the pedagogical strategies deemed necessary if equitable engagements with participating countries are to be achieved. In addition the writers express concern that current approaches to international medical electives are at risk of nurturing colonialist ideas in the relationship between countries in the north and south.

Acknowledging the lack of evidence concerning the effectiveness of preparatory programmes, Xu et al (2011) identify five essential components of pre-departure training for elective healthcare students. These comprise personal health, travel safety, cultural awareness, linguistic competency and ethical considerations. The findings of Jeffrey et al (2011) share the concerns expressed above about personal health and travel safety as well as the limited resources and faculty inexperience in supporting elective students. Nevertheless they claim that electives contribute to a well-rounded training and help medical students to become culturally competent. Lough (2011) warns that acquiring such competence requires certain preconditions and these issues are discussed further in *Chapter 2*.

Decades earlier, Ruben and Kealey (1979) identified several interpersonal communication skills deemed important in acquiring cross-cultural adaptation. These include empathy, respect, role behaviour flexibility, orientation to knowledge, and tolerance of ambiguity. These attributes could well serve in helping with both selection and preparation of potential elective students and healthcare consultants who aspire to cross cultures.

Emanating from examining issues affecting the health of Dutch medical students undertaking electives, Sharafeldin et al (2010) recognise that limited medical experience and an unfamiliar healthcare setting combine to expose students to health risks including blood-borne viral infections and malaria. They report the development of an integral set of measures including a mandatory global health module designed to prepare and protect the health of all their medical students planning electives overseas. Some of the main issues to consider in preparing for an elective or overseas assignment are summarised in *Table 1.2*.

Table 1.2. Preparing for an assignment or elective in a low resourced or developing country			
Subject	**See chapter**	**Subject**	**See chapter**
Essential insights			
Cross-cultural competence	2	Linguistic ability	1, 3, 4, 7, 9
Major cultural contrasts	4, 5, 6, 9, 10	Adapting interpersonal	
Minimising culture shock	4	and communication skills	3, 5, 10
Political awareness and		Minimising reverse culture	
correctness	3, 4	shock	10
Professional ethics	1, 4		
Survival and safety			
Travel safety, personal		Travelling and working	
security	7, 6, 9	alone	7
Personal health	2, 8	Personal support	2, 6, 10
Minimising jet lag	6		
Background knowledge			
Locality data: Historical,		Skilled attendance	1, 2, 3, 6, 8, 9
geographical, political	throughout	Management of change	2, 8
Millennium Development		Tropical health and	
Goals	1, 6, 8, 10	medicine	8
The Safe Motherhood		Traditional approaches to	
Initiative	1, 5	health and medicine	1, 3
Modernisation and		Cultural differences in	
development, bridging the		educational approaches	2, 4, 5, 7
'epoch gap'	2, 6, 10	Essentials of team work	8
Gender issues	1, 3, 5, 7–10	International consultancy	1, 10
Practice issues			
Clinical skills	1, 2, 6, 9	Coping with the 'quality gap'	6, 7, 10
Evidence-based practice	3, 5, 7–9	HIV/AIDS	1, 2, 8
Administrative issues			
Terms of reference,		Reporting back at	
contracting, accountability	10	conferences, study days	2, 10
Report writing and making			
recommendations	1–3, 5, 8–10		
Additional knowledge and skills useful to consultants			
Evaluation skills	10	Evidence-based advocacy	8, 9
Capacity development	2, 7	Rights-based approaches	3, 8
Sustainable development	7, 10		

International consultancy: Facets and functions

International consultancy is a multifaceted occupation and requires those who embark upon it to function in countless and sometimes contrasting capacities. Various titles have been used to describe health and other professionals who cross international borders to share their specialist knowledge, skills or expertise in the cause of development. They may be known as consultants, development workers, technical advisers or assistants and may be required to fulfil a complexity of roles in this process (*Figure 1.2*).

In addition to their specialised knowledge and experience, international consultants are usually expected to possess the personal attributes that not only qualify them to advise or assist in this context, but also commend them to their clients. The task calls for personal as well as professional qualities. A number of qualities that make short-term consultants acceptable or unacceptable as they work in an international context have been identified (Maclean, 1998) and a number of these are shared in this book, particularly in *Chapters 2, 3, 6 and 10*.

In carrying out my research, when posing two direct questions concerning the acceptability of consultants, without exception respondents addressed the issue of unacceptability first. Evidence suggests that history as well as experience accounts for some of the pre-existing attitudes towards development workers apparent today. Benavides (1992) passionately declares his animosity towards oppressive colonial powers dating back centuries, regarding them as invaders, imposers and robbers, claiming that their real intention was 'to make us like them'. In offering advice and making recommendations, consultants dare not assume that such an interpretation of their intent will not occur. Wherever appropriate, nurturing indigenous innovation and creativity may go some way towards denying any inclination or indication of attempts to impose one culture upon another. This issue is raised in *Chapter 5* and considered in some detail in *Chapter 8*.

Nonetheless, pathways into cultures that at first present as alien have been made and successes have been noted. An example is cited from within a Mexican society where outsiders were dubbed 'coyotes', however, an indigenous population discovered that such people were not inevitably evil. A Nahua Indian gives this explanation:

> *There are individuals who manage to bridge the cultural gap between the two social realities. They know the good and the bad. Where it is safe to tread and where not. At the beginning of this present century a coyote came and settled down in my community. He respected our traditions, our people and our Nahauti culture in general.*
>
> *(Hernández, 1987: 187)*

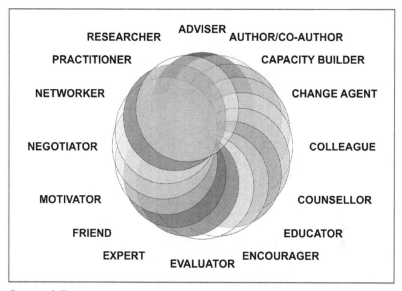

Figure 1.2. The complexity of roles required of an international consultant. Sources: Bingham, 1954; Bruner, 1975; Goldhamer, 1978; Fry and Thurber, 1989; Forss et al, 2006; Maclean, 2011.

The aspiration of both consultants and students must surely surround being able to discern the good from the bad and know where it is safe to tread. Maybe the key is veiled within the three 'R's of cross-cultural acceptability: an ability to show and earn respect, establish and maintain relationship and provide evidence of reliability. The key should help interpret a route map into the unknown. Such a map needs to identify the areas that are safe to tread and those that are best avoided (*Figure 1.3*). The wisdom needed to discern these issues is a precious commodity.

Policy makers and political commitment

In my research, policy makers confided that the consultants they found most unacceptable were those who were critical, bossy or argumentative. It was also the emotional, culturally insensitive or inflexible consultants and those who could not work independently that posed problems. Sending agencies, responsible for the selection, support and specifics of the task of the consultant expressed concern about the acceptability of recommendations offered on behalf of their organisation. Creativity and innovation needed to take second place to usability, with the latter depending not only on the content and context but also on the spirit with which the suggestions

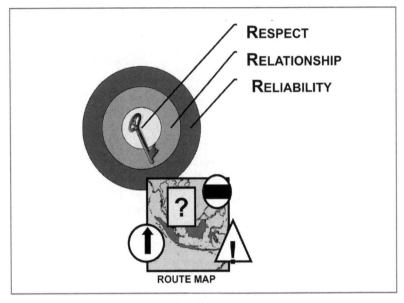

Figure 1.3. The three 'R's that are key to cross-cultural acceptability.

were offered. Recommendations that are in harmony with the policies and practice of the stakeholders were deemed desirable (Maclean, 1998). Democratic governance, gender issues and poverty alleviation were high on the international aid agenda a quarter of a century before the advent of the Millennium Development Goals and have not lost significance in a more recent context (Arthur et al, 1996; Sveriges Riksdag, 2005; UN, 2011). The aspiring consultant would be wise to consider formulating recommendations within a framework of history, culture and the prevailing emphasis of national and international stakeholders. The art and skill of making recommendations is further discussed in *Chapters 8 and 10*. Acquiring a timely and appropriate approach as well as the correct emphasis is a prime task for national professionals, and consultants frequently have opportunities to augment the efforts that their colleagues are making in this respect.

Soon after the launch of the Safe Motherhood Initiative, Royston and Armstrong (1989) highlighted the paucity of government inactivity:

> *It is only very recently that people have started to challenge – loudly and clearly in international forums – the stifling mix of personal fatalism and political disregard for women's needs that has condoned inaction in many poor countries.*

> *(Royston and Armstrong, 1989: 9)*

Yet apathy towards addressing maternal mortality still needs to be challenged. Fathalla (2006), echoing the sentiment of his challenge 15 years earlier, categorically claims that pregnancy-related deaths occur not because of difficulty in managing the causative conditions but because societies do not find it fitting to invest in the required resources to save lives. He maintains that the question revolves around whether the lives of women are considered worth saving. Framing the issue within the human rights context, he concludes that a woman's right to safe motherhood is attainable 'with political commitment and international cooperation' (Fathalla, 2006: 419).

There is considerable evidence that political commitment is essential in successfully addressing maternal mortality (Araujo and Diniz, 1990; Department For International Development, 2007; Gill et al, 2007). Countries such as Malaysia and Bolivia with maternal mortality up to 400 per 100000 halved their death tolls in less than 10 years. Chile, Columbia, Egypt and Sri Lanka similarly reduced their maternal mortality in 6–7 years and Honduras, Nicaragua and Thailand halved their maternal morality at an even quicker pace (WHO, 2005). Indeed, securing political commitment is not just fundamental, it is crucial to making progress in reducing this shameful and largely preventable death toll. In the absence of such commitment, women continue to die and suffer needlessly.

Personal reflections on practice

* Standards of practice may be severely challenged by numerous issues including a lack of equipment, limited clinical skills, staff shortages and pressures of an overstretched health service.
* My personal and professional ethical framework may not find resonance within a very different culture and setting.
* Colleagues may not have had the same opportunities that I have had in receiving teaching and supervision during clinical practice to enable them to acquire the necessary skills.
* Delay can be a deadly foe and it appears in numerous forms, denying many life-saving interventions.

Some lessons learned and shared

* Learning to avoid making snap judgements of the reasons for inefficiency, ineffectiveness or seemingly unethical decisions is needful. The truth may not be immediately obvious and such matters often do not respond to simple or easily attainable solutions.

- Ignoring our own weaknesses will only allow them to be accentuated in another culture and practice environment. You may never feel ready, but attempt to prepare yourself as thoroughly as possible for your elective or assignment by dealing with those areas of your practice which you know you need to address.
- Consultants may be required at short notice, but keeping a reflective diary and learning from experience as well as availing oneself of any preparatory courses can be advantageous. Students would do well to aim at allowing time for preparation by planning an elective as far ahead as possible.

Reflective exercises

- Reflect on the clinical skills that you anticipate being required of you during a forthcoming elective or assignment. Identify any that you may wish to learn, enhance or update. Prioritise them and compile an action list to address them during your preparation.
- Think about a recent incident in practice which called for an ethical judgement.
  - What personal and professional frameworks did you, your colleagues or supervisors use from which important decisions were made?
  - How might the final decision have varied if the responsible practitioner had been using a very different ethical framework within a divergent legislative and practice environment?
- You might find it useful to consider one of the case studies cited in the World Medical Association's medical ethics manual (WMA, 2009). Select a case relevant to your practice area that you anticipate could be viewed differently within a contrasting culture and discuss your reflections with a colleague or supervisor.

References

Ahmed S, Creanga AA, Gillespie DG, Tsui AO (2010) Economic status, education and empowerment: Implications for maternal health service utilization in developing countries. *Open Access PLoS ONE* 5(6): e11190. doi:10.1371/journal.pone.0011190

Alisjahbana A, Williams C, Dharmayanti R, Hermarwen D, Kwast BE, Koblinsky M (1995) An integrated village maternity service to improve referral patterns in a rural area in West Java. *International Journal of Gynaecology and Obstetrics* 48(Suppl): S83–S94

Analen C (2007) Saving mothers' lives in rural Indonesia. *Bulletin of the WHO* 85(10): 740–1

Annual Action Programme (2012) *Country registers over 54,000 traditional healers.*

ANGOP Health, Agencia Angola Press, Luena, 15 July 2012. Available from: http://www.portalangop.co.ao/motix/en_us/noticias/saude/2012/6/28/Country-registers-over-000-traditional-healers,17324675-c880-4917-ba6a-4a0fd5a36f5e.html [last accessed 17.07.2012]

Anwar I, Sami N, Akhtar N, Chowdhury ME, Salman U, Rahman M, Koblinsky M (2008) Inequity in maternal health-care services: Evidence from home-based skilled birth attendant programmes in Bangladesh. *Bulletin of the WHO* **86**(4): 252–9

Araujo M, Diniz SG (1990) The Campaign in Brazil: From the technical to the political. In: *Maternal mortality and morbidity: A call to women for action*. Amsterdam: Women's Global Network for Reproductive Rights and the Latin American and Caribbean Women's Health Network/ISIS International. Special Issue 56 (28 May)

Arthur L, Preson RA, Negahu C, le Breton SS, Theobold D (1996) *Quality in overseas consultancy, understanding the issues*. International Centre for Education and Development, University of Warwick, published by the British Council

Benatar SR, Daar AS, Singer PA (2003) Global health ethics: The rationale for mutual caring. *International Affairs* **79**(1): 107–38

Benavides M (1992) Lessons from 500 years of a 'New World Order' towards the 21st century: Education for quality of life. *Convergence* **XXIV**(2) 37–43

Bergström S, Goodburn E (2001) The role of traditional birth attendants in the reduction of maternal mortality. In: De Brouwere V, Van Lerberghe W (Eds) *Safe motherhood strategies: A review of the evidence. Studies in Heath Services Organization and Policy* **17**: 77–96

Bingham J (1954) *Shirtsleeve diplomacy. Point 4 in Action*. John Day, New York.

Black RE, Allen LA, Bhutta ZA et al (2008) Maternal and child undernutrition: Global and regional exposures and health consequences. *Lancet* DOI:10.1016/S0140-6736(07)61690-0 www.lancet.com [last accessed 02.10.2012]

Bruner J (1975) The role of the researcher as an adviser to the educational policy maker. *Oxford Review of Education* **1**(83): 183

Department for International Development (2007) *DFID's maternal health strategy on reducing maternal deaths: Evidence and action. 2nd Progress Report, April 2007.* Department For International Development, London

Department of Health (1995) *Breastfeeding: Good practice guidance to the NHS.* Department of Health, London

Elit L, Hunt M, Redwood-Campbell L (2011) Ethical issues encountered by medical students during international health electives. *Medical Education* **45**(7): 704–11

Family Care International (1998) *The Safe Motherhood Initiative. Safe Motherhood Fact Sheet.* Family Care International, New York

Fathalla MF (2006) Human rights aspects of safe motherhood. Best practice and research. *Clinical Obstetrics and Gynaecology* **20**(3): 409–19.

FIGO (2011) *Global competency-based fistula surgery training manual*. FIGO and Partners. FIGO/UNFPA. Available from: http://www.figo.org/files/figo-corp/FIGO_Global_Competency-Based_Fistula_Surgery_Training_Manual.pdf [last accessed 16.07.2012]

FIGO (2012) *Fistula initiative*. Available from: http://www.figo.org/projects/fistula_initiative [last accessed 16.07.2012]

Fleming JR (1994) What in the world is being done about TBAs? An overview of international and national attitudes to traditional birth attendants. *Midwifery* **10**(3): 142–7.

Forss K, Vedung E, Kruse SE, Mwaiselage A, Nilsdotter A (2006) *Can evaluations be trusted? An enquiry into the quality of Sida's evaluation reports*. Sida, Stockholm, Sweden

Fry GW, Thurber CE (1989) *The international education of the development consultant: Communicating with peasants and princes*. Pergamon Press, Oxford

General Medical Council (2006) *Good medical practice*. General Medical Council. Available from: http://www.gmc-uk.org/static/documents/content/GMP_0910.pdf [last accessed 25.07.2012]

Gill K, Pande R, Malhotra A (2007) Women deliver for development. *Lancet* **370**(9595): 1347–57

Goldhamer H (1978) *The adviser*. Elsevier, New York

Hanson L, Harms S, Plamondon K (2011) Undergraduate international medical electives: Some ethical and pedagogical considerations. *Journal of Studies in International Education* **15**(2): 171–85.

Hernández N (1987) Indigenous images, assumptions and prejudices. *Adult Education and Development* **48**: 179–201

Houweling TAJ, Ronsmans C, Campbel OMR, Kunst AE (2007) Huge poor–rich inequalities in maternity care: An international comparative study of maternity and child care in developing countries. *Bulletin of the WHO* **85**(10): 745–54

Jeffrey J, Dumont RA, Kim GY, Kuo T (2011) Effects of international health electives on medical student learning and career choice: Results of a systematic literature review. *Family Medicine* **43**(1): 21–8

Jokhio AH, Winter HR, Cheng KK (2005) An intervention involving traditional birth attendants and perinatal maternal mortality in Pakistan. *New England Journal of Medicine* **352**(20): 2091–9

Koblinsky MA, Campbell O, Heichelheim J (1999) Organizing delivery care: What works for safe motherhood? *Bulletin of the WHO* **77**(5): 399–406

Kwast BE (1995) Building a community based program. *International Journal of Gynaecology and Obstetrics* **48**(Suppl): S67–S82.

Kwast BE (1996) Reduction of maternal and perinatal mortality in rural and peri-urban settings: What works. *European Journal of Obstetrics, Gynaecology and Reproductive Biology* **69**: 47–53

Lough BJ (2011) International volunteers' perceptions of intercultural competence. *International Journal of Intercultural Relations* **35**(4): 452–64

Maclean GD (1998) *An examination of the characteristics of short-term international midwifery consultants.* Thesis submitted for the degree of Doctor of Philosophy. University of Surrey, Guildford, England

Maclean GD (2011) Short-term international midwifery consultancy: Discussing the need. *British Journal of Midwifery* **19**(6): 387–91

Marmot M, Friel S, Bell R, Houweling TAJ, Taylor S (2008) Commission on Social Determinants of Health. Closing the gap in a generation: Health equity through action on the social determinants of health. *Lancet* **372**: 1661–9. doi:10.1016/S0140-6736(08)61690-6

Nie J-B (2011) *Medical ethics in China, a transcultural interpretation.* Routledge, London

Nursing and Midwifery Council (2010) *Standards of Conduct, Performance and Ethics for Nurses and Midwives.* Available from: http://www.nmc-uk.org/Nurses-and-midwives/Standards-and-guidance1/ [last accessed 25.07.2012]

O'Rourke K (1995) The effect of hospital staff training on management of obstetrical patients referred by traditional birth attendants. *International Journal of Gynaecology and Obstetrics* **48**(Suppl): S95–S102

Perkins HS, Supik JD, Hazuda HP (1998) Cultural differences among health professionals: A case illustration. *Journal of Clinical Ethics* **9**(2): 108–17

Royston E, Armstrong S (1989) *Preventing maternal deaths.* WHO, Geneva

Ruben BD, Kealey DJ (1979) Behavioral assessment of communication competency and the prediction of cross-cultural adaptation. *International Journal of Intercultural Relations* **3**: 15–47

Safe Motherhood Initiative (1987) Preventing the tragedy of maternal deaths. A report of the international Safe Motherhood conference, Nairobi, Kenya. World Health Organization, Geneva

Save the Children (2012) State of the World's mothers 2012. The 2012 Mothers' Index. Save the Children, Available from: http://www.savethechildren.org/ [last accessed 28/07/2012]

Sharafeldin L, Soonawala D, Vandenbroucke JP, Hack, Visser LG (2010) Health risks encountered by Dutch medical students during an elective in the tropics and the quality and comprehensiveness of pre and post travel care. *BMC Medical Educational* **10**(1): 89. doi:10.1186/1472-6920-10-89 http://www.biomedcentral.com/1472-6920/10/89

Sibley LM, Sipe TA (2006) Transition to skilled birth attendance: Is there a future role for traditional birth attendants? *Journal of Health, Population and Nutrition* **24**(4): 472–8

Sibley LM, Sipe TA, Brown CM, Diallo MM, McNatt K, Habarta N (2009) Traditional birth attendant training for improving health behaviours and pregnancy outcomes (Review). *The Cochrane Library.* Available from: http://www.thecochranelibrary.com [last accessed 02.10.2012]

Starfield B, Birn AE (2007) Income redistribution is not enough: Income inequality, social welfare programs, and achieving equity in health. *Journal of Epidemiology and Community Health* **61**: 1038–41. doi: 10.1136/jech.2006.054627

Sveriges Riksdag (2005) *Sweden's New Policy for Global Development.* Sveriges Riksdag, the Swedish Parliament, Stockholm

UN (2010) *United Nations Standing Committee on Nutrition (SCN). 6th Report on the World Nutrition Situation.* United Nations, New York

UN (2011) *The millennium development goals report 2011.* United Nations, New York

UNFPA (2011) *The state of the World's midwifery 2011: Delivering health, saving lives.* UNFPA, New York. Available from: www.stateoftheworldsmidwifery.com [last accessed 02.10.2012]

UNICEF (2012) *The state of the World's children 2012.* UNICEF, New York

Veatch RM (2000) *Cross cultural perspectives in medical ethics* (2nd Edn). Jones and Bartlett Publishers International, London

WHO (1978) *Declaration of Alma Ata.* World Health Organization, Geneva

WHO (1996) *Midwifery education modules. Education for safe motherhood. Educational material for teachers of midwifery.* World Health Organization, Geneva

WHO (1999) *Reduction of maternal mortality: A joint WHO/UNFPA/UNICEF/ World Bank Statement.* WHO, Geneva

WHO (2004) *Making pregnancy safer: The critical role of the skilled attendant. A joint statement by WHO, ICM and FIGO.* World Health Organization, Geneva

WHO (2005) *World health report: Make every mother and child count.* World Health Organization, Geneva

WHO (2006) *Midwifery education modules. Education for safe motherhood. Educational material for teachers of midwifery* (2nd Edn) World Health Organization, Geneva

WHO (2008) *The Beijing Declaration adopted by the WHO Congress on Traditional Medicine, Beijing, China, 8 November 2008.* Available from: http://www.who.int/ medicines/areas/traditional/congress/beijing_declaration/en/ [last accessed 18.07.2012]

WHO (2010) *10 facts on maternal health. WHO Fact File.* Available from: http://www. who.int/features/factfiles/maternal_health/maternal_health_facts/en/index1.html [last accessed 13.07.2012]

WHO (2012a) *Trends in maternal mortality 1990 to 2010.* WHO, UNICEF, UNFPA and World Bank. World Health Organization, Geneva. Available from: http://www.who. int/reproductivehealth/publications/monitoring/9789241503631/en/ [last accessed 13.09.2012]

WHO (2012b) *Emergency and essential surgical care. Pregnancy-related complications.* Available from: http://www.who.int/surgery/challenges/esc_pregnancy_more/en/ [last accessed 16.07.2012]

World Medical Association (2006) *World Medical Association Declaration of Geneva editorially revised by the 173rd WMA Council Session Divonne-les-Bains, France, May 2006*. Available from: http://www.wma.net/en/30publications/10policies/g1/ [last accessed 25.07.2012]

World Medical Association (2009) *Medical ethics manual of the World Medical Association*. Available from: http://www.wma.net/en/30publications/30ethicsmanual/index.html [last accessed 25.07.2012]

Wollast E, Renard F, Vandenbussche P, Buekens P (1993) *Detecting maternal morbidity and mortality by traditional birth attendants in Burkina Faso*. Health Policy and Planning **2**: 161–8

Xu JJ, Pereira IJ, Liu WW, Herbert CP (2011) *Assessing the effectiveness of pre-departure training for healthcare students working in resource limited settings*. University of Toronto Medical Journal **88**(3): 199–204

Yadav H (1987) Utilisation of traditional birth attendants in MCH care in rural Malaysia. *Singapore Medical Journal* **28**(6): 520–5

Zere E, Oluwole D, Kirigia JM, Mwikisa CN, Mbeeli T (2011) Inequities in skilled attendance at birth in Namibia: A decomposition analysis. *BMC Pregnancy and Childbirth* **11**: 34

Chapter 2

Into Africa

He who offends forgets but he who suffered from the offence does not.
(Tswana Proverb)

Unlike western societies, in a culture where oral tradition exists the ability to memorise tends to take priority initially over seeking understanding – but this is a complex issue extending beyond the practice of rote learning

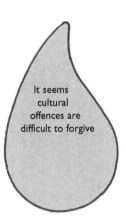

It seems cultural offences are difficult to forgive

Subject strands introduced

- Initiating change
- General health issues
- Culturally different approaches to learning

- Infant feeding issues
- Capacity development
- Individualist and collectivist societies
- Cultural competence

Practice points

- Survival
- Working where 'they' work and sitting where 'they' sit

- The power of friendship
- Reflection

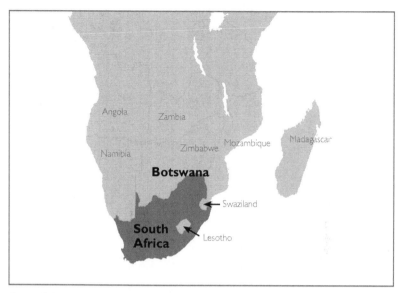

Figure 2.1. Botswana and South Africa.

Botswana: Background

Botswana

The Republic of Botswana is a democratic landlocked country bordered by South Africa, Namibia, Zambia and Zimbabwe. Botswana is named after the country's leading ethnic group, the Tswana. The country covers an area of 581 730 km², the capital is Gaborone; Francistown is the other large city. It was a British Protectorate before independence in 1966. The population is around 2 million (estimated 2012), 60% living in urban areas. Botswana struggles with one of the highest incidences of HIV/AIDS in the world but also has one of the most progressive and comprehensive programmes addressing this issue. The predominant religion is Christianity (70%) whilst a minority adhere to the indigenous African religion of Badimo. There are 14 recognised languages; Setswana is the official national language and English is widely spoken. Botswana has experienced decades of stability and economic growth. Traditionally known for cattle farming, diamond mining has become a principal industry. There is also a growing tourist industry, whilst a significant portion of the country is covered by the Kalahari Desert; the beautiful inland delta of the Okavango graces the northern region. Botswana is developing one of the highest rates of technology penetration in sub-Saharan Africa and top exports as well as diamonds include vehicles, nickel, copper and meat.

South Africa: Background

South Africa

The Republic of South Africa occupies the southern tip of the African continent, flanked by the Atlantic and Indian Oceans whose waters meet at Cape Agulhas. Its northern neighbours are Namibia, Botswana, Zimbabwe and Mozambique. South Africa completely encircles Lesotho and partially surrounds Swaziland. Its coastline stretches for more than 2500 km although the country covers 1 219 090 km². Pretoria is the administrative, Cape Town the legislative and Bloemfontein the judiciary capital. South Africa is a multiparty democracy with an independent judiciary and a free press. Until 1994 the country was known for apartheid, but in 1997 the New Constitution which is declared as the highest law in the land came into force, promoting and protecting equality and freedom. The population is around 49 million (estimated 2012) with 57% living in urban areas and the vast majority being of black African origin. Almost 80% of the population profess to be Christian, 15% claim no belief and small minorities adhere to other faiths. There are 11 recognised languages, IsiZulu being the most widely spoken, by almost a quarter of the population. Afrikaans and English are also spoken. Mining is one of the key industries; others include automobile assembly, textiles, iron and steel. The country is the world's largest producer of platinum and chromium.

Botswana and South Africa: Data

Botswana	South Africa
HDI*: medium (118)	HDI*: medium (123)
MMR (2010): 160	MMR (2010): 300
MMR: proportion related to HIV/AIDS: 56.4%	MMR: proportion related to HIV/AIDS: 59.9%
Lifetime risk of maternal death: 1 in 220	Lifetime risk of maternal death: 1 in 140
Mothers index ranking (2012)**: 58 (Tier II)	Mothers index ranking**: 33 (Tier II)
Births attended by skilled personnel: 95%	Births attended by skilled personnel: 91%

HDI: Human Development Index, MMR: Maternal Mortality Ratio
*Assessed according to life expectancy, educational and economic factors
**Ranked globally (within 3 tiers: I = more developed, II = less developed, III = least developed) according to health, education, economic and political status of women

Background and data sources: UN Development Program, 2011; Africa.com, 2012; Index Mundi, 2012; South Africa Info, 2012; Save the Children, 2012; UNICEF, 2012; WHO, 2012
Linguistic note:
Setswana/Tswana = the language; Batswana = the people of Botswana; Motswana = one person of Botswana

Exploring experience

Straddling continents

Experiences early in my career had taken me to India where, for some years, I had studied language and lived among the people. Working with a Christian mission, my responsibilities had included teaching obstetric nursing as well as English and other subjects to student nurses. I am aware that I learned more than I ever taught. As well as learning to communicate in other languages and assimilate other cultures I learned some critical survival skills including how to 'bath' with just a mugful of water, and how to survive by circulating water from drinkable status to hot water bottle, to washing and ultimately toilet flushing. These skills were essential while living in an environment where electricity and water supplies were intermittent at best. A few vacuum flasks became crucial allies in the fight for survival in a semi-desert area that was subject to extreme heat and cold in the different seasons.

My personal introduction to Africa therefore was very much easier. In my particular role I was privileged to enter at a different stratum of society. My initial invitation to act as an external examiner to the midwifery programme in Botswana came with the privilege of accommodation in a good standard hotel. How grateful I was that I had moved in a favourable direction from my youthful experiences, although such experiences were to stand me in good stead in this, as in other countries, in the years ahead. With the proximity of the Kalahari Desert there seemed to be a relative absence of insect life, at least surrounding my habitation, although a shower of much longed for rain would soon bring out these other forms of life. In Kolkata (Calcutta) I had learned to share a bathroom with the largest spider I have seen. My well-practised skill of eliminating all creatures that threatened my safety or stability with one swipe of a flip-flop sandal was defied by this one. I had to acknowledge defeat and learn a different level of tolerance. Botswana, a country that can experience years of drought, posed no threats from insect life on my early visits. The intense poverty that had been so evident whilst living in India seemed not to plague this diamond-rich little country of just over a million people at that time. However, I was to discover that there was of course poverty; there were street children and other social challenges with which my colleagues and acquaintances were only too familiar.

My experience of South Africa was more limited. It was a number of years before I entered the country rather than simply changing planes in Johannesburg in order to access other countries in the region. This rapidly developing country, which has been called 'the rainbow state' since the outlawing of apartheid, has undoubtedly made strides on the world map in recent years.

Engaging in examining

My initial encounter with the midwifery professional examining system in Botswana saw me literally knee deep in examination papers. One hundred students each wrote six three-hour papers. In addition there were practical and oral examinations. I could of course only sample the 600 papers, but it would take time to sort out the areas of greatest potential need, not an easy task for one uninitiated in the examination system then in use. Having made a start at this and knowing that I had three weeks in which to complete the task, I decided to tackle the papers in small doses and spend the majority of the daytime hours that often extended into night shifts, observing the practical and oral examinations. This, I decided would give me a better idea of what I really needed to establish, 'Are they fit to practice?' This question rightly challenges every examiner monitoring entry onto a register of professional practitioners.

It soon became apparent that although practical examinations in such a format had long since been discontinued in the West, their continuation here provided a very useful insight for the external examiner and indeed for my national counterpart with whom I worked very closely. The principal midwifery tutor endeavoured to make available everything I asked to observe. We worked together and laughed and cried together as we shared the joys of success and the tears of near disaster. I discovered that like the Asian learners to whom I had become accustomed, these African students relied much on rote learning. Unlike Western societies, in a culture where oral tradition exists, it seems that the ability to memorise tends to take priority initially over seeking understanding. Certainly the memories of the Batswana students far surpassed mine. Whilst there were distinct advantages in such an art it did not always serve them well; they could so easily become slaves to the order and sequence they had diligently learned. The skill of knowing what to omit and when to make haste escaped some students who laboriously followed an A to Z order that could not be adjusted whatever happened, especially in a final examination.

One student, who was admitting a multiparous woman with a large pendulous abdomen in advanced labour, was demonstrating how to carry out a physical examination. She was determined to demonstrate her very best. Commencing with excluding any parasites in the woman's hair, she proceeded with skill and total commitment to examine the conjunctivae, mouth and neck. When she reached the breasts and proceeded to expel some fluid, I could resist it no longer. 'What are you doing?' I asked 'Looking for colostrum' she replied knowingly, 'And what will that tell you?' I enquired, 'That she's pregnant!' she announced. 'Well' I offered 'I think we know that she's pregnant, don't we?' My Motswana colleague fortunately shared my sense of humour and never forgot the incident. 'Make it snappy!' she urged the student fearing, as I did, that the woman so obviously pregnant would give birth long before the student reached the abdomen! This emphasised to me the need to teach not only students, but some of the midwives too, the skill of knowing how to prioritise and take expedient action in urgent or emergency situations. It was to take years to work on such issues through clinical teaching sessions and training trainers in these skills.

I was to discover on a later visit that my every action was observed by my colleagues and noted down in detail. I once discovered a tutor accompanying me on a clinical venture compiling a list of the questions I asked and writing down what I said and did in the various situations. I realised that, as the old dictum goes, 'What you do speaks so loudly, I cannot hear what you say.' In this case, though, the proviso could have been added, 'Yet what you say speaks loudly enough that I need to record it in every detail.' Whichever way I looked at it, my report was going to offer much less wisdom than my example and I just hoped and prayed that the latter would be worth remembering. My decision to focus my attention in the practice area was valuable to me as an examiner, but it became a critical learning time for my colleagues too. It helped me to enter their real world in a way nothing else could have done. Midnight vigils to see women through complications of labour were not infrequent and enabled me to feel the pulse of my profession as well as experience the tears of my fellow women.

Initiating change

The halo effect experienced when first arriving in a country, receiving a warm welcome and discovering what is going well is gradually or suddenly displaced as reality sets in. Nationals often confide more in a consultant or colleague they know well, giving the opportunity to share the real problems, the deeper issues on which they really need and want a fresh mind. This is not achieved overnight and I have always found that a continuing relationship with colleagues over a period of years, albeit in short assignment periods, allows for much more meaningful interaction. My early impressions that allowed me to think 'Anything is possible here', gradually have a habit of evolving into wondering whether any change is possible. The reality usually lies somewhere in between.

My experiences of examining in Botswana taught me a lot and I would like to think that it taught my national colleagues a lot too. It is helpful to get feedback from them, but one must be realistic and know that some offences that we will inevitably have committed we may never discover. Here was a culture that showed deference to an older person and I ranked in that league. Students undertaking electives will be younger and sometimes under the supervision of cooperating university personnel. However, outside of Western society, open criticism is unlikely to be offered to a visitor, even if it is constructive. Therefore, reflective practice is an essential tool in international consultancy as in any professional practice and can be invaluable during student elective experiences too. I kept quiet for some time about my initial reaction to the hours of examinations to which the one-year midwifery students were subjected. There were other issues that concerned me, such as the necessity of learning the skills of examination question setting and the art of marking papers too. Balancing safe practice against the unacceptability of actually failing or discontinuing a student in a culture where this did not seem a viable option presented an inevitable challenge to me as an external examiner. Years of partnership with midwifery colleagues resulted eventually in curriculum reviews and lengthening of the midwifery programme to 18 months for registered nurses, a fact that even now Batswana professionals regard with pride as a 'first' in Africa. Hopefully they consider it as something they achieved themselves. As the Chinese proverb warns 'Do not fear going forward slowly; fear only to stand still'; undoubtedly introducing change takes time and patience and is always best when initiated from within. The greater the ownership of any changes, the greater the impact is likely to be.

Initiating change has been a major issue in the newborn state of South Africa. My first assignment in this country involved consideration of the health of babies from birth through the critical first year of life. Issues surrounding infant feeding focus high on the agenda in many countries; and the ever constant battle between formula milk companies and advocates of total breastfeeding was very evident in South Africa. Efforts to redress the balance were no doubt being influenced by financial issues in the business sections of the large cities of this vast land.

Examining the evidence

Entering and engaging

Those who cross international borders need to consider numerous issues. Experiencing living where clients or colleagues live, engaging with them, learning to understand their culture, and having skills in introducing change are just a few of the issues that need to be considered. There is always much to be learned. It is important for anyone entering a new environment to become familiar with the situations in which colleagues both work and live. In my personal research on the subject, one Asian respondent commented that if a consultant was serious about learning what it is like in her country, she should stay where local people stay, rather than in 'a posh hotel' (Maclean,

1998). Especially for those without prior experience of living in a low-income country, there is much to commend this view. Living in an international standard hotel ensures that foreign visitors lead a separate existence in their own protective bubble, which, although comfortable, will seriously damage their ability to identify with national colleagues and their problems. Gap year and elective students often have more opportunity to live in the real situation, although wise precautions obviously need to be taken concerning safety and health. The British Foreign and Commonwealth Office (FCO, 2012) offers current advice about particular countries and situations and visiting their website is an essential part of preparation for an overseas assignment or elective. Ultimately, in choosing accommodation, a number of matters need to be taken into consideration. Identifying with local colleagues is important as well as the personal health and safety issues, but access to a reliable source of electricity and the internet, at least for a significant portion of the time, can, in certain assignments, also be critical in getting the job done. I experienced no such problems with these in Botswana or South Africa, but in some other countries challenges can abound in this sphere.

For the consultant, forming friendships with colleagues who are clients can be viewed from differing perspectives. Decades ago, in considering the work of expert expatriates in Africa, Seers (1980) emphasised that the approach of a good colleague simulated that of a good friend> He stresses:

What is important is the style of work – that one should limit one's role to that of a friend who can point to some considerations which may have been overlooked, rather than offering solutions, especially solutions based on European models.

(Seers, 1980: 156)

Forss et al (2008), in undertaking a quality evaluation of technical assistance, stress that the influence of the personality of the consultant and of friendships formed can be overlooked. They claim that:

Friendship can be a prime factor in processes of structural and normative change.

(Forss et al, 2008: 38)

Student elective experiences offer opportunities to make new friends, but since it usually takes time to establish meaningful relationships, some university lecturers actively encourage their students to visit an area where such relationships may be initiated and continued in the future for the mutual benefit of host country and sending university. Exchange visits may subsequently be arranged and a continuing professional relationship established. It has been acknowledged that with proper planning and supervision, medical electives hold the potential to offer valuable healthcare services and opportunities to learn lessons as well as providing a strategic resource for health diplomacy (Banerjee, 2010).

Preparation for an elective period in a low or middle income country needs to start well in advance and a few texts have been prepared to assist in this process. The Christian Medical Fellowship (CMF) offers advice for students from various healthcare disciplines and useful documents can be downloaded from the internet. There is information about institutions offering electives and some such opportunities are offered to non-Christian students too who are in sympathy with the principles and aims of the organisation with which they will work (CMF, 2011).

Life after birth

During the early years of the new millennium Botswana was identified among three countries that had made significant progress in improving skilled care and reducing maternal mortality. The country's profile was presented in a handbook designed to assist programme planners and managers at all levels (Family Care International, 2002). However, between 1990 and 2010, Botswana and South Africa were among five countries in sub-Saharan Africa that experienced the greatest percentage increase in maternal mortality. Significantly this area experiences the highest HIV prevalence in the world; however maternal mortality began to decline there with the introduction of antiretroviral therapy (WHO, 2012). Whilst some efforts in Botswana to reduce maternal and child mortality have been successful, including antenatal care attendance, 'skilled attendance at delivery', prevention of mother-to-child transmission of HIV, and immunisation coverage, other areas have been deemed to need further attention. A low percentage of mothers were found to be exclusively breastfeeding (32%) and since this practice has been shown to reduce under-nutrition (Mahgoub et al, 2006) the government has needed to address this issue urgently. Concern about low utilisation of various preventive and therapeutic approaches to killer diseases stimulated the government of Botswana to launch an accelerated child survival and development strategy in 2009 (UN Development Group, 2012). Since its implementation, vitamin A supplementation has increased across the country (UNICEF Botswana, 2011). There are recommendations advocating concentration of efforts on maternal employment and economic activities that do not compromise important practices such as breastfeeding (Mahgoub et al, 2006).

South Africa has faced numerous challenges since democracy and there has been little improvement in infant mortality (UN, 2010), a major cause being gastro-intestinal infections. In 2011 only around 25% of women were reported as breastfeeding exclusively for the first six months of life, although this was the highest recorded figure since 1994. Modernisation and aggressive marketing of formula feeds in the country have been blamed for this situation (Department: Health, Republic of South Africa, 2011).

Botswana and South Africa, as well as Angola and Namibia, are home to indigenous Bushmen, but these people have too often paid a heavy price for progress when lucrative diamond mines and safari camps have taken precedence over their needs, denying them the right to water and hunting. Kalahari Bushmen in Botswana have been forcibly removed into resettlement camps and the toll on the health of these communities has been considerable (Survival International, 2012). While money-making business initiatives may contribute to a country's economy, such changes can prove costly to the indigenous peoples.

Introducing change: its theories, thrills and threats

In examining the theories and practice of change, Hogg and Terry (2000) point out that radical change will disrupt the need for identity, consistency and continuity as well as a sense of self-esteem. The cultural context in this process therefore becomes critical, especially in an environment where continuity with the past assumes great importance. In studying the Igbo people of Nigeria within a rapidly changing society, Duru (1983) questions whether a renewed awareness of the significance of traditional values accentuates continuity. She proposes therefore that observed change may in fact be superficial. She maintains that although a gradual erosion of traditional rural lifestyle influenced also by the introduction of Western technology has occurred, attitudes and beliefs acquired during the process of socialisation are likely to last a lifetime. She comments that:

> *The cultural theme of human interdependence and beneficial reciprocity has its source in the mutual interdependence of the world of humans and the world of spirits.*
>
> *(Duru, 1983: 8)*

In Botswana it has been claimed that the country has used its colonial heritage wisely in promoting democracy and economic development, with the implicit assumption that 'continuities with its indigenous state culture' were not allowed (Maundeni, 2001: 108). However, there is recognition that 'the Batswana proceeded modestly and prudently, blending the traditional and the modern in a pragmatic way (Landell-Mills, 1992: 544). Maundeni (2001: 120) recognised that the country enjoyed the rare phenomenon of an 'invited colonisation', and Botswana as a Protectorate rather than a colony had managed to protect Tswana culture. Dr David Livingstone heralded the missionary era in the region and Christian chiefs ruled the then named Bechuanaland, with missionaries acting as advisers long before the Protectorate was established in 1885. The history and political stance of Botswana may well have contributed to the difference in approach experienced in its attitude towards change, the development of the country and of its modern midwifery profession. It is salutary to consider that although trends can be identified across continents, it is erroneous to assume similarities. I recall a missionary who had worked for many years in Africa stating that whenever someone referred to the Congo in general they were thinking of one place in particular. How much more so does this apply in attempting to consider a continent. The influence and effects of colonialism are considered in more detail in *Chapter 6*.

Fiol and O'Connor (2002), accepting that radical change is likely to threaten the fundamentally held beliefs and assumptions reasoned by Huy (1999), question whether a group would ever voluntarily engage in change. They assert that external intervention is necessary to introduce radical change since the tendency of a group to protect its identity frequently inhibits this process. They explain:

If threatened by these external interventions, however, identity beliefs can become emotionally heated and resistant to the cognitively rational efforts of outsiders. At the same time, the insider group's emotional energy is essential to mobilize and sustain radical change.

(Fiol and O'Connor, 2002: 532)

They construe that a shift in identity rather than a shift from negative to positive perceptions within a group are required, and to facilitate this, external agents need to begin with a very positive view of those inside the organisation. They conclude that a relatively long period of time is necessary to implement radical and sustainable change and that there may not be any shortcuts. However, in the context of achieving the Millennium Development Goals, Pedercini and Barney (2010) suggest that, in the latter part of the 20th century, initiatives were driven by what has been described as the 'Washington Consensus' and there has been little room for developing countries to devise their own pathways of change. Such a consensus was believed to constitute a 'universal convergence' comprising 'the common core of wisdom embraced by all serious economists' (Williamson, 1993: 1334). Gore (2000: 800) reiterates the sentiment expressed above that:

Change should not be imposed from outside but requires ownership, participation, partnership and consensus building.

Change may well be at the heart of consultancy, but it is not an easy process and most certainly cannot be forced by well-intentioned expatriates. Little, cited in Goulet (1977: 64), recognised long ago that consultants in the management of change must be in the business of facilitating 'the optimal blending of change with continuity'. In considering this, the value of seeking local opinion cannot be overstressed. Chambers (1981) recognised many decades ago that the real experts are the nationals who know the problems very well and often also the best solutions. A little later, Ross (1988) described a 'collaborative approach' in providing technical assistance where 'substantive contact' between expatriate analysts and nationals is maximised. Ross insists that joint decisions by nationals and visiting consultants in considering recommendations for policy change are more likely to offer changes appropriate to the local setting. In the context of attitude, as well as advice, the words of a team director of US advisors serve as a salutary warning that can be applied far beyond American borders:

> *Every American should realise that he is here to assist and not to run. It is a common failing of the American technical personnel to attempt to control rather than advise. Everything must be done, on the contrary, to assure our counterparts that the responsibility for running the institution is theirs. Our hosts are so sensitive about this point.*
>
> *(Cited in Fry and Thurber, 1989: 95)*

In my own research I was informed of consultants being unacceptable because of personality issues, a critical spirit and imposing ideas. One respondent commented that a consultant:

> *'...tried to tell us what to do!' adding, 'You cannot transfer things directly from one country to another.'*
>
> *(Maclean, 1998: 285)*

Another remarked that consultants' behaviour is not always appropriate, stating:

> *'They do not discuss with the decision makers; they do not understand our problems. Sometimes they do not form good relationships.'*
>
> *(Maclean, 1998: 296)*

In examining change in educational practice, Gess-Newsome et al (2003) assert that in order to create and sustain fundamental change, there needs to be dissatisfaction with existing teaching and learning goals. The process also requires a belief in the effectiveness of new strategies to meet the revised educational goals in the context of how students learn. It was just such a belief which ushered in the new midwifery curriculum in Botswana. It is encouraging to note too that from Botswana comes the recognition of the importance of the role of the external examiner with respect to reviewing and updating curricula. Recommendations emanate from this study surrounding the selection, preparation and guidance of such personnel and the wisdom of establishing a register of external examiners in the region (Magobe, 2012).

How do people learn?

My experience in Botswana caused me to reflect on how people learn. Approaches inevitably vary, and different is neither necessarily better nor worse. An extensive literature review has emphasised the need for further research into educational approaches embracing the profound influence of culture on learning, and the issue of memorisation versus understanding. The researchers urge appreciative thinking in respect of approaches to learning in order to identify the epistemological and ontological dimensions involved (Tavakol and Dennick, 2010).

Numerous educational researchers towards the end of the last century concurred that approaches to learning can be regarded as either deep or superficial (Marton and Säljö, 1976; Biggs, 1987; Entwistle, 1987, 1990; Richardson, 1994). The deep approach usually represents the desire to understand the meaning, with the superficial merely adopted to reproduce the information, often for the purpose of assessment.

Kember (1996) uses the terms 'rote learning' and 'memorisation without understanding' interchangeably, although considers emerging evidence for a learning approach that encompasses the intention to both memorise and understand. In a phenomenological study of how Nepalese students learn, Dahlin and Regmi (1997) make a clear distinction between the terms and assert that memorising is not incompatible with understanding. Whereas rote learning is considered trivial, memorisation is very different. In the Nepali language rote learning has been dubbed 'throat learning' ('*kantastha garnu*' literally: to put into the throat), implying that one merely learns to say things mindlessly. Respondents explained that rote learning could be used for examination purposes, but was likely to be forgotten afterwards. Memorisation by contrast conveys a sense of keeping in mind the meaning once it has been grasped '...and this is at the same time what one understands, or develops into understanding' (Dahlin and Regmi, 1997: 477). The researchers reveal that in the Nepali context such memorisation is associated with matters of great significance such as sacred texts and mytho-historical events. Watkins and Regmi (1990) underline the significance of language itself, suggesting that learning in other than a student's first language stimulates the search for meaning. Kember (1996) concludes that there is a possibility that Asian students who perform well academically may have a greater predisposition towards combining memorising and understanding, and that their ability in this could be linguistic and/or cultural. This subject is further explored in other chapters and the theme of preferred individual learning styles is considered in *Chapter 9*.

An innovative environment and approach to learning has been explored in the Eastern Cape of South Africa. In a groundbreaking pilot study a trans-disciplinary collaborative training for doctors and midwives has been advocated to hold promise in enhancing the competence and confidence of midwives. It is expected to improve the public image of midwives and hopefully the uptake of care in a geographical area where maternal mortality remains unacceptably high. It is also anticipated that increased teamwork and mutual respect will emerge from such an educational process (James et al, 2012).

Capacity development, community divergence

If an assignment is to be fruitful, the task of the international consultant demands venturing beyond education issues or the process of change to developing local capacity and encouraging indigenous talent. 'Capacity development' has become a watchword of development assistance. This has been defined as:

> ...the process whereby people, organisations and society as a whole unleash, strengthen, create, adapt and maintain capacity over time.
> *(OECD/DAC, 2006:12).*

The extent and specific responsibilities of personnel who provide technical assistance has been considered and debated over decades, but the need to enhance methods and approaches to building capacity is increasingly emphasised. Indeed the need to recognise capacity development as 'a distinct area of development practice, within which technical cooperation should be considered one of several possible inputs' has been stressed (Land et al, 2007: 2). The short-term visitor should bear this in mind whatever his or her particular role in the developmental process. It is also essential to be mindful of the considerable differences that exist in the structure and function, attitudes and values of different societies.

In considering cross-cultural encounters in the business world, Ferraro (1998: 59) identifies nine critical dimensions of contrasting values and divergent attitudes between different communities, namely those of the USA and other cultures. These comprise: individualism, precise recognition of time, a future orientation, work and achievement, control over the natural environment, youthfulness, informality, competition, and relative equality of the sexes. These reflect some of the issues that were raised by Hofstede (1997) who, having traced the development of human societies for more than 10 000 years, proceeds to study the key differences between individualist and collectivist societies. He defines individualistic societies as those:

...in which ties between individuals are loose; everyone is expected to look after himself or herself and his or her immediate family.

(Hofstede, 1997: 261)

Whilst collectivist societies are those:

...in which people from birth onwards are integrated into strong, cohesive groups, which throughout people's lifetime continue to protect in exchange for unquestioning loyalty.

(Hofstede, 1997: 260)

Hofstede (1997) has identified several cultural dimensions that have formed the basis of numerous theories relating to national identity. While there have been challenges to this concept, particularly concerning evidence of variations within cultures of individualism and collectivism (Dutta-Bergman and Wells, 2002), it has also been acknowledged as a priority in guiding cross-cultural research, psychology and anthropology (Kim, 2005). However, one must be careful not to stereotype either nations or individuals, as Kim (2008: 359) points out:

In the dizzying interface of national, ethnic, linguistic and religious traditions, the once clear definitions of 'us and them' are being blurred.

However, from Hofstede's study of IBM employees in 50 countries and three regions of the world, some of the contrasts between these diverse societies can be well illustrated. For example, the collectivist society regards harmony as very important and so confrontation is usually unacceptable. In an individualistic society 'speaking one's mind' and 'telling the truth' are considered most desirable. It is understandable therefore that truth and lies can be perceived from totally different perspectives in different societies. Again, the concept of shame in a collectivist society portrays dishonour brought upon the community by the misdemeanour of a member of that group, whilst in an individualistic society, it is more likely to be perceived as guilt borne solely by the individual responsible. A later work of Hofstede et al (2010) incorporates six dimensions of culture that offer much food for thought for the serious cross-cultural student. The issues raised by these and other scholars can form a useful reference point and checklist for anyone seeking to explore cross-cultural differences (*Box 2.1*) and these issues are explored further in *Chapter 4* in the East Asian context.

Box 2.1. Some key areas where there are differences in perception across diverse societies

- Precision and relevance of time
- A future orientation versus significance of the past and present
- The importance of work and achievement
- Degree of control over the natural environment
- Youthfulness versus respect for age and experience
- Degrees of formality or informality
- The relevance of competition
- Degree of equality between the sexes
- Levels of equality and inequality in state and society
- Preference for structured or unstructured situations
- The concept of shame and losing face
- The importance of harmony in society
- The tendency towards self-direction and self-achievement
- The importance of conformity
- Evidence of the relative magnitude of secularism, materialism, consumerism and religion in society

Derived from: Hofstede, 1997; Ferraro, 1998; Maclean, 1998;
Kim, 2005; Hofstede et al, 2010

Cultural competence

In the realm of international exchange, the visitor needs to develop some degree of cultural competence. An old Setswana proverb states that 'the faeces of a visitor are offensive whilst those of the host are of no significance' (*Sepa legolo ke la moeng, la monggae pipitlwane*). The inference is that the mistake made by the visitor or expatriate is more serious than that of the local person (Merriweather, 1992: 77). It certainly seems that cultural offences are difficult to forgive, not only in Botswana, but wherever one is unfortunate or thoughtless enough to overstep the boundary of cultural propriety. In my own research, asking clients a direct question concerning the unacceptable characteristics of international consultants, I learned that these were numerous, but cultural offences and attitudinal problems prevailed (Maclean, 1998). An air of superiority was difficult to tolerate, and one respondent commented:

If they criticise or write reports with severe criticisms. This is like the effect which the media have; people read the bad and then ignore the good points.
(Maclean, 1998: 286)

I have learned the importance of this too in reporting back at conferences and study days. I have cringed when I have heard short-term visitors belittle their colleagues or ridicule what they have seen. It happens, but it is a considerable insult to our hosts, colleagues and clients and a poor reflection on those of us who visit and observe, often without proper insight into the reasons underlying the differences in culture and professional standards. As an old American Indian proverb goes: 'Do not judge a man until you have walked for two moons in his moccasins'.

The acquisition of cultural competence has been described as adopting 'a set of congruent behaviours, attitudes, and policies'. The aspiration is that these will fuse into a system that enables professionals to work effectively in cross-cultural circumstances (Cross et al, 1989). Intercultural or cultural competence has been recognised as an increasingly necessary skill for healthcare workers returning to practice in their own multicultural society, and nursing students who have undertaken exchange visits have been recognised as a critical resource in a profession facing cross-cultural challenges (Kokko, 2011). However, Lough (2011) maintains that, in spite of the fact that numerous international voluntary sending agencies claim that volunteering will increase intercultural competence, such learning will only occur if certain pre-conditions exist. These relate to service duration, cultural immersion, guided reflection and contact reciprocity, adding that guided reflection tends to moderate the relationship between duration and intercultural competence. This underlines the importance of reflective practice for short-term professionals as well as students; both student and consultant benefiting most if reflection can be guided by an experienced mentor either on the field or back at the home base.

Fry and Thurber (1989) long ago recognised the demand for international experts who can become 'genuine multicultural protean individuals'. They depict these desirable persons as those who are able to relate effortlessly with peasants and princes. The objective is high, but if we are mindful of that need and the inherent risk of causing offence rather than offering assistance, then surely we are less likely to transgress and more likely to transmit mutually acceptable targets. Elective and gap year students have a great opportunity to develop attitudes that will serve them well throughout their professional careers in a world that is rapidly becoming smaller and that may be described as 'a global village' (McLuhan, 1962) – a term more apt in the 21st century than when it was first coined.

Tackling the task of understanding culture is doubtless an enormous one and a lifelong process. It is however essential to attempt to make sense of the cross-cultural experiences to which we are exposed on a daily basis. In considering how occupational therapists educated in the USA make sense of their lived cross-cultural experiences, Humbert et al (2011) conclude that practitioners need to embrace and assimilate the ability to integrate layers of cultural awareness, complexity and connectedness into their practice. These were the three central themes that emerged from the study. They report that 'cultural awareness' comprises the recognition and understanding of a different culture, then comparing the insights gained with one's own culture and responding to the differences. 'Complexity' embraces the concept of cultural differences being multifaceted and dynamic as well as intricate. 'Connectedness', in this context, relates to relationship formation during cross-cultural experiences. It behoves the cross-cultural visitor, in whatever capacity, to penetrate these layers of cross-cultural behaviour and acquire a cultural competence that undoubtedly demands an enduring process of learning. Steixner (2011) maintains that intercultural competence is derived from multidimensional learning processes and cannot be acquired through merely learning the cultural do's and don'ts. She suggests that a core competency in this context comprises the ability to manage change whilst remaining in control in situations of added intercultural complexity. Such a skill lies at the heart of many cross-cultural consultancies undertaken by healthcare workers and electives embarked upon by students. It would certainly seem worth aspiring towards.

Personal reflections on practice

- Adaptation is a key survival skill – I learn or I perish!
- The basic principles of my profession may well be the same wherever I practise, but their application cross-culturally is likely to be very different. My ability to make adaptations both personally and professionally is crucial.
- What I do is noted in its every detail. If I do not wish to see it emulated – I should not do it!
- It takes time to move towards constructive change and there is always at least one right way and many wrong ways to introduce change.
- Seniority is a very important attribute in a time-honoured culture and there are no short cuts. In Batswana culture, I learned that an offending person is expected to give a chicken to an offended elder. It is

nowadays sometimes joked about among the educated, but the practice is rooted in tradition. The principle matters. There are no short cuts, but there are roads in and it is my job to find them.

Some lessons learned and shared

- Ensuring adequate drinking water, making use of recycling principles whenever possible, acquiring survival skills – these are the first essentials of cross-cultural work. If you do not manage that, you will not manage anything else.
- What you are and what you do are observed in every detail; any formal lessons taught will take second place to that.
- Before proposing change, remember that things are inevitably done for a reason, even if that reason is no longer valid. Nationals in any country are the natural experts to know the whys and wherefores of any practices and can usually advise as to how, when and whether proposed changes are likely to be considered.
- Keep capacity development in mind – local people need to manage well long after we leave, so trying to facilitate and strengthen colleagues in this respect is important. Sincere encouragement can be a valuable catalyst.
- Be aware of recognised cultural differences, but take care not to stereotype, the exceptions may surprise you.
- Aspire towards acquiring cultural competence, remember it is a lifelong learning process, and so endeavour at the least to avoid causing cultural offence.

Reflective exercises

- It has been purported that developing reflective practice involves valuing oneself as a practitioner and that: 'Thoughtfulness and purposeful communication and action reside at the heart of what matters in effective practice' (Taylor, 2010: 10). With this in mind, consider a recent experience in your own area of practice that you feel good about.
  - What criteria made it a positive experience?
  - What communication strategies did you use? Could they be described as 'purposeful'?
  - How might these strategies have been (or how were they) challenged in a cross-cultural situation?
  - What preparation might you need to make in order to transfer that experience into a different culture?

- Imagine that you were being 'shadowed' by a colleague of a different cultural background and experience during a recent day's work. Stand back from the situation and try and see yourself objectively.
  - Make notes that may have been taken by the person shadowing you and hoping to learn from you.
  - What queries might that person raise about your actions and how you handled situations?
  - How would you try to respond to such queries?
  - Are there things that you would do differently on another occasion given similar circumstances?

Resources

Some valuable resources when considering travel in low income countries include:

- Christian Medical Fellowship: http://www.cmf.org.uk/
- The British Foreign and Commonwealth Office: http://www.fco.gov.uk/en/

References

Africa.com (2012) *Botswana Facts and Figures*. Available from: Africa.com: http://www.africa.com/botswana/facts [Last accessed 03.10.2012]

Banerjee A (2010) Medical electives: A chance for international health. *Journal of the Royal Society of Medicine* **103**(1): 6–8

Biggs J (1987) *Student approaches to learning and studying*. Australian Council for Educational Research, Melbourne

Chambers R (1981) Rural poverty unperceived: Problems and remedies. *World Development* **9**: 1–19

Christian Medical Fellowship (2011) *Student electives, planning and preparation. Information for medical, nursing and midwifery, dental and therapy electives.* Christian Medical Fellowship. Available from: http://www.cmf.org.uk/ [last accessed 23.08.11]

Cross T, Bazron B, Dennis K, Isaacs M (1989) *Towards a culturally competent system of care*. Vol 1. CASSP Technical Assistance Center, Georgetown University Child Development Center, Washington, DC

Dahlin B, Regmi MP (1997) Conceptions of learning among Nepalese students. *Higher Education* **33**(4): 471–93

Department: Health, Republic of South Africa (2011) National Breastfeeding Week (1–7 August 2011) Fact Sheet. Department: Health, Republic of South Africa. Available from: http://www.unicef.org/southafrica/SAF_pressrelease_breastfeed2011facts.pdf [last accessed 19.05.2012]

Duru MS (1983) Continuity in the midst of change. Underlying Themes in Igbo Culture. *Anthropological Quarterly* **56**(1): 1–9

Dutta-Bergman MJ, Wells WD (2002) The values and lifestyles of idiocentrics and allocentrics in an individualist culture: A descriptive approach. *Journal of Consumer Psychology* **12**(3): 231–42

Entwistle N (1987) A model of the teaching–learning process. In Richardson JTE, Eysenk MW, Warren Piper D (Eds). *Student learning: Research in education and cognitive psychology* (pp. 13–28). SRHE and Open University Press, Milton Keynes

Entwistle N (1990) *Handbook of educational ideas and practices*. Routledge, London

Family Care International (2002) *Skilled care during childbirth*. Country profiles. New York

Ferraro GP (1998) *The cultural dimension of international business* (3rd Edn). Prentice Hall, Upper Saddle River, NJ

Fiol CM, O'Connor EJ (2002) When hot and cold collide in radical change processes: Lessons from community development. *Organization Science* **13**(5): 532–46

Foreign and Commonwealth Office (2012) *Travel and living abroad: Staying safe and healthy*. British Foreign and Commonwealth Office, London. Available from: http://www.fco.gov.uk/en/travel-and-living-abroad/staying-safe/ [last accessed 03.10.12]

Forss K, Vedung E, Kruse SE, Mwaiselage A, Nilsdotter A (2008) *Can evaluations be trusted? An enquiry into the quality of Sida's evaluation reports*. Sida, Stockholm, Sweden

Fry GW, Thurber CE (1989) *The international education of the development consultant: Communicating with peasants and princes*. Pergamon Press, Oxford

Gess-Newsome J, Southerland SA, Johnston A, Woodbury S (2003) Educational reform, personal practical theories, and dissatisfaction: The anatomy of change in college science teaching. *American Education Research Journal* **40**(3): 731–67

Gore C (2000) The rise and fall of the Washington consensus as a paradigm for developing countries. *World Development* **28**(5): 789–804

Goulet D (1977) *The uncertain promise: Value conflicts in technology*. Transfer, New Horizons Press, New York

Hofstede G (1997) *Cultures and organizations: Software of the mind*. McGraw-Hill, New York

Hofstede G, Hofstede GJ, Mikov M (2010) *Cultures and organizations: Software of the mind* (Revised and expanded 3rd Edn). McGraw-Hill, New York

Hogg MA, Terry DJ (2000) Social identity and self-categorization processes in organizational contexts. *Academy of Management Review* **25**(1): 121–40

Humbert TK, Burket A, Deveney R, Kennedy K (2011) Occupational therapy practitioners' perspectives regarding international cross cultural work. *Australian Occupational Therapy Journal* **58**(4): 300–9

Huy QN (1999) Emotional capability, emotional intelligence, and radical change. *Academy of Management Review* **24**(2): 325–45

Index Mundi (2012) *Country comparison > population.* Index Mundi. Available from: http://www.indexmundi.com/g/r.aspx [last accessed 28.09.2012]

James S, Mabenge M, Rala N (2012) Transdisciplinary collaborative training: A midwifery need. *African Journal of Midwifery and Women's Health* **6**(4): 167–70

Kember D (1996) The intention to both memorise and understand: Another approach to learning? *Higher Education* **31**(3): 341–54

Kim YY (2005) Inquiry in intercultural and development communication. *Journal of Communication* **55**(3): 554–77

Kim YY (2008) Intercultural personhood: Globalisation and a way of being. *International Journal of Intercultural Relations* **32**: 359–68

Kokko R (2011) Future nurses cultural competencies. What are their learning experiences during exchange and studies abroad? A systematic literature review. *Journal of Nursing Management* **19**(5): 673–82

Land T, Hauck V, Baser H (2007) *Aid effectiveness and the provision of TA personnel: Improving practice. Policy Management Brief 20.* European Centre for Development Policy Management, The Netherlands

Landell-Mills P (1992) Governance, cultural change, and empowerment. *Journal of Modern African Studies* **30**(4): 543–67

Lough BJ (2011) International volunteers' perceptions of intercultural competence. *International Journal of Intercultural Relations* **35**(4): 452–64

Maclean GD (1998) *An examination of the characteristics of short term international midwifery consultants.* Thesis submitted for the degree of Doctor of Philosophy. University of Surrey, Guildford, England

McLuhan M (1962) *The Glutenberg Galaxy, the making of typographic man.* University of Toronto Press, Canada

Magobe KD (2012) Quality assurance through the external examiner system. *African Journal of Midwifery and Women's Health* **6**(4): 177–82

Mahgoub SEO, Nnyepi M, Bandeki T (2006) Factors affecting prevalence of malnutrition among children under three years of age in Botswana. *African Journal of Food, Agriculture, Nutrition and Development* **6**(1): 1–15

Marton F, Säljö R (1976) On qualitative differences in learning. I: Outcome and process. *British Journal of Educational Psychology* **46**: 4–11

Maundeni Z (2001) State culture and development in Botswana and Zimbabwe. *Journal of Modern African Studies* **40**(1): 105–32

Merriweather AM (1992) *Medical phrasebook and dictionary* (English and Setswana). Pula Press, Gaborone, Botswana

OECD/DEC (2006) *The challenge to capacity development: Working towards good practice.* OECD, Paris

Pedercini M, Barney GO (2010) Development analysis of interventions designed to achieve Millennium Development Goals: The case of Ghana. *Socio-Economic Planning Science* **44**: 89–99

Richardson JTE (1994) Cultural specificity of approaches to studying in higher education: A literature survey. *Higher Education* **27**: 449–68

Ross LA (1988) Collaborative research for more effective foreign assistance. *World Development* **16**: 233–4

Save the Children (2012) *State of the World's mothers 2012. The 2012 Mothers' Index.* Save the Children. Available from: http://www.savethechildren.org/ [last accessed 13/07/2012]

Seers D (1980) The international context within which European experts work. In: Stone JC (Ed) *Experts in Africa, Proceedings of a Colloquium at the University of Aberdeen, African Studies Group.* Aberdeen, Scotland

South Africa Info (2012) *About South Africa.* Available from: www.southafrica.info/about/facts.htm [last accessed 04.10.2012]

Steixner M (2011) Intercultural competence: Describing a developmental process – methods and processes of intercultural development in training and coaching. *Gruppendynamik und Organisationsberatung* **42**(3): 237–51

Survival International (2012) *Survival for tribal peoples: The Bushmen of Botswana.* Available from: http://www.survivalinternational.org/tribes/bushmen [last accessed 19.05.2012]

Tavakol M, Dennick R (2010) Are Asian international medical students just rote learners? *Advances in Health Science and Education* **15**(3): 369–77

Taylor BJ (2010) *Reflective practice for healthcare professionals* (3rd Edn). OU Press, McGraw Hill, Berks

UN (2010) *Levels and trends in child mortality report 2010. Estimates developed by the UN Inter-Agency Development Group for Child Mortality Estimation.* UNICEF/WHO/World Bank/UNDESA. UNICEF, New York

UN Development Group (2012) *Botswana Accelerated Child Survival and Development Strategic Plan.* Available from: http://mdgpolicynet.undg.org/ext/MDGoodPractices/mdg4/MDG4A_Botswana_Accelerated_Child_Survival_and_Development_Strategic_Plan.pdf [last accessed 19.05.2012]

UN Development Program (2011) *International human development indicators, United Nations Development Program.* Available from: http://hdr.undp.org/en/statistics/ [Last accessed 13.02.2012]

UNICEF (2012) *State of the world's children 2012*. UNICEF, New York

UNICEF Botswana (2011) *Vitamin A supplementation improving lives of children*. UNICEF Botswana. Available from: http://www.unicef.org/botswana/7285.html [last accessed 19.05.2012]

Watkins D, Regmi MP (1990) An investigation of the approach to learning of Nepalese tertiary students. *Higher Education* **20**: 459–69

WHO (2012) *Trends in maternal mortality 1990 to 2010*. WHO, UNICEF, UNFPA and World Bank. WHO, Geneva

Williamson J (1993) Democracy and the Washington consensus. *World Development* **21**(8): 1329–36

Chapter 3

Island encounters

This time, like all times, is a very good one, if we but know what to do with it.

(Ralph Waldo Emerson)

Peoples of various ethnic origins often observe very different cultural practices, religions and languages.
A smile may have a thousand different meanings in Indonesian culture.

The fluidity of time can be interesting, but it can also cost lives

Subject strands introduced

- Grasping some language basics
- Human rights and freedom
- Regulation of practice
- Respecting indigenous experience

- Traditional medicine
- Promoting indigenous research

Practice points

- Utilising time wisely
- Listening and learning
- Noting body language

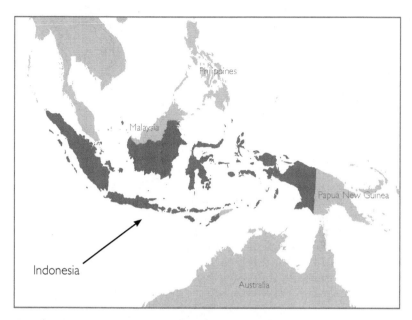

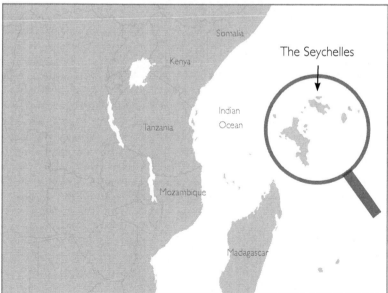

Figure 3.1. Indonesia and The Seychelles.

Indonesia and The Seychelles: Background

Indonesia

The archipelago is the largest in the world and comprises more than 17000 islands covering 1 919 440 km² that straddle the equator. Indonesia is bordered by East Timor, Malaysia and Papua New Guinea. The name of the country is probably derived from Indian or Indies Islands. The capital is Jakarta on the island of Java and originating from its colonisation the republic practices a system of civil law based on the Roman-Dutch model and influenced by customary law. Indonesia has a population of around 249 million (2012), 46% living in the urban areas. Indonesia's position on the trade routes has produced a cultural diversity with influences of Animism, Hinduism, Buddhism and Christia nity, although Islam is the prevailing religion today. There are around 300 different ethnic groups and an equivalent number of languages. Bahasa Indonesia, a form of Malay, is the official language. Dutch, emanating from the colonial past, is spoken along with some English. Natural resources include petroleum, coal and some precious and semiprecious metals. Agricultural products include rice, peanuts, cocoa, coffee and rubber. Main exports comprise oil, gas, electrical appliances, plywood and textiles.

The Seychelles

The archipelago comprises 115 islands covering 455 km² in the middle of the equatorial area of the Indian Ocean, northeast of Madagascar. The name of the country is derived from Séchelles, a finance minister to King Louis XV of France. Historically, a long battle over sovereignty between France and Britain ended in the early 19th century. The Seychelles gained independence from the UK in 1976 and practices a system of law comprising English common law, French civil law and customary law. The islands are home to around 90 000 people (estimated 2012), 50% living in the urban areas. The inner islands are the cultural and commercial centres; the capital is Victoria on the island of Mahé. The Seychellois comprise peoples of Creole, African, Chinese, Indian, French and British ethnic origin. The religion is predominantly Roman Catholic with some other Christian denominations and a small percentage of other religions. Creole is spoken by more than 90% of the population, but English is the official language. Tourism has been a major contributor to economic growth whilst the government has encouraged development of farming, fishing and small scale manufacturing. Agricultural products include vanilla, cinnamon and coconuts.

Indonesia and The Seychelles: Data	
Indonesia	**The Seychelles**
HDI: medium (124)	HDI: high (52)
MMR: 220 (2010)	I maternal death reported in 2008
Lifetime risk of maternal death: 1 in 210	Lifetime risk of maternal death: data not available
Mothers index ranking (2012)**: 59 (Tier II)	Mothers index ranking** (not ranked)
Births attended by skilled personnel: 79%	Births attended by skilled personnel: 99%
HDI = High Development Index, MMR: Maternal Mortality Ratio *Assessed according to life expectancy, educational and economic factors **Ranked globally (within 3 tiers: I = more developed, II = less developed, III = least developed) according to health, education, economic and political status of women	
Background and data sources: Indonesia Fact File, 2012; Index Mundi, 2012; Ministry of Foreign Affairs, Seychelles, 2010; Save the Children, 2012; United Nations Development Programme, 2011; UNICEF, 2012; World Atlas, 2012; World Bank, 2012; World Factbook, 2012; WHO, 2012a, 2012b; WHO/AFRO, 2009; World Population Review, 2012	

Exploring experience

Touching down, touching ground

Arriving in a new country always fills me with excitement tinged with anxiety. What opportunities and new experiences lie ahead? What challenges will confront me? What will these new people, totally unknown to me, be like? Will they welcome me or meet me with suspicion?

My first encounter with the mighty archipelago that comprises Indonesia was no exception. The assignment was to last for three months and my task was to address issues relating to midwifery education and legislation. With a considerable number of objectives to accomplish, I was eager to get started. Having got my bearings, I was ready for 'off'. However, my hosts viewed things from a different perspective. They, no doubt, needed to get to know me too and establish whether I could really help them in the challenges they faced; understandable and, indeed, appropriate. During my first two weeks in these islands I was therefore allocated to two colleagues, a doctor and a midwife, who would take me to various parts of the country providing an orientation that would offer me insights into the Indonesian situation. This, I thought, was most helpful and would give me the opportunity to observe and ask questions that would provide a good basis from which to work.

One problem remained; my guides, who greeted me warmly with their charming Indonesian smiles, spoke and understood no English. I therefore very quickly decided that my first priority was to learn some of the local language. If I was going to utilise this time to good advantage, I needed to establish a relationship that went beyond the charm of smiles and my powers of observation. I was reminded of my first experience of language learning in India. Initially delegated to work in the Mizo Hills, and facing the task of learning the language, I had been allocated a teacher in Kolkata (Calcutta) who spoke only Mizo and Bengali. This had called for both innovation and imagination – and since the only phrase book available contained such 'useful' phrases as 'This bull has a bad cough' and 'Who cut off his head?' – both innovation and imagination were needed.

To my delight, I discovered that the national language, Bahasa Indonesia, had its linguistic roots in some of the major languages I had learned in India. This was a great bonus; I just needed to be aware that although some words were the same, their meaning was different. For instance, *'masala'* related to a hot curry in the Indian context whereas in Indonesia it meant 'problem'. Since fiery spices had presented me with problems of a digestive kind, it was not too difficult for me to remember this new meaning. Of course, other words were not nearly so obliging, but to my relief I discovered that here was a language with just one tense – the present. Past and future became apparent in context, but did not present the novice with the agonies of declining verbs.

Therefore, my first fortnight in Indonesia was devoted to language learning that took on a sense of urgency as I anticipated encountering experiences that would need all the understanding I could muster. I was, of course, at a later point partnered with a national to facilitate translation during my working day, but insights into the language nevertheless stood me in good stead for the months and years ahead that I was to visit and work in this country. My national counterpart gave me three words of advice in language learning. In response to my request for her to teach me further, she advised, 'Listen! Listen! Listen!' These proved to be words of unquestionable wisdom.

Through my attempts at language learning, I gained much more than the limited linguistic skills I could possibly hope to acquire in such a short time. I gained by developing a relationship with the colleagues who were my initial guides and who really appreciated my faltering efforts, taking pride in teaching me new words at every opportunity and taking pains to ensure that I understood what I was observing.

The inexplicable and the unexpected, skirting with the sacred and the secular

Returning to Indonesia on another occasion I faced a very different challenge. This time I had the privilege of working with a British colleague and all anxieties as well as inspiration could be shared. Our first challenge was to meet us sooner than expected; Jakarta had been struck by severe flooding at the time of our arrival from the UK. Having acquired a little of the language on my previous visit, my colleague urged me to go out and see if there was a taxi we could hire. I was not optimistic. Leaving my baggage, I sallied forth to see what I could achieve. The airport was full of pessimists, some had been there all day, and there was no movement of traffic in or out of Jakarta. I was prepared to return and report our plight. However, miraculously a taxi appeared from nowhere. I told the driver our destination and he offered to take us on a route that would bypass the floods. I made a deal and we accepted the offer. We drove through the night catching glimpses of flood waters and partly submerged buildings, arriving at the hotel after a rather prolonged but successful journey. The receptionist greeted us with amazement: 'Madam, where have you come from?' My reply telling him that we had come from the airport was greeted with disbelief: 'No madam! That is impossible! No-one has come from the airport in the last 24 hours!' I was too tired to debate the issue, but the evidence stood before him.

Entering The Seychelles presented no linguistic problems. The island's history and place names provide evidence of French possession in the mid-18th century before the islands offered a whaling base for America, Britain and later Norway until the First World War. Touching down into this beautiful archipelago brought one rather closer to the mighty Indian Ocean than would seem desirable since the airport runway has been entirely reclaimed from the sea. However, no floods complicated my arrival and I proceeded to my destination unhampered by the elements, although later I was to discover the perils of tropical storms that would occasionally make the roads hazardous. The greatest challenge when it came to water was to acquire the art of jumping from one boat to another during the numerous inter-island expeditions that were to form part of the assignment in The Seychelles.

Both these archipelagos, although differing in everything from extent to emphasis, display freedom of religion enshrined in their legislation. Although a majority Muslim population, the national constitution in Indonesia proclaims the right of all to their religion. Any faith can be tolerated, what cannot be understood, the tourist guides warn, is no faith at all. The latter seems to provide an enigma in many countries across Africa and Asia where secularism has not taken hold. The predominantly Roman Catholic population of The Seychelles, as well as the minority groups, enjoy freedom of religion which is protected, greatly respected and accounts for the lack of divisiveness in society (US Department of State, 2010). However, news items from various countries backed by studies by international agencies, indicate that freedom of religion enshrined in legislation is not in reality guaranteed. Such issues did not impinge on my movements or activities in either of these archipelagos, but one cannot be sure of this in political hotspots where human rights are constantly being thrown into question.

Education for practice

My task in The Seychelles was to advise on midwifery education. Evidence-based practice had not taken root at the time and some of the issues were met with some degree of disbelief. Where tradition holds strong, as it does in many parts of the world, new ideas, even though well researched, may not be welcomed.

I recall during one of the many island hops, reviewing midwifery practice and consequent educational needs with a Seychellois colleague. She could not tolerate the thought that 'salt in the bath', a once almost sacred midwifery ritual for the puerperal woman, could not be shown to be effective in promoting perineal comfort or healing (Sleep and Grant, 1988). My colleague was convinced that regular bathing in the crystal clear waters of the Indian Ocean was effective, in her professional experience that had straddled a quarter of a century. Dogmatism has never been my style and it seemed very obvious here that the best approach was to encourage indigenous research on the topic. After all, research undertaken in Western urban society may not provide the ultimate word in guiding practice thousands of miles away in a different context, climate and culture. Imported ideas must surely always show deference in favour of indigenous evidence, providing it meets the usual expectations of credibility, reliability and validity. In Indonesia I was shown evidence of research into the safety and effectiveness of indigenous plants that are used in traditional medicine. These are popular among many communities and used to bring healing by numerous traditional practitioners as part of an entirely different and often ancient system of medicine.

My initial task in Indonesia involved helping with the selection of suitable candidates to undertake a programme in the UK to enhance the education of midwifery teachers (*guru bidan*). There were several challenges, the first related to the fact that many of those teaching midwifery did not hold a midwifery qualification themselves. The other issue was with regard to the value of rooting studies in the country of practice rather than in an overseas environment, which at best will only offer some solutions. The Ministry ultimately agreed that Module One of the programme, specifically designed for the teachers of midwifery, would be carried out in Jakarta. My hopes to implement the final module in-country were never realised, but sometimes one has to settle for what is possible, and funding agreements between governments is but one factor that may make the ideal from the professional perspective impossible to achieve in practical terms.

We faced other educational challenges in introducing mature women to a totally different approach to education. Initially I considered that there was a language problem that we needed to address. 'I think we need to teach them some more English!' I confided in my colleague early in the programme.

With due reflection she replied: 'I think we need to teach them how to think!' Her observations were astute. The students' linguistic abilities advanced more rapidly than their ability to approach learning from a very different perspective. Thinking, in this educational context, was tinged with an unfamiliar flavour; there were many aspects that we needed to explore if we were going to understand and work with our oriental colleagues. As in Africa, rote learning or memorisation was the norm and here the academic style of challenging information and questioning facts was almost unthinkable. I felt it necessary at one point to establish that professional textbooks and articles should be questioned. Facts indeed become questionable in the light of new discovery and emerging evidence. It was a hard truth to swallow and I am not sure that we managed to convince our most respectful students in those early days that we welcomed academic debate.

Regulating practice, realigning concepts

The second half of my initial Indonesian assignment related to advising on legislation to regulate midwifery practice, and presented even more challenges. An American consultant on another assignment had greeted the information with delight when enquiring what I was doing. 'Gee! You're just like Moses!', she had announced, leaving me with a somewhat thankful feeling that at least what I would prepare would never be written on tablets of stone. Indeed, I questioned many times during those early months whether anything would ever be written on paper, leave alone in stone.

From my experience of Statutory Body work in the UK, I was very aware that legislating for any one profession could not be considered in isolation. I therefore set out to establish a working group comprising relevant medical specialists as well as a pharmacist and the indispensable lawyer. My first difficulty related to the fact that neither of the two available lawyers could work in English and my Bahasa Indonesia most certainly could not rise to the Statute Book. Progress was slow and I never did manage to get a full working group together whilst I was in the country. When the end of my assignment was looming I felt it appropriate to leave the team with guidelines and options that they could hopefully work with, pending my next visit. Quite how things eventually progressed I shall never know, but the required documents seemed to emerge eventually, maybe because of my help, but maybe also in spite of my limitations. In my experience, plans to return to a country in the future offer the opportunity to leave some tasks unfinished. Providing lifelines in the form of written guidance, continued support via the internet and the willingness to return assists in getting the job done. Undoubtedly in any first assignment, establishing a mutually trusting relationship is the paramount task, because without that there can be no progress.

Subsequent years found me returning to Indonesia many times, sometimes alone, sometimes with one or two colleagues. We evaluated the various midwifery programmes and a well-established relationship with local colleagues made the task much easier, especially on the occasions when reports had to highlight many areas that needed addressing. It was obvious that my colleagues were keen to improve the quality of education and provide a better maternity service for their women. They welcomed new ideas and sought ways of addressing what they knew were shortcomings. Government policy to train one midwife for each village had proved difficult to achieve in the early years. Obtaining sufficient clinical experience frequently defied realisation given the large numbers of medical and midwifery students who were competing for such opportunities. Along with our national counterparts, we needed to look at ways of making available that experience which could lead to the acquisition of essential hands-on skills. Not an easy task, but ways forward needed to be found. Had I not known and cared so deeply for these people it would not only have been far more problematic but also, without establishing that essential working relationship marked by mutual respect, it is possible that recommendations would never have been implemented. Consultancy reports tend to have a variable 'shelf life' and if they are shelved for any length of time the consultant risks being a costly investment without being effective.

While there are no quick and easy solutions, the serious cross-cultural visitor, whether student or professional, needs to adopt a process of continued learning. Each concept learned or realigned can contribute to this. Colloquialisms too can reveal relevant concepts in a culture and are worth noting. In Indonesia for example, I learned the idiomatic term 'rubber time' in connection with delays and missed appointments. In a city like Jakarta where traffic jams could literally hold up anyone for hours, I was informed that time is like rubber – you have to be flexible! Similarly, I learned the local word '*belum*'. This could be translated as 'later', and could indicate soon, next week, next year or any time – but not now. Functioning within a language that only uses a present tense somehow fitted the picture. Going with the flow in Asia takes the visitor in a totally different and often unexpected direction. The concept of time and the different cultural orientations to it are explored in the next chapter.

Examining the evidence

A learning experience

John F Kennedy is credited with the words:

> *He that travelleth into a country before he hath some entrance into the language goeth to school and not to travel.*

Language learning is a challenge for any consultant or visiting student on a short-term placement, and in most cases time alone does not permit it. For this reason, universities most usually arrange electives in countries where English is widely spoken or else ensure that the student is fluent in the language most widely used in education and in professional communications. However, the willingness to learn what one can in the local vernacular will often commend the visitor to the host. Concerning the acceptability of consultants, in my own research one Indonesian respondent commented:

If they learn the language, this shows great interest, they are serious in wanting to solve the problem. We trust them.

(Maclean, 1998: 308)

Whilst fluency is not a viable option during the usual timeframe afforded for consultancy or elective assignment, learning words of greeting and 'thank you' can be very useful and could scarcely be beyond the most inept linguist. Terms enquiring, 'How are you?', would seem valuable to the healthcare professional, but the replies will obviously call for careful interpretation if one is providing care or advising on it. The expatriate visitor also needs to appreciate that the words do not necessarily convey accurate meaning. The standard answer to the question, 'How are you?', in Indonesia was inevitably 'Fine!' This was stated whatever the circumstances and was usually accompanied by a smile which formed part of the traditional greeting. I learned that in order to establish the true situation one needed to probe more deeply and ask other questions. I also learned that a smile may be nothing to do with the feelings of the person behind it, since it may be used to convey goodwill, smooth over conflicts or to bridge gaps in language and culture, thus the visitor is urged not to be deceived (Barker, 1990). Other body language is worth noting in order to avoid offence since aggressive postures which include pointing at someone, standing akimbo or with folded arms are not acceptable. The student or professional aspiring to work in Indonesia would be wise to note these points that are identified in many tourist guides and to look out for them in other countries too. However, moving into a new environment has been identified as an important life event (Kim, 2001) and it has been acknowledged that exposure to a new culture provides opportunities for students to improve cross-cultural communication skills (Brown, 2009), always remembering that communication goes beyond words.

A question of freedom

In considering human rights and religious freedom the visitor needs to be aware of many issues that can change situations overnight. It is helpful to examine some of the historical as well as the contemporary issues that relate to this aspect of cross-cultural experience. Marshall (1950), in his classic work, proposes an evolving threefold typology of human citizenship comprising civil rights, political rights and social rights. In tracing development in Britain he perceives citizenship establishing a relationship with capitalism through conflict and collusion. Marshall describes civil rights developing during the 18th century and coinciding with the establishment of the judiciary; political rights developing during the 19th century in line with parliamentary institutions of governance; and social rights during the 20th century as the welfare state and educational system were established. Roy (2005) points out that this process did not occur over the same timescale in other parts of the world, indeed colonisation of many countries interfered with civil rights and these issues only began to be addressed in the 20th century with the withdrawal of colonial rule. Roy, perceiving the situation from an Indian perspective, emphasises the inequalities that exist in societies disadvantaged by exploitive systems whether these relate, for example, to class, caste, race or gender, and the inability of those persons 'to participate in the community of citizenship in which they have legal membership' (Roy, 2005: 16).

Waldron (1998) describes 'participation' as the 'right of rights' in depicting the basic right of people to influence the decisions that will affect their lives. In considering the Indonesian situation and acknowledging the different kinds of rights cited above, Halabi (2009) urges vigilance in maintaining a unified perspective on human rights:

> *...resisting the persistent tendency to separate and prioritise civil and political rights over economic, cultural and social rights.*

He further maintains that

> *Political participation alone is no panacea for improving other rights such as the highest attainable standard of health.*
>
> *(Halabi, 2009: 54)*

These concepts are summarised in *Figure 3.2*.

Arat (2003) argues that liberalists do not advocate the inclusion of social and economic rights as human rights at all, since rights can be perceived as either negative or positive. Civil and political rights are viewed as negative since they relate to what governments are forbidden to do, including torture, making arbitrary arrests and preventing meetings or freedom of speech. Conversely, social and economic rights relate to what governments are required to do and are considered positive as they relate to the quality of life and include the provision of essentials such as food, shelter, medical care

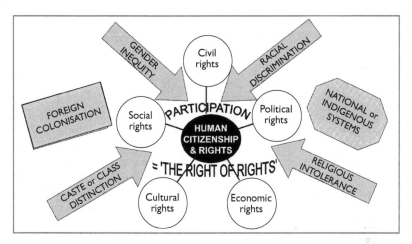

Figure 3.2. Some basic human rights of citizenship and factors associated with exploitive systems that mitigate against 'the right of rights'. Derived and developed from concepts stated by Marshall, 1950; Waldron, 1998; Roy, 2005; and Halabi, 2009.

and preventing unemployment. Arat maintains that socioeconomic rights are often regarded as group rights since they can only be maintained at the expense of individual civil-political rights. This issue has been explored more recently in the East Asian context (UNESCO, 2004) and is further examined from an ethical perspective in *Chapter 4*.

Human rights have been clearly linked to the quality of healthcare provision in the context of the Millennium Development Goals (MDGs) (Action for Global Health, 2009) and a rights-based approach has been advocated in development work. This identifies rights holders and their entitlements and corresponding duty bearers and their obligations (UN, 2006). The concept of rights-based approaches is explored further in *Chapter 8*.

Establishing ethnic evidence

Evidence-based practice has become the norm in healthcare in many industrialised countries in recent decades. This is apparent from the substantial investment in infrastructure to increase the likelihood that the healthcare provided is based on the best existing evidence, and such endeavours can be observed for example in the UK, USA and Australia (Rycroft-Malone et al, 2004). This is also evident in Western-style curricula and the plethora of publications that currently exists. In respect of evidence-based medicine, Sackett et al (1996) maintain that this relates to individual clinical expertise being integrated with the best available clinical evidence derived from systematic research. They define 'individual clinical expertise' as:

...the proficiency and judgement that individual clinicians acquire through clinical experience and clinical practice'.

(Sackett et al, 1996: 71)

In considering the etymology of the word 'evidence', Upshur (2001) maintains that this is rooted in the concept of experience and relates to what is obvious and manifest. The wisdom of relying too much on evidence has been challenged and the art of reflection advocated as an initial approach to care with the utilisation of research afterwards in order to justify the approach (Rolfe, 1999). Rycroft-Malone et al (2004) emphasise the importance of four types of evidence in the delivery of effective nursing care; these comprise research, clinical experience, patient experience and information in the local context. The Seychellois solution to perineal healing complied with the latter three criteria and, in line with Rolfe's proposal, I had considered it expedient to prompt the first, in the form of indigenous research.

The use of evidence to guide practice has traditionally been met with attitudes among experienced staff varying from suspicion to rejection. Undoubtedly, research needs to be carefully evaluated if it is to promote a change in professional practice. Barriers to using evidence-based midwifery care in one area of England have been related to several shortages, namely of time and support, as well as a lack of knowledge and confidence (McSherry et al, 2006). Clearly these barriers have to be overcome in any country; and where resources in education and practice are severely limited, the barriers become even more prohibitive. My experience in The Seychelles alerted me to recognise such barriers but also to give credit for the other criteria identified by Rycroft-Malone et al (2004) and cited above, especially when imported evidence is viewed with suspicion and may indeed not be transferable into a totally different environment. Research evidence may not be clear cut. Morley (2011), in considering the conflicting evidence relating to the administration of cholesterol-reducing drugs in the elderly, cites Aristotle who claimed that the highest level of wisdom is that known as 'phronesis'. This concept, he explains, relates to the ability to discern the correct action when there is a dearth of scientific evidence to facilitate discovery of the absolute truth. Such wisdom may have been the inspiration for my Seychellois colleague's approach in postnatal care and until evidence dictated otherwise, in the absence of any contraindicating factor, I was prepared to acknowledge the existing local wisdom on the topic. Maybe a healthy cocktail of phronesis and reflection could help to promote safe practice until such a time as research evidence substantiates or refutes it.

Figure 3.3.The 'SOBS' and 'SODS' of an international consultant. Derived from Maclean (1998).

Early on in my time consulting in Indonesia, my experience outweighed any accessible evidence on many of the topics in question. Interviewing a medical colleague at the Ministry about acceptable approaches of consultants, she urged me to provide a number of options on the way forward adding:

> *'You need to explain clearly: If you do this...this may happen', justifying her comment by stating, 'Because we do not necessarily know the details and implications of our decisions.'*

> *(Maclean 1998: 334)*

I learned many sobering facts from listening to the wise words of my colleagues. There were clearly areas that could cause offence; sometimes in word, sometimes in deed, but sometimes merely by the manner of being (see *Figure 3.3*).

Biodiversity and its application in traditional medicine

Both these archipelagos have a considerable biodiversity and uniqueness in flora and fauna (Fauna and Flora International, 2012; Ministry of the

Environment and Energy, 2012). Records from the early navigators to The Seychelles reveal that 80 out of the 2000 tropical and equatorial plants listed in the 18th century were unique to these islands (Pavard, 1992). The government has a long history of conservation and management initiatives dating back to the 1770s and maintained to this day (Ministry of the Environment and Energy, 2012).

For centuries, plants have been used to treat disease (Schulz et al, 2001). There is evidence that plants native to Japan were classified in a pharmacopoeia in the 9th century (Saito, 2000) whilst the Ayurveda medical system, primarily practised in India, has incorporated the use of plants for the past 3000 years (Encyclopaedia Britannica, 2012). It has been claimed that Ayurvedic medicine represents a unique holistic approach, which can in no way be equated merely to herbal medicine (WHO, 2004). Vandebroek et al (2004) assert that traditional remedies play an important part in the primary healthcare of indigenous communities in Bolivia and the Amazon; this is because of their importance in the Bolivian Andean cultural context and the lack of healthcare facilities in the Amazon region. They conclude that:

> ...not only the use but also knowledge about medicinal plants is influenced by physical isolation of communities and use of pharmaceuticals.
>
> *(Vandebroek et al, 2004: 249)*

A desire to recapture the virtues of the traditional systems of medicine has led to an increased interest in alternative approaches and herbal medicine across the world, notably in Europe and North America (Tyler, 2000). Today, the World Health Organization (WHO) acknowledges the importance of the use of traditional medicines, recognising that they are used by 70–80% of the world's population and that the associated revenue runs into billions of dollars. WHO notes that new antimalarial drugs were developed from a plant that has been used in China for almost 2000 years. However, WHO warns that there are numerous challenges. These comprise the reality of the international diversity of herbal remedies and a lack or limitation of national policies and regulations that test their safety, effectiveness and quality in most countries. WHO is committed to supporting the integration of such medical systems into national health strategies but strongly emphasises issues relating to their safety (WHO, 2008).

Since traditional herbal medicines, typically derived from naturally occurring plants, may be accompanied by minimal or no processing, and given that they are used as part of local healing practices, they are gaining significant attention globally in the 21st century (Cravotto et al, 2010; Oloyede, 2010). These issues assume relevance to academic communities in considering the merits or menace of many traditional remedies and Etkin and Elisabetsky (2005) claim that, by definition, ethnopharmacology lies at the intersection of three disciplines, namely the medical, natural and social sciences. However, Reyes-García (2010) embraces the total concept of such approaches to healing and emphasises that:

> *...traditional medical systems are holistic in nature and often consider illness, healing, and human physiology as a series of interrelationships among nature, spirits, society, and the individual.*
>
> *(Reyes-García, 2010: 7)*

However, since the original holders of indigenous knowledge may be least able to benefit from it in view of a lack of availability, Reyes-García highlights a moral obligation in claiming that:

> *Ethnopharmacologists can be instrumental in working with healthcare providers in the developing world for practical implementation of ethnopharmacological research results.*
>
> *(Reyes-García, 2010: 10)*

But it is issues of safety that overwhelmingly confront the overseas visitor in this context and I have known national colleagues to be concerned about safe dosages of herbal remedies and also about their surreptitious administration by relatives to women during labour. The latter is sometimes the reason given for prohibiting visitors to the labour wards since preparations with uterotonic properties can prove fatal where a well-meaning family decides to hasten the end of a lengthy labour using traditional remedies (Maimbolwa et al, 2001).

Regulation

Professional regulatory mechanisms are promoted in order to protect the public by ensuring that health professionals practice safely and competently to provide a high standard of care. The need to regulate pharmaceutical products has been discussed above in the context of natural remedies.

Alongside the regulation of physicians and provision of specialist obstetric training, the regulation of midwifery education and practice has historically been linked to progress in maternity care (Högberg, 2004). In the light of global efforts to reduce maternal mortality through the use of skilled attendance during childbirth, this matter becomes ever more relevant (De Brouwere, 2007). In this context the International Confederation of Midwives

(ICM) offers a professional framework comprising three key components that contribute to skilled midwifery care, namely global standards for midwifery education, essential competencies for basic midwifery practice and global standards for midwifery regulation. The aim of the latter is to assist midwives to work autonomously within their scope of practice (ICM, 2011). However, the regulation of midwifery has not experienced an easy path and in the USA, Butter and Kay concluded back in 1988 that states without legislation to control midwifery may actually provide better opportunities for midwifery practice than those with so-called 'enabling laws'. Nevertheless, historically, the mortality rate has been reduced in Europe as a result of cooperation between doctors and midwives who were highly competent and available locally (De Brouwere et al, 1998).

A dilemma presents in many countries where no enabling legislation exists and maternal mortality remains high. This can result in midwives and nurses in the absence of doctors having to perform some functions that are not catered for in legislation and regulation and where no supervision is available either. This may include more advanced procedures and can include the prescribing and dispensing of lifesaving drugs (Miles et al, 2006). The World Health Organization states that:

Whether the need is to develop new legislation, or amend legislation that presently exists, it is a fundamental fact that appropriate legislation is part of the essential foundation for the effective development of health services.

(WHO, 2011: 7)

Existing resources from ICM and WHO now make a consultant's task much easier if called upon to advise on the regulation of midwifery and other professional healthcare education and practice. Information relating to accessing these resources is given below.

Personal reflections on practice

- Time is only wasted if I choose to waste it. Learning the art of utilising waiting time is a valuable skill.
- Time devoted to language learning when I could do nothing else teaches more than just the language and helps to establish relationships which may prove worthwhile in the weeks and years ahead.
- My task is always set within a context of culture, religion and tradition that is likely to be very different from my own. It is helpful whenever I can, to find similarities and initially attempt to seize these rather than the differences.

- Differences in beliefs have to be acknowledged, but it is essential to show respect with the same sincerity as I would wish to be shown.
- Where a different set of rights exists within a society this can conflict with my own ethical stance. It is useful to remember that the MDGs promote rights-based approaches, and this may be a condition of the donor that I can utilise to the advantage of the disadvantaged in the context of my task and in making recommendations.

Some lessons learned and shared

- Utilise time wisely, even that which could quite easily be wasted needs to be harnessed into useful activity whatever the situation.
- Attempt to learn some basic words in the local language. A greeting and word of thanks are not beyond most. Write words down phonetically as they are heard and check them with a local speaker. Correct spelling is not helpful for learning pronunciation when the language, even using roman script, does not have the same sounds as English. Efforts at language are inevitably appreciated and can indicate the visitor's attempts to help and to relate to his or her national colleagues.
- Learn the body language of the country and be careful not to offend. Using the left hand which is perceived as unclean in some countries (including Indonesia and India), pointing the feet towards someone, and adopting aggressive postures can undo any good relationship that has been established. If in doubt don't. Ask a colleague if you are interpreting these things correctly.
- 'Listen! Listen! Listen!' not only to the language, but to what your colleagues are trying to tell you. Sometimes the messages are subtle and would not be expressed overtly (as in some Western cultures) especially if the message might be perceived as disrespectful. 'No' does not always mean 'no' in some Asian cultures when it could cause offence. Use every sense in listening to the most important messages being communicated to you – use all your senses in raising your level of awareness.

Reflective exercises

- Observe someone (or several persons) for a few hours without them being aware of your objective. Note the body language they use. From your understanding of such communication in other countries, which postures or actions might offend in a different culture? Reflect on how else the messages or attitudes could have been communicated, then set aside a few hours to note your own body language and modify it so that it would not offend in a culture with very different sensitivities from those to which you are accustomed.

- Phronesis, as identified by Aristotle, relates to the wisdom of discerning the correct action when there is a dearth of scientific evidence to facilitate discovery of the absolute truth. Keep this in mind during your next working day. When did you or another professional practitioner or supervisor need this form of wisdom? What was the outcome? What did you learn from the experience?

Resources

Some valuable resources when considering education and regulation of midwifery practice include:

- International Confederation of Midwives Global Standards for Midwifery Education and Regulation: http://www.internationalmidwives.org/Policyandpractice/ ICMGlobalStandardsCompetenciesandTools/tabid/911/Default.aspx
- World Health Organization Strengthening Midwifery Toolkit: http://www.who.int/maternal_child_adolescent/documents/ strenthening_midwifery_toolkit/en/index.html

References

Action for Global Health (2009) *Right to Health and the Health MDGs. Position Paper. Action for Global Health.* http://www.actionforglobalhealth.eu/uploads/media/Right_to_Health_ position_paper_AFGH_03.pdf [last accessed 21.01.12]

Arat ZF (2003) *Democracy and Human Rights in Developing Countries.* iUniverse Inc Lincoln NE 68512.

Barker J (1990) *Practical Indonesian – a communication guide.* 7th edition, Apa Productions Hak Pengarang Dilundungi, Undang Undang

Brown L (2009) The Transformative Power of the International Sojourn: An ethnographic study of the international student experience. *Annals of Tourism Research* **36**(3): 502–21

Butter IH, Kay BJ (1988) State Laws and the practice of lay midwifery. *American Journal of Public Health* **78**(9): 1161–69

Cravotto G, Boffa L, Genzini L et al (2010) Phytotherapeutics: an evaluation of 1000 plants *Journal of Clinical Pharmacology and Therapeutics* **35**: 11–48

De Brouwere V, Tonglet R, Van Lerberghe W (1998) Strategies for reducing maternal mortality in developing countries: what can we learn from the history of the industrialized West? *Tropical Medicine and International Health* **3**: 771–82

De Brouwere V (2007) The comparative study of maternal mortality over time. The role of the professionalisation of childbirth. *Social History of Medicine* **20**(3): 541–62

Encyclopaedia Britannica (2012) *Ayurveda*: Encyclopaedia Britannica on line. Available from: http://www.britannica.com/EBchecked/topic/46631/Ayurveda [last accessed 18.06.2012]

Etkin NL, Elisabetsky E (2005) Seeking a transdisciplinary and culturally germane science: The future of ethnopharmacology. *Journal of Ethnopharmacology* **100**: 23–6

Flora and Fauna International (2012) *Indonesia*. Available from: http://www.fauna-flora.org/ explore/indonesia/ [last accessed 18.06.2012]

Halabi SF (2009) Participation and the right to health: Lessons from Indonesia. *Health and Human Rights* **11**(1): 49–59

Högberg U (2004) The decline of maternal mortality in Sweden. The role of the community midwife. *American Journal of Public Health* **94**(8): 1312–20

Indonesia Fact File (2012) *The Business Travel Report*. Available from: http://www.thebtr. com/pages/countryfactfiles/indonesiafactfile.htm [last accessed 12.05.2012]

Index Mundi (2012) *Country comparison > population*. Available from: http://www. indexmundi.com/g/r.aspx [last accessed 28.09.2012]

International Confederation of Midwives (2011) *Global standards for midwifery regulation*. ICM. Available from: http://www.internationalmidwives.org/Policyandpractice/ ICMGlobalStandardsCompetenciesandTools/tabid/911/Default.aspx [last accessed 21.01.12]

Kim YY (2001) *Becoming intercultural: An integrative theory of communication and cross-cultural adaptation.* Sage, Thousand Oaks, CA

Maclean GD (1998) *An examination of the characteristics of short-term international midwifery consultants.* PhD Thesis, University of Surrey, Guildford

McSherry R, Artley A, Holloran J (2006) Research awareness: an important factor for evidence-based practice? *Worldviews on Evidence-Based Nursing* **3**(3): 103–15

Maimbolwa MC, Sikazwe N, Yamba B et al (2001) Views on involving a social supportperson during labour in Zambian maternities. *Journal of Midwifery and Women's Health* **46**(4): 226–34

Marshall TH (1950) *Citizenship and social class.* (Reissued with foreword by Butterworth T January 1987). Pluto Press, London

Miles K, Seitio O, McGilvray M (2006) Nurse prescribing in low-resource settings: professional considerations. *International Nursing Review* **53**(4): 290–6

Ministry of the Environment and Energy (2012) *Seychelles biodiversity, environment*. Ministry of the Environment and Energy, Republic of Seychelles. Available from: http://www.env. gov.sc/index.php/homepage/biodiversity [last accessed 18.06.2012]

Ministry of Foreign Affairs, Seychelles (2010) *Seychelles Millennium Development Goals: Status report 2010.* Ministry of Foreign Affairs, Seychelles

Ministry of Foreign Affairs, Seychelles (2012) *General information*. Ministry of Foreign Affairs, Republic of Seychelles. Available from: http://www.mfa.gov.sc/content. php?content_id=16 [Last accessed 18.06.2012]

Morley JE (2011) The cholesterol conundrum. *Journal of the American Geriatric Society* **59** (10): 1955–6

Oloyede O (2010) Epistemological issues in the making of an African medicine: Sutherlandia (Lessertia Frutescens). *African Sociology Review* **14**(12): 74–88

Pavard C (1992) *The Seychelles archipelago*. Richer/Hoa-Qui Editions, Paris

Reyes-García V (2010) The relevance of traditional knowledge systems for ethnopharmacological research: theoretical and methodological contributions. *Journal of Ethnobiology and Ethnomedicine*. doi:10.1186/1746-4269-6-32: http://www. ethnobiomed.com/content/6/1/32 [last accessed 12.10.2012]

Rolfe G (1999) Insufficient evidence: the problems of evidence-based nursing. *Nurse Education Today* **19**(6): 433–42

Roy A (2005) *Gendered citizenship - historical and conceptual explorations*. Orient Longman, Hyderabad

Rycroft-Malone J, Seers K, Titchen A, Harvey G, Kitson A, McCormack B (2004) What counts as evidence in evidence based practice? Nursing and Health Care Management and Policy. *Journal of Advanced Nursing* **47**(1): 81–90

Sackett DL, Rosenburg WMC, Muir Gray JA, Haynes RB, Richardson WS (1996) Evidence based medicine: what it is and what it isn't. *British Medical Journal* **312**(7023): 71–2

Saito H (2000) Regulation of herbal medicines in Japan. *Regulatory Pharmacology* **41**: 515–9

Save the Children (2012) *State of the World's mothers 2012, The 2012 Mothers' Index*. Save the Children. Available from: http://www.savethechildren.org/ [last accessed 13/07/2012]

Schulz V, Hänsel R, Tyler VE (2001) *Rational phytotherapy. A physician's guide to herbal medicine* (4th edn). Springer-Verlag, Berlin

Sleep JM, Grant A (1988) Routine addition of salt or savlon bath concentrate during bathing in the immediate post-partum period – a randomised controlled trial. *Nursing Times* **84**(21): 55–7

Tyler VE (2000) Herbal medicine: From the past to the future. *Public Health Nutrition* **3**: 447–52

UN (2006) *Frequently asked questions on a human rights-based approach to development cooperation*. United Nations, New York and Geneva. Available from: http://www.ohchr. org/Documents/Publications/FAQen.pdf [Last accessed 26.01.12]

UN Development Programme (2011) *International Human Development Indicators*. United Nations Development Programme. Available from: http://hdr.undp.org/en/statistics/ [Last accessed 13.02.2012]

UNESCO (2004) *Promoting human security: Ethical, normative and educational frameworks in East Asia*. Korean National Commission for UNESCO, Seoul, Republic of Korea

UNICEF (2012) *State of the World's children 2012*. UNICEF, New York

Upshur REG (2001) The status of qualitative research as evidence In Morse JM, Swanson JM, Kuzel AJ (eds) *The nature of qualitative evidence* (pp. 5–26). Sage, Thousand Oaks, CA

US Department of State (2010) *2010 Report on International Religious Freedom, Seychelles, 17 November 2010*. Available from: http://www.unhcr.org/refworld/docid/4cf2d06b82. html [last accessed 9 January 2012]

Vandebroek I, Caelwaert J-B, Stijn DJ et al (2004) Use of medicinal plants and pharmaceuticals by indigenous communities in the Bolivian Andes and Amazon. *Bulletin of the WHO* **82**(4): 243–50

Waldron J (1998) Participation: the right of rights. *Proceedings of the Aristotelian Society* **98**: 307–37

WHO (2004) *Traditional medicine in the South East Asia region:* Report of the regional working group meeting, New Delhi, India 16-17 August, WHO Project No: IND EDM 050. WHO (SEARO), New Delhi

WHO (2008) *Traditional medicine. Fact Sheet No: 134*. WHO. Available from: http://www. who.int/mediacentre/factsheets/fs134/en/ [Last accessed 18.06.2012]

WHO (2011) *Strengthening midwifery toolkit module 2: Legislation and regulation of midwifery - Making safe motherhood possible*. WHO, Geneva

WHO (2012a) *Global health data repository*. WHO. Available from: http://apps.who.int/ ghodata/?theme=country [last accessed 06.09.2012]

WHO (2012b) *Trends in maternal mortality 1990 to 2010*. WHO, UNICEF, UNFPA and World Bank. WHO, Geneva

WHO/AFRO (2009) *WHO Country Cooperation Strategy 2008–2013 Seychelles*. WHO Regional Office for Africa, Brazzaville

World Atlas (2012) *Countries of the World*. Available from: http://www.worldatlas.com/aatlas/ populations/ctypopls.htm [last accessed 03.07.2012]

World Bank (2012) *World development indicators*. Available from: http://data.worldbank.org/ country/indonesia [last accessed 02.07.2012]

World Factbook (2012) *Seychelles*. CIA. Available from: https://www.cia.gov/library/ publications/the-world-factbook/geos/se.html [Last accessed 12.06.2012]

World Population Review (2012) *Indonesia*. Available from: http://worldpopulationreview. com/population-of-indonesia-2012/ [last accessed 12.06.2012]

Chapter 4

Eastern enigmas (of orchids, ethics and automatons)

Enthusiasm is the mother of effort, and without it nothing great was ever achieved.

(Ralph Waldo Emerson)

Time is perceived very differently depending on its cultural context

Where extreme poverty contributes to mortality and morbidity, resourcefulness and commitment break through the tears

Subject strands introduced

- Ethics in cross-cultural contexts
- Differing educational approaches
- Work ethic
- Filial piety

- Concepts of time
- Appreciating cultural diversities
- Culture shock

Practice points

- Adaptation
- Expectation
- Cultural norms

- Personal preparation

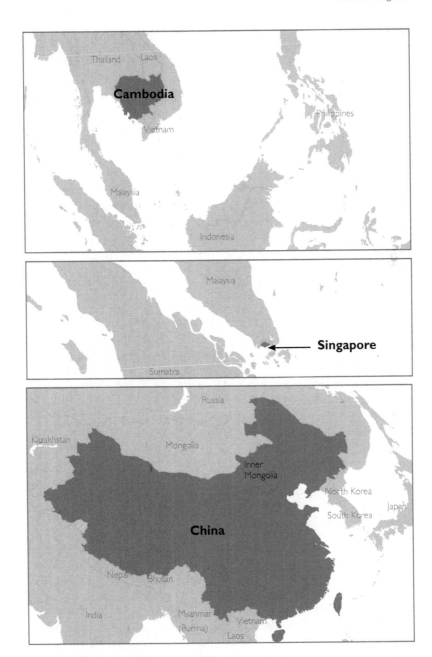

Figure 4.1. Cambodia, Singapore and China.

Cambodia, Singapore and China: Background

Cambodia

Cambodia is situated on the Indochinese peninsula, bordered by Laos, Thailand and Vietnam. The name is thought to derive from the Sanskrit 'Land of the Kambojas' inferring the sense of 'enjoyers of beautiful things'. Cambodia stretches for 181 035 km²; the capital city is Phnom Penh. The country obtained independence from France in 1953. It is a constitutional monarchy headed by a democratically elected Prime Minister. The legal system is influenced by French law, royal decree and customary law with remnants of communist theory. It is home to around 15 million people (estimated 2012), 19% living in the urban areas. Ninety five per cent of Cambodians follow Theravada Buddhism. The main language is Khmer and some French, Vietnamese, Chinese and English are also spoken. Cambodia's main waterway is the Mekong River and 66% of the country is comprised of forests and woodland, its chief agricultural products being rice, rubber, wood and corn. Other natural resources include gem stones, timber, manganese and phosphates.

Singapore

Singapore is an island territory lying between Malaysia and Indonesia. The Malay name 'Singapura' is derived from the Sanskrit meaning 'Lion City' and covers a land area of 637.5 km². It is a parliamentary republic that was founded as a British trading colony in 1819, joined with Malaysia in 1963 and became independent in 1965. Singapore uses a legal system based on English common law. The population of Singapore numbers around 5 million (estimated 2012), 100% living in this entirely urbanised state. Chinese constitute more than 75% of the population, Malay and Indian being the largest of the minority groups. Major religions include Buddhism and Islam with some Christian as well as Indian and other Chinese religions. The official languages are Chinese, Malay, Tamil and English. It is a focal point for SE Asian sea routes and its natural resources include deep sea ports and fish. There is a successful free market economy with electronics and chemicals being major exports.

Inner Mongolia, China

Inner Mongolia is an autonomous region comprising about 12% of China and is bordered internationally by Mongolia and Russia. The name China may have been derived from the Sanskrit Chin, but is often considered to originate from the Qin dynasty (221–206BC). China is the fourth largest country in the world covering around 9.6 million km². Inner Mongolia covers 1 183 000 km², with the grassland region accounting for a quarter of the total grasslands of China. The national capital is Beijing and the capital of Inner Mongolia is Hohhot. Genghis Khan is credited with having unified the Mongol tribes in 1206 and with establishing the Mongol Empire. His memory is greatly revered in the region of Inner Mongolia.

China: Background (cont)

China has an estimated 1.3 billion total population (estimated 2012) while Inner Mongolia has a population of around 24 million (estimated 2004). Fifty one per cent of the population are estimated to reside in the urban areas. China is officially an atheistic state with a communist government. Several languages are spoken, including Mandarin and Cantonese. The Han Chinese form the largest ethnic group in Inner Mongolia as well as in China, and Mongolians in the region speak various dialects of Mongolian. Inner Mongolia constitutes one of the livestock husbandry bases of China and has well-developed farming. Industries include coal and iron. China's largest export markets are to the EU, USA, Japan and S Korea with major goods including office, telecommunication and electrical equipment.

Cambodia, Singapore and China: Data

Cambodia	Singapore
HDI*: medium (139)	HDI*: very high (26)
MMR (2010): 206	MMR (2010): 3
Lifetime risk of maternal death: 1 in 165	Lifetime risk of maternal death: 1 in 25 300
Mothers index ranking (2012)**: 6 (Tier III)	Mothers index ranking**: not rated
Births attended by skilled personnel: 71%	Births attended by skilled personnel: 100%

China (national)
HDI*: medium (101)
MMR (2010): 37
Lifetime risk of maternal death: 1 in 1700
Mothers index ranking (2012)**: 14 (Tier II)
Births attended by skilled personnel: 99%

HDI: Human Development Index, MMR: Maternal Mortality Ratio
*Assessed according to life expectancy, educational and economic factors
**Ranked globally (within 3 tiers: I = more developed, II = less developed, III = least developed) according to health, education, economic and political status of women

Background and data sources: Cambodia Demographic and Health Survey, 2011; Go China, 2012; Index Mundi, 2012; Mekong.net, 2012, Save the Children, 2012; United Nations Development Programme, 2011; UNICEF 2012, World Facts and Figures, 2012; WHO 2012.

Exploring experience

In the beginning

I spent my early childhood in a working class area of a town in Wales before it was recognised as a city. Times were not easy and hard work was the order of the day. I have no regrets about that. It gave me perspective. I learned what was important in life – its depth not its possessions and I learned to value what had been hard earned.

Journeys from primary school for my twin sister and me were often coloured by flowers which we would pick for our Mum. We did not cross flowering meadows on our way to school, and they were not from anyone's garden, rather they grew out of the dreary grey walls along the street. They were dandelions, in all their golden splendour! Our Mum always received them graciously. Our intention was to present her with the only bouquet available and the flowers were received in the same spirit.

Decades later, entering countries in East Asia, I was surrounded by orchids in the same abundance as my childhood dandelions. Arriving at the airport in Singapore was like landing in some enchanted garden; masses of orchids of numerous varieties, colours and sizes greet the traveller. Some of the airlines and hotels present these beautiful blooms to arriving visitors. However, life and work in that demanding environment was no bed of roses – nor orchids. The work ethic has to be experienced to be believed.

I had agreed to help a colleague run a refresher course for midwives. We were to run two courses each day: the first from 7am until 1pm and the second would start at 2pm and end at 8pm. That way those attending in the morning would work the afternoon shift and vice versa. Everyone could attend, night staff included. I discovered that this work ethic perpetrated all of Singaporean society. There seemed to be no free time and everything and everybody seemed to function 24 hours a day. My observation and experience of the work ethic at that time was confirmed years later in a letter from a colleague. She wrote:

> *Singapore is a very competitive country. Every one of us is expected to work extra hard and long hours and produce 'best results', so we are constantly under stress, lacking sleep and rest.*
>
> *(Yee, 2012)*

My colleague proceeded to explain that the only day of 'rest' is Sunday and that that is spent doing housework, laundry, cooking and shopping.

The media in the West have recently focused on 'tiger mothers' of Chinese origin who, as well as being very strict disciplinarians, expect their children to be the best in all they do (Chua, 2011). There are various definitions and opinions about the ills and virtues of the approach but 'tiger mothers' put extreme pressure on their offspring to study hard in order to achieve the coveted first place. It seems that in some countries, 'tiger mothers' who have produced their own 'tiger cubs' may also function as 'tiger managers' in the running of many of the institutions. Certainly the 'tiger economies' of the region have become well known. Whatever the origin, there is most certainly a very strong work ethic apparent in this part of the world and working two days in one was our personal experience during the assignment. Despite not having been reared by 'tiger mothers' we did our very best to fulfil the expectations of our hosts.

Organisation, automatons and ethics

At the time of our visit, Singapore practised strict timing, not only with work schedules but with regard to births too. Induction of labour was commonplace with births planned for the daytime 'office hours' such as had been the trend in the 1960s in the UK. Hospitals were run with clockwork precision and efficiency. Indeed, clockwork would be an outdated phrase even towards the end of the 1990s as technology had already taken a firm hold. I was amazed when visiting a large city hospital to discover robots roaming the corridors and delivering laundry and other supplies to the wards. Encountering these 'creatures' en route was quite an experience. There was no risk of being taken unawares either. The automatons slowed down when approaching any other moving object, politely reciting 'Excuse me! Excuse me!' I have never seen anything like them before or since, but the assistance of these robotic workers enhanced the already tip-top system of organisation.

One of the subjects that I had agreed to teach in the refresher course embraced professional ethics. I had prepared carefully and attempted, as always, to make the session as interesting as possible. During group work I asked the participants to discuss an ethical dilemma and come to a decision. The scenario I used was a standard situation that generally initiated substantial debate and consideration from various angles. Not so in Singapore. The situation cited was not clear cut and various options were theoretically possible. The decision revolved around whether or not offering one captive to die was acceptable in order to be sure of the release of the others. There was no debate, only decision by my Singaporean colleagues. The one should die for the good of the group – no question about it. No 'What if?' or 'Just suppose ...' – that was it. It was a silly question as far as the participants were concerned and I never used it again in that part of the world. Ethics in East Asia were a world away from Western ideology. Here was a place where the good of the group always took precedence over that of the individual. On the topic of individual rights, a senior politician at the Ministry of another country in the region was later to inform me during my own research: 'Sometimes the individual can sing so loudly, he can put all the others out of tune!' (Maclean, 1998: 36). In this part of the world it seemed, the tune can never be tampered with.

Catastrophe and commitment in Cambodia

Undertaking a consultancy assignment in Cambodia gave insights into the experiences of a country in long-term recovery, many years after the horrors of the Pol Pot regime in the 1970s. Cambodia had numerous programmes in operation and I was asked to work with a colleague to evaluate an obstetric life saving skills programme. I had completed such evaluations in several countries, and each one brought its own challenges. I usually opted to assess those who had completed the course during their clinical practice. This my colleague and I attempted in Cambodia, although opportunity was limited and we had to resort to demonstration with models for many of the skills. We were able to identify considerable achievements in the training efforts. What stands out in my mind was the course arrangement for one-to-one mentoring of trainer with trainee. I had not come across this in any other country, but as far as we could establish it seemed to be functional here. The competency-based programme had been designed to overcome the lack of clinical skills with which the midwives had been struggling.

The country could not have been more of a contrast to the high-tech busyness of Singapore. Here was an Asian kingdom that had known terrible atrocities and bloodshed and decades later was still making heroic efforts to build up an infrastructure and a health service for all. I was told at the Ministry of Health of the need to train doctors in three months in the early years following the massacres; a little training was better than none since most of their educated people had been slaughtered. Cambodia had come a long way in the ensuing decades, but I observed appalling conditions across the country with people living in trees in the rural areas and poverty that was painful to perceive.

A focus group meeting with various cadres of healthcare workers as well as village people revealed not only the catastrophes with which they wrestled but also the commitment with which they worked. In response to the question as to what would make childbirth safer in the area, the answer was that the government needed to build roads in order to facilitate referral. Other things they could work on themselves. I recall the agreement within one village where a cooking pot could be borrowed if a woman had to be admitted to hospital. Without this, the family of the woman could not eat if she took the only vessel with her into hospital, as was expected.

Early afternoon, one of the traditional birth attendants asked if she might be excused from a meeting; she had walked for six hours through the jungle to attend the meeting and wanted to return before sunset because of the wild animals en route. She was all of 70 years old and may have been more. Such commitment put any discomforts I suffered to shame. This was indeed a very different world.

Chinese puzzles

My only appointment with China to date has consisted of a visit to Inner Mongolia, briefly stopping over in Beijing. A Westerner visiting the Orient cannot fail to notice the vast difference in culture, and of course the same is true when those from the East travel West. Culture shock can be a very real experience, but preparation can help to minimise it. In spite of preparation for my visit to Inner Mongolia, I felt ill-equipped for the short but interesting experience which was to be mine. Being an honoured guest and regarded as one of the 'international experts' at a conference was a new experience in this particular context. Since my visit was very short, it would be inappropriate for me to even pretend that I could understand or interpret my experiences. It was, for me, another of those steep learning curves where one learns much more than one imparts and where more questions than answers emerge.

Because of the international nature of the event I had not included a phrase book in my baggage; after all, Chinese languages are not known for their simplicity. This was my first mistake. Since around one fifth of the world's population are Chinese, it should not really have surprised me that no English seemed to be spoken at the 'international hotel' where we were boarded or at the conference centre, except in the confines of the seminar room allocated to the international visitors. The Chinese script is for the long-term visitor to wrestle with and so, as a matter of urgency, I concentrated on learning the most essential survival language to see me through. The technology was advanced and since the standard answer at the hotel could be expressed in one of three English phrases, 'Not possible!' 'There is a problem!' or 'I don't understand!', I had to figure out for myself how to connect to the internet from my room and how to produce that very essential cup of tea.

I was particularly interested in discovering the facts behind China's success in reducing the maternal mortality ratio seemingly without discrimination between the better off and the poor, or between urban and rural communities (Yanqiu et al, 2009). Discovering the reality remained beyond my reach, although a visit to the grasslands provided me with an opportunity to interview one of the residents and establish some information about the policy of everyone giving birth in hospital. Even from the more remote areas of the grassland community, my informant, a young married woman, assured me that, by car or cart, access to assistance was available to all at the time of birth or in emergency.

It was noteworthy that solar panels graced the roofs of the yurts, their indigenous houses, and mobile phones seemed always to be available. Flying over the vast grassland areas and remote hamlets of Inner Mongolia left a sense of wonder about quite how travelling to hospital in some of the emergencies that challenge obstetric and midwifery practice was possible. I left with the feeling that there remained numerous unlearned lessons from this region.

Examining the evidence

East Asian ethics

Whilst it must be accepted that cultural values and priorities may vary significantly between nations within a region and even within some countries, there remain issues that emanate from common historical origins. Experience has shown that Eastern and Western understanding of ethics can be poles apart. Becker (1997, 2002), a researcher and teacher of medical ethics for many years in Japan, cites six broad rules of East Asian ethics (see *Box 4.1*). He acknowledges that such a code of ethics has enabled Asian societies to function 'with great harmony and continuity for thousands of years' and urges that Westerners should not attempt to impose their standards in an imperialistic style in an oriental domain.

Box 4.1. Six principles of East Asian ethics

- Interdependence over independence
- Hierarchy over equality
- Obligations over rights
- Others over self
- Harmony over confrontation, resignation over protest
- Stability of form over change

Derived from Becker 1997, 2002

Recognising that the six principles are by no means comprehensive, Becker (1997) proceeds to explain the fundamental issues that underlie the ethical stance in the region. The first championing 'interdependence over independence' is rooted in a collectivist society. This concept has been described extensively by anthropologists and was considered in the context of examining the contrasts between collectivist and individualist societies in *Chapter 2*. 'Hierarchy over equality' dictates both order and etiquette. On this issue Becker (2002) comments:

In Japanese and Korean language, raising of questions is tantamount to challenging the authority of the listener ...in short we should not question our superiors.

(Becker, 2002: 318)

This concept was my experience too in Indonesia (*Chapter 3*) where encouraging course participants to approach education with a questioning mind was not familiar and doubtless would seem discourteous and even unethical in this part of the world. However, in South Korea at least, changes in this respect are reported to have accompanied increasing exposure to the Western world along with the advent of the internet, so that young employees are encouraged to express their views even if they differ from their superiors. Nowadays they may well be promoted ahead of their seniors. However, children are still taught to respect the elderly and heed their advice (Lim, 2012).

The maxim to think about obligations before rights is considered the correct sequence in cultures where there is no private territory, and where territories overlap. Becker (2002: 319) comments:

Nothing belongs to us privately except the thoughts which we never voice; words and deeds are all potentially public.

Eastern ethics directs 'others over self'. When a decision is needed and a precedent exists, then the norm is to follow it. Where there is no precedent, then the expectation is that elders, seniors or colleagues should be consulted and their advice followed. In traditionally crowded East Asian societies the principle of 'harmony over confrontation, resignation over protest' is considered appropriate. Becker (2002: 319) notes that:

...silence is golden; 'not making waves', 'not losing face', 'not rocking the boat', 'not sticking out', is critically important.

Here is a society where lying is considered better than telling the truth where the truth would hurt, and where protecting others is considered more important than telling the truth or giving full disclosure. Disagreements, it seems, are best kept to oneself.

Lastly, 'stability of form over change' maintains that it is tradition rather than law that assures one's standing.

However, the theories behind oriental ethics have been questioned formally from within society (UNESCO, 2004). As expounded above, it is acknowledged that the ethical stance in East Asia focuses on the common good through emphasis on the necessities of overall society, but warns that this may be at the expense of the needs and rights of the individual. The traditional approach has been challenged contending that it:

...rests on the assumption that respect for each individual is ethically good, and if so, then clearly the logic in forgoing human security through the neglect of individual human rights for the sake of national stability is exposed to some ethical flaws.

(UNESCO, 2004: 40)

Herein lies another enigma, but one that doubtless needs a solution from within rather than without society. However, international visitors in any capacity need to be aware of these ethical norms that impinge on educational strategies and infiltrate national and professional politics, policies and practice.

Challenges in education

In the light of the questions raised in examining East Asian frameworks (UNESCO, 2004), perhaps the group ethics exercise that I used in the educational setting in Singapore would at least have justified some debate a decade later. Whether debate would be an appropriate form of educational approach is another issue where persons of differing degrees of seniority are involved.

The contrasts in Eastern and Western educational methodology are widely recognised and have been mentioned in previous chapters. In considering these discrepancies, Kim (2005) claims that educational systems emerge from cultural expectations and ideologies and that they reflect the strengths and weaknesses of those cultures. In comparing education in the USA with that in Asian countries, Kim (2005) maintains that educationalists can learn from each other. She contends that what American students lack in enthusiasm they possess in creativity, whereas in East Asian countries where there is unquestioned commitment to learning, creativity is sacrificed to rote learning and repetition. On the subject of creativity, Park and Kim (1999) cite the issue of Korean students being motivated by social tradition. Chong and Michael (2000) maintain that such motivation is extrinsic and, in accordance with the theories propounded by Torrance (1963), hold that whereas intrinsic motivation is conducive to creativity, extrinsic motivation is detrimental to it.

Haynes and Chalker (1998) describe how East Asian students enrol in privately run 'cram schools' to augment their studies and to help them gain entry into the best colleges. I observed many students proceeding from one school to another late at night during a visit to South Korea and appreciate that intense pressure is put on these students to excel. It has been widely recognised that East Asian parents believe that success emanates from hard work, endurance, perseverance and persistence rather than from a gifted mind (Henderson, 1990; Haynes and Chalker, 1998; Park and Kim, 1999; Kim, 2005) and this is exemplified in the arguments put forward by Chua (2011) in respect of the parenting style that she advocates.

Work ethic and enthusiasm

The Eastern educational philosophy backed by the popular parenting style could be assumed to have something to do with the vigorous work ethic evident in the region. The success of the five 'dragon' or 'tiger economies' as they are sometimes dubbed comprising Hong Kong, South Korea, Japan, Taiwan and Singapore has been attributed to the virtues of hard work, skill acquisition, patience, study and perseverance (Chen and Chung, 1994; Hahm, 2003).

Yu (2002) perceives the East Asian work ethic and enterprise spirit to be a contrast to the individualism that has driven Western modernisation. In East Asia, business success is rooted in a society where individuals can only find significance 'in the network of interpersonal relations', so that in the workplace

> *...everyone must scrupulously abide by his or her duties and obligations in organisations and pay attention to mutual cooperation.*
>
> *(Yu, 2002: 14)*

The work ethic in the region has been deemed to emerge from Confucianism (Hofstede, 1984, 2001; Yum, 1988; Franke et al, 1991; Robertson, 2000) and has been dubbed 'Confucian dynamism' (Bond, 1988). This quality observed in the oriental environment is not unlike that which was recognised long ago in the West as the Protestant work ethic where the honest performance of a good day's work was considered the highest form of Christian obedience (Weber, 1958). Although this concept, in its secular guise, has been associated with personality traits (Mudrack, 1999), managers have been reported to relate success with a strong work ethic and attribute declining business to its deterioration (Nord et al, 1988). Ralston et al (1999) claim that the rapid economic developments in China since the 1970s have caused work managers to become less compliant with Confucian values and more individualistic than their predecessors. It is interesting to note that Protestantism has also been associated with the rise of individualism in the West (Daly, 1980), although Burnett (1990) argues that it is the mechanical model of man proposed in the secular worldview that ultimately led to the individualistic concept. The truth probably lies somewhere in between and Yu (2002) maintains that in modern economic development, these countries 'have not consciously created a new ethics and spirit' (Yu, 2002: 15), rather they have absorbed those features considered desirable from the West. This, however, has not been done without careful analysis. Yu explains:

> *But just as colorless light is refracted into an entire spectrum through a prism, Western culture is bound to be filtered through Eastern culture resulting in quite different styles and features.*
>
> *(Yu, 2002: 15)*

Yu acknowledges that, conversely, transformation of Eastern culture may also ensue so that new developments evolve.

Traversing the time lines

Time can be as difficult to define as it is to capture. Aristotle (*circa* 350BC) debated much about the concept of time and purported that

> ...*not only do we measure change by time, but time by change, because they are defined by one another.*
>
> *(Aristotle, Physics Book IV 220b: 14–15)*

Philosophers, mathematicians, linguists and others approach the debate from their own, often opposing, corners. However, time takes on a different significance for those who would not only cross international time lines but also traverse and seek to understand the cultural barriers that can beset professional, business and student interactions alike. Such conflicting concepts of time are capable of intercepting both aid and trade. Time orientation, which relates to whether there is a marked emphasis on the past and its tradition or more on the present and investing in the future, has become an issue in cross-cultural studies and experience. Decades ago, Kluckhohn and Strodtbeck (1961) purported that people adopt a time orientation that emanates from their culture. This, they suggest, through a complex process of socialisation, may be described as a past or future orientation. A psychologist considers another viewpoint. Considering that behaviour is influenced by several dimensions of what is anticipated in the future including goals, hopes, wishes and fears, Trommsdorf (1983: 384) interprets the complex nature of future orientation as being 'a multi-dimensional cognitive-motivational-cultural construct'.

Hofstede (2001), following his numerous studies defining and deliberating culture and its consequences, confirms that people carry a mental programming that is defined early in life and reinforced later by schools and organisations. He also maintains that such mental programmes possess a component of national culture and proceeds to explore how these differ across numerous nations. Hofstede (2001) revisits and renames the concept of 'Confucian dynamism' (Bond, 1988) cited above in view of the fact that respondents from no more than six out of the 23 countries participating in research on the topic had ever heard of Confucius. He therefore refers to this concept, which he regards as the fifth dimension of culture, as 'long-term versus short-term orientation'. In summary, long-term orientation demonstrates a preference towards persistence as opposed to obtaining quick results. It also favours saving rather than spending, and personal adaptability over steadfastness, with stability and status assuming significance in establishing relationships. East Asian countries tend to score high on the long-term orientation scale.

Hofstede's work has been a focal point for debate through the years (Yeh and Lawrence, 1995; Tang and Kovios, 2008). However, that the concept of time or time orientation differs greatly in different cultures is not an issue for debate but rather is readily experienced by the cross-cultural visitor. The Chinese view of time has been linked with the concept of Tao, with the suggestion that just as all that fish need to do is to get lost in water, so all man needs to do is to get lost in time. To live in the Tao is to practise '*wu-wei*' which means living by the law of reversion within the harmony of opposites. *Wu-wei*, rather than doing absolutely nothing, involves instead doing nothing that is unnecessary and unnatural. It calls for humility, not being attached to the fruit of one's labours and withdrawing from it once the work is done (Legge, 1962).

Time, and an apparent shortage of it, does not faze people from such a different cultural background as it does the Westerner. Proverbs that are instilled in the psyche early in life stand testimony to some of these concepts. Individuals brought up in an atmosphere where such maxims as 'Time and tide wait for no man' and 'A stitch in time saves nine' are held in regard may well have problems in adopting a conflicting attitude to time. Encountering greatly differing cultural perspectives along the river of life can be challenging, especially when they relate to some of the fundamental concepts of one's life and one's labour. Attempting to understand not only how the flow of events proceeds, but also discovering their source and point of origin can be helpful not only in project work but also in establishing the relationships that are fundamental to making progress. Wasting time would surely find marked differences in definition across international timelines.

Filial piety

Undoubtedly some of the principles of East Asian ethics infiltrate into all aspects of societal and family life. The concept of filial piety (*xiao*) perpetrates the region and has many interpretations. One interpretation emanates from the Chinese characters representing the old '*lao*' and the son '*zi*'. In the Mandarin script when the characters are combined to form '*xiao*' the '*lao*' is supported by the '*zi*' and can be seen as the younger generation supporting the elders (*Figure 4.2*). Others perceive it as the young being burdened or even oppressed by the old (Ikels, 2004).

However, the extended family remains a feature in much of the world and offers undeniable advantages that have long been lost in many parts of Western society. Nevertheless, for all its virtues, a family-centred society faces increasing challenges in the 21st century. Fan (1997) describes a concept of autonomy that is culturally specific in East Asia upholding

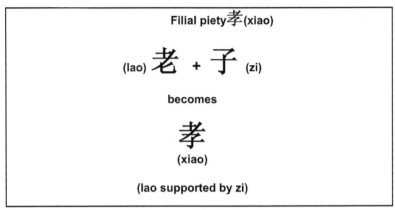

Figure 4.2. Filial piety (xiao). Courtesy of Annie Wang-Evans.

the concept of harmonious dependence. This is described as 'a family-determination-oriented principle' (Fan, 1997: 315). Fan describes family as an 'autonomous unit as a whole' (Fan, 1997: 317) and it is evident that marriage constitutes one example of being a family matter rather than a personal one in the experience of many Asians. Since harmony is highly regarded, a family-centred society sometimes calls for self-suppression.

Filial piety calls for respect and obedience and an affection that is sometimes likened to worship (Lin, 1992; Chao and Roth, 2000; Hsu et al, 2001). The concept of filial piety is promoted by the Government of Singapore as one of the five shared family values (Phua and Loh, 2008). The ideal has been noted to influence maternity care in Singaporean culture where mothers-in-law have considerable influence over women at the time of childbirth. It is more likely to ensure that traditional birth practices are followed, although modern internet access and mass media have changed the search for knowledge and are influencing women's choices as they become aware of perinatal practices on a global scale (Naser et al, 2011). As mothers and midwives become better informed, the climate could be more conducive to introducing change, not least in the area of evidence-based practice.

In search of the truth and tangible tactics

While I searched for evidence of equity in achieving safer childbirth across China, my doubts were shared by other researchers who have considered the available evidence. Beyond the report by Yanqiu et al (2009), more recent evidence is not so convincing. While reports inevitably acknowledge the tremendous progress that China has made towards the fifth Millennium Development Goal (MDG5), they question the equity of the success across society (Wagstaff et al, 2009; Feng et al, 2010) and express uncertainty as to whether the gap in maternal health care has been reduced between rich and poor across this vast land (Xing et al, 2011). In a rapidly developing nation where technology is advanced and motivation high in achieving excellence, it will be interesting to see how China emerges in achieving each of the MDGs in the global league tables.

In the quest for tactics that are likely to be functional in another country, it is salutary to seek out local wisdom. Thinking about the logical approaches in situations deep rooted within a community, I am reminded of the solutions offered by Cambodian villagers. It has long been recognised that the real experts are likely to be those residing within the situation (Chambers, 1981) and we do well to listen to them; poor, uneducated they may be, but they are still likely to hold the keys to what will work in their own environments. We can ignore them at their cost and ours, or respect them and heed them in our efforts to meet their very real needs.

Minimising culture shock

The matter of culture shock needs to be taken seriously by any traveller who seeks to traverse cultural boundaries. Culture shock has been linked with the psychological consequences associated with unfamiliar surroundings and may include variable degrees of depression and even paranoia. Since the condition can be distressing, the etymological link between the words 'travel' and 'travail' have been perceived as significant (Furnham and Bochner, 1986). Culture shock has also been identified with physical symptoms (Hofstede, 1994) and may take many forms. Pre-existing medical conditions may become exacerbated.

Given the increasing amount of international travel and migration and its potential toll on health, alongside culture shock, cultural adaptation has received increasing attention in recent years. The ultimate goal is achieved when the traveller acquires an ability to live with change and difference (Anderson, 1994). Smith and Bond (1998) compare this process to the experience of adapting to other life changes, such as bereavement, starting college or giving up an addiction. Writers and researchers across several decades have variously described cultural adaptation as incorporating learning, journeying or obtaining equilibrium. The learning model emphasises the need to acquire the necessary knowledge and skills to function in a different sociocultural environment (Guthrie, 1975; Taylor, 1994). The journeying model focuses on passing from ignorance and rejection of the alien culture towards an understanding and acceptance of the differences

(Bennett, 1986). Whilst Grove and Torbiörn (1985) advocate the equilibrium model requiring 'a dynamic process of tension reduction' which produces a modified behaviour as the disturbed person ultimately realises a state of subjective harmony.

In examining the effects of studying abroad on nursing students, Ruddock and Turner (2007) conclude that developing cultural sensitivity is a complex process enhanced by the decision to adopt the customs of the host culture. This approach leads to an understanding that sensitivity to a different culture calls for a willingness to acknowledge its political and social structures and incorporate indigenous beliefs about health and illness.

In considering ways of minimising culture shock Furnham (1993) reckons that training in social skills is the most effective antidote. Ward et al (2003) emphasise that essential social skills may be learned through mentoring, behavioural training and studying historical, sociopolitical and philosophical aspects of the new culture. Further they underline the importance of appropriate selection, training and support for individuals who are crossing cultures. It therefore behoves the elective student or aspiring consultant to note these issues and take appropriate steps to minimise this potentially traumatic condition.

Personal reflections on practice

- Time has a totally different meaning in an Eastern environment. A visitor's time orientation is likely to be poles apart from that of national counterparts.
- Teaching subjects such as ethics in a totally different culture introduces very different issues. It would seem that the subject would have been better addressed by a national. A trial run with a group of course organisers may have forestalled the problem.
- Obtaining the 'best results' is more of a standard than an ideal, it would seem that there is no such word as 'can't' in this part of the world where excellence is an expectation.
- Commitment in remote parts of the world can be life threatening. Reflecting on some of the situations faced by the indigenous populations in rural areas of Cambodia, it is clear that these people not only form the backbone of their communities, but also hold many of the keys to solving major issues. However, so often they are powerless and their voices remain unheard.
- It is a mistake ever to travel without some guide to the language. At the minimum, a 'picture phrase book' would have solved a number of problems (Pearse et al, 1987; Franklin, 2005).

Some lessons learned and shared

- Whenever possible, checking out practical exercises with a national before utilising them in education programmes is wise, especially if they relate to ethical situations where expectations and norms can be diametrically opposed to your previous experience.
- It seems that a clear-cut decision in professional practice in the West may be no such thing in the Orient where the ethical stance may be totally different.
- It is necessary to appreciate that your own time orientation may be very different from that of colleagues in the host country. Sometimes this can cause serious practical problems, other times inconvenience. It is helpful to distinguish between these.

Reflective exercises

- Identify an ethical dilemma that you have experienced or observed in your area of professional practice: how was it resolved? Using the Six Principles of East Asian Ethics (*Box 4.1*) attempt to view the situation again through an Eastern prism as described by Yu (2002) and cited above. Does this reveal differences in perspective on the situation and might it influence the outcome when viewing through an 'oriental prism' by comparison with an 'occidental prism'?
- Oriental wisdom in respect of time regards it important to do nothing that is unnecessary or unnatural, to adopt an attitude of humility, not to focus on the fruit of one's labours and to withdraw when the work is completed (Legge, 1962). Consider a task or project that you have recently completed or a day's work or study. Viewing it from such a perspective, how many aspects of your work may be considered appropriate and what may be deemed inappropriate or unnecessary to an Eastern colleague?
- Imagine that you hold a different opinion from one of your national colleagues. Do this in the light of the observation of Becker (2002) where 'not making waves', 'not losing face', 'not rocking the boat' and 'not sticking out' are considered to be 'critically important'. How would this affect your situation as a consultant required to recommend change or a student seeking to practise within the requirements set out by your university? Consider any recommendations you make or actions you wish to take in the light of how they will affect you and how they are likely to be perceived by your host. Draft out your approach.
- Make an action list of how you will prepare for your assignment in order to minimise culture shock.

References

Anderson LE (1994) A new look at an old concept: Cross-cultural adaptation. *International Journal of Intercultural Relations* **18**: 293–28

Becker CB (1997) Social ethics in East Asia. *Drug Information Journal* **31**: 1089–96

Becker CB (2002) Good clinical practice? Can East Asia accommodate Western standards? In Barnhart M (ed) *Varieties of ethical reflection. New Directions for ethics in a global context* (pp. 317–20). Lexington Books, Oxford

Bennett MJ (1986) A developmental approach to training for intercultural sensitivity. *International Journal of Intercultural Relations* **10**: 179–96

Bond MH (1988) Finding universal dimensions in individual variation in multicultural studies of values. The Rockeach and Chinese Value Surveys. *Journal of Personality and Social Psychology* **55**: 1009–15

Burnett D (1990) *Clash of worlds*. MARC, Monarch Publications, Eastbourne.

Cambodia Demographic and Health Survey (2011) *2010 Cambodia Demographic and Health Survey: Key Findings*. National Institute of Statistics, Directorate General for Health and ICF Macro. Phnom Penh, Cambodia and Calverton, Maryland, USA.

Chambers R (1981) Rural poverty unperceived: problems and remedies. *World Development* **9**: 1–19

Chao S, Roth P (2000) The experiences of Taiwanese women caring for parents-in-law. *Journal of Advanced Nursing* **31**(3): 631–8

Chen GM, Chung J (1994) The impact of Confucianism on organizational communication. *Communications Quarterly* **42**: 93–105

Chong S, Michael WB (2000) A construct validity study of scores on a Korean version of an academic self-concept scale for secondary school students. *Education and Psychological Measurement* **60**: 17–30

Chua A (2011) *Battle hymn of the tiger mother* (1st edn). Penguin Press, London

Daly G (1980) *Transcendence and imminence: A study in Catholic modernism and integralism*. Clarendon Press, Oxford

Fan R (1997) Self-determination vs family determination: Two incommensurable principles of autonomy. *Bio-ethics* **11**: 309–22

Feng XL, Zhu L, Song L et al (2010) Socio-economic disparities in maternal mortality in China between 1996 and 2006. *British Journal of Obstetrics and Gynaecology* **117**(12): 1527–36

Franke RH, Hofstede G, Bond MH (1991) Cultural roots of economic performance. A Research Note. *Strategic Management Journal* **12**: 165–73

Franklin M (2005) *The universal phrasebook: A picture dictionary for international travelers*. Sterling Publishing, NY

Furnham A (1993) Communicating in foreign lands: The causes, consequences and cures of culture shock. *Special Issue: Culture and Language Learning in Higher Education. Language, Culture and Curriculum* **6**(1): 91–109

Furnham A, Bochner S (1986) *Culture shock: Psychological reactions to unfamiliar surroundings.* Methuen, London and New York

Go China (2012) *China's key statistics at a glance.* Available from: http://gochina.about. com/od/factsfigures/ [last accessed 20.02.2012]

Grove CJ, Torbiörn I (1985) A new conceptualisation of intercultural adjustment and the goals of training. *International Journal of Intercultural Relations* **9**: 205–33

Guthrie GM (1975) A behavioural analysis of cultural learning. In Brislyn RW, Botcher S, Lonner WJ (eds) *Crosscultural perspectives on learning* (pp. 95–115). Wyley, New York

Hahm C (2003) Law, education and the politics of Confucianism. *Columbia Journal of Asian Law* **16**: 254–301

Haynes RM, Chalker DM (1998) The making of a world class elementary school. *Principal* **77**: 5–9

Henderson ZP (1990) Myth of native ability hurts American education. *Human Ecology* **19**: 29–30

Hofstede G (1984) *Cultures consequences: International differences in work related values.* Sage, Newbury Park, CA

Hofstede G (1994) *Cultures and organizations: Intercultural co-operation and its importance for survival. Software of the Mind.* Harper Collins, London

Hofstede G (2001) *Cultures consequences: Comparing values, behaviors, institutions and organizations across nations* (2nd edn). Sage, London and New Delhi

Hsu H, Lew-Ting C, Wu S (2001) Age, period, and cohort effects on the attitude toward supporting parents in Taiwan. *Gerontologist* **41**(6): 742–50

Ikels C (ed) (2004) *Filial piety, practice and discourse in contemporary East Asia.* Stanford University Press, California

Index Mundi (2012) *Country comparison: population.* Available from: http://www. indexmundi.com/g/r.aspx [last accessed 28.09.2012]

Inner Mongolia Database (2012) *Inner Mongolia Database.* Available from: http://www.unescap. org/esid/psis/population/database/chinadata/innermongolia.htm [last accessed 20.02.2012]

Kim KH (2005) Learning from each other: Creativity in East Asian and American Education. *Creativity Research Journal* **18**(4): 337–47

Kluckhohn F, Strodtbeck FL (1961) *Variations in value orientations.* Row, Peterson, Evanston IL

Legge J (1962) *The texts of Taoism: Part I, The Tao Ti Ching and Lao Tzu. The writings of Chuang Tzu. The Sacred Books of China.* Translated by James Legge, Dover Publications Inc, New York

Lim J (2012) Personal communication

Lin A (1992) *Study of filial piety in Confucian thought.* Wen Jin, Taipei

Maclean GD (1998) *An examination of the characteristics of short-term international midwifery consultants.* PhD Thesis, University of Surrey, Guildford

Mekong.net (2012) *Cambodia facts, figures and statistics.* Available from: http://www.mekong.net/cambodia/facts.htm [last accessed 20.02.2012]

Mudrack PE (1999) Time structure and purpose, Type A behavior and the Protestant work ethic. *Journal of Organizational Behavior* **20**: 145–58

Naser E, Mackey S, Arthur D, Klainin Yobas P, Chen H, Creedy DK (2011) *An exploratory study of traditional birthing practices of Chinese, Malay and Indian women in Singapore.* Available from: http://www.sciencedirect.com/science/article/pii/S0266613811001501 [Acessed 16.01.2012]

Nord WR, Brief AP, Atieh JM, Doherty EM (1988) Work values and the conduct of organizational behavior. *Research in Organizational Behavior* **10**: 1–42

Park YS, Kim U (1999) The educational challenge of Korea in the global era: The role of family, school and government. *Chinese University Education Journal* **26**: 91–120

Pearse RS, Rowe B, James J (1987) *The traveller's picture phrase-book: Speak any language in pictures.* Vacation Work, Oxford

Phua V, Loh J (2008) Filial piety and intergenerational co-residence: The case of Chinese Singaporeans. *Asian Journal of Social Science* **36**: 659–79

Ralston DA, Egri CP, Stewart S et al (1999) Doing business in the 21st century with the new generation Chinese managers. A study of generational shifts in work values in China. *Journal of International Business Studies* **30**(2): 415–28

Robertson CJ (2000) The global dispersion of Chinese values: A three-country study of Confucian dynamism. *Management and International Review* **40**(3): 253–68

Ruddock H, Turner D (2007) Developing cultural sensitivity: Nursing students' experiences of a study abroad programme. *Journal of Advanced Nursing* **59**(4): 361–9

Save the Children (2012) *State of the World's mothers 2012. The 2012 Mothers' Index.* Available from: http://www.savethechildren.org/ [last accessed 13/07/2012]

Smith PB, Bond MH (1998) *Social psychology across cultures* (2nd edn). Prentice Hall Europe, London and Paris

Tang L, Kovios PE (2008) A framework to update Hofstede's cultural value indices: economic dynamics and institutional stability. *Journal of International Business Studies* **39**: 1045–63

Taylor EW (1994) A learning module for becoming interculturally competent. *International Journal of Intercultural Relations* **18**: 389–408

Torrance EP (1963) *Education and the creative potential.* University of Minnesota Press, Minneapolis

Trommsdorf G (1983) Future orientation and socialization. *International Journal of Psychology* **18**: 381–406

United Nations Development Programme (2011) *International Human Development Indicators*. Available from: http://hdr.undp.org/en/statistics/ [Last accessed 13.02.2012]

UNESCO (2004) *Promoting human security: Ethical, normative and educational frameworks in East Asia*. Korean National Commission for UNESCO, Seoul, Republic of Korea

UNICEF (2012) *State of the World's children 2012*. UNICEF, New York

Wagstaff A, Yip W, Lindelow M, Hsiao WC (2009) China's health system and its reform: a review of recent studies. *Health Economics* **18**: S7–23

Ward C, Bochner S, Furnham A (2003) *The psychology of culture shock* (2nd edn). Routledge, Sussex

Weber M (1958) *The Protestant ethic and the spirit of capitalism* (Translated by Parsons, T. from the original work published 1904–1905) Scribner, New York

WHO (2012) *Trends in maternal mortality 1990–2010*. WHO, UNICEF, UNFPA and World Bank. WHO, Geneva. Available from: http://www.who.int/reproductivehealth/publications/monitoring/9789241503631/en/ [last accessed 13.09.2012]

World Facts and Figures (2012) *World Facts and Figures: Singapore*. Available from: http://worldfactsandfigures.com/countries/singapore.php [last accessed 20.02.2012]

Xing LF, Xu L, Guo Y, Ronsmans C (2011) Socio-inequalities in hospital births in China between 1988 and 2008. *Bulletin of the WHO* **89**: 432–41

Yanqiu G, Ronsmans C, Lin A (2009) Time trends and regional differences in maternal mortality in China from 2000 to 2005. *Bulletin of the WHO* **87**: 913–20

Yee PF (2012) Personal communication received 12 January 2012

Yeh RS, Lawrence JJ (1995) Individualism and Confucian dynamism: A note on Hofstede's cultural root and economic growth. *Journal of International Business Studies* **26**(3): 655–9

Yu X (2002) *Cultural impact on international relations: Chinese Philosophical Studies XX*. Council for Research in Values and Philosophy, Washington

Yum JO (1988) The impact of Confucianism on interpersonal relationships and communication patterns in East Asia. *Communication Monographs* **55**: 374–88

Chapter 5

From creative resources to refugees

The greatest virtues are those that are most useful to other persons.

(Aristotle)

Values vary and a multitude of communication strategies are mobilised across diverse cultures. Africa can boast centuries of experience not only in education but in moving a multitude of messages through such means as dance, drumbeat or dialogue

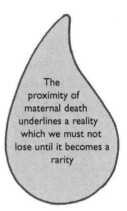

The proximity of maternal death underlines a reality which we must not lose until it becomes a rarity

Subject strands introduced

- Education for practice
- Indigenous initiatives
- Communication strategies

- Appreciative Inquiry
- Refugee issues
- Values

Practice points

- Meeting real needs
- Encouraging indigenous creativity
- Recognising local know-how

- Learning different ways of communication

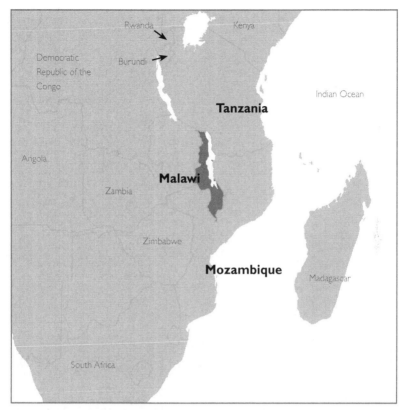

Figure 5.1. Malawi, Mozambique and Tanzania.

Tanzania: Background

Tanzania

Tanzania is situated in central east Africa bordered by eight other African countries and meets the Indian Ocean on the eastern side. The country covers 947300 km². The capital is Dodoma, although Dar Es Salaam is one of the largest cities. Tanzania is home to Africa's highest mountain, Mount Kilimanjaro. Tanganyika was colonised by the British until 1961. The island of Zanzibar had become the centre of the Arab slave trade and Tanganyika and Zanzibar merged to form Tanzania in 1964. Tanzania has a five level judiciary combining jurisdictions of tribal, Islamic and British common law. The population is around 47 million (estimated 2012) with 35% living in urban areas. Christianity and Islam each account for 40% of the national religions. Swahili and English are widely spoken. The main exports are cashew nuts, cloves, cotton, coffee and tea.

Malawi and Mozambique: Background

Malawi

Malawi in central east Africa is bordered by Tanzania, Mozambique and Zambia. The name of the country means 'glitter of the sun rising across the lake'. It covers 118484 km². Within this landlocked territory, Lake Malawi is 587 km long and 84 km wide. The mountainous areas of the country surround the Rift Valley plateaus. The capital Lilongwe is one of the two largest cities, the other being Blantyre. Malawi was colonised by the British from the late 19th century until 1964. The population exceeds 16 million (estimated 2012) with 16% living in the urban areas. Eighty per cent of the population are Christian and others practise Islam or local religions. English is spoken along with Chichewa and other local languages. Tobacco, sugar cane, coffee and tea are among the main exports.

Mozambique

Mozambique in south eastern Africa is bordered by seven other African countries and meets the Indian Ocean on the eastern side. The name of the country is thought to originate from that of an Arab ruler Sheik Mussa Ben Mbiki. The country covers 801591 km². The capital Maputo is one of several large cities. Colonised by the Portuguese in 1505, Mozambique became independent in 1975. The country has a mixed legal system comprising Portuguese civil law, Islamic and customary law. The population is around 23.5 million (estimated 2012) with 36% living in the urban areas. Half of the population are Christian, the majority being Roman Catholic. Muslims constitute almost 30%. Portuguese is widely spoken along with Swahili, Makhua and Sena. Aluminium, timber, cotton and bulk electricity are exported as well as cashew nuts, sugar and prawns.

Tanzania, Malawi and Mozambique: Data

Tanzania	Malawi
HDI*: low (152)	HDI*: low (171)
Estimated MMR: 460 (2010)	Estimated MMR: 460 (2010)
MMR: proportion related to HIV/AIDS: 18%	MMR: proportion related to HIV/AIDS: 29.3%
Life time risk of dying in childbirth: 1 in 23	Life time risk of dying in childbirth: 1 in 36
Mothers Index ranking (2012)**: 17(Tier III)	Mothers Index ranking (2012)**: 3(Tier III)
Births attended by skilled personnel: 49%	Births attended by skilled personnel: 54%

Mozambique
HDI*: low (184)
Estimated MMR: 490 (2010)
Proportion related to HIV/AIDS: 26.8%
Life time risk of dying in childbirth: 1 in 37
Mothers Index ranking (2012)**: 10(Tier III)
Births attended by skilled personnel: 55%

HDI: Human Development Index, MMR: Maternal Mortality Ratio
*Assessed according to life expectancy, educational and economic factors
**Ranked globally (within 3 tiers: I = more developed, II = less developed, III = least developed) according to health, education, economic and political status of women

Background and data sources: Africa.com 2012; Index Mundi, 2012; Save the Children, 2012; UN Development Program, 2012; UNICEF 2012, World Factbook, 2012; WHO, 2012

Exploring experience

Touching ground in Tanzania

My initial encounter with Tanzania occurred when I conducted a preliminary field test on some of the educational material I had written for the World Health Organization (WHO, 1996). The work represented one of the many and varied attempts to address issues relating to the Safe Motherhood Initiative (SMI, 1987). Having worked with one of the Tanzanian leaders in midwifery education in Asia as well as another African country, this was an enormous help in establishing a workshop to facilitate the field test. A British colleague advising on another educational project worked alongside me.

We spent the first night in Dar-es-Salaam at an international hotel and then were offered the option of continuing there or moving to a rural area where the workshop participants were residing. To stay in the capital would have involved travelling daily to the site, but identifying with our hosts in the village conference centre obviously had much to commend it. Without hesitation we chose to join them. The discomforts of the rural environment were outweighed not only by our proximity to the participants, but also our move brought us nearer to the reality of life from an African perspective.

I was to experience once again the inconvenience of intermittent electricity supplies and the reality of needing to improvise for everything not included in my resource pack.

My colleagues and I sought to utilise the educational materials and assess their limitations as well as their scope. Having designed the learning games at home, but with mind and heart flying between Africa and Asia, I now set about testing them to see whether what had worked in Botswana would find resonance elsewhere in the continent. Having improvised for the dice that I had omitted from my packing, I proceeded to test the game 'Walking where Mrs X walked'. Would it be relevant here I wondered? Was it possible to fulfil my obligation from Geneva to design a global template for these modules? Time would tell.

The game forms part of the Foundation Module and highlights situations with which pregnant women and communities wrestle in trying to achieve a safe birth. The groups soon became immersed in the various scenarios. 'Oh, I'm HIV positive!', 'Travel is impossible because of storms!', 'The vehicle has a puncture!', 'I'm living below the poverty line!' came the various cries with the occasional cheer as someone managed to reach a health centre, acquire antibiotics or live in a village where a nutritious diet was possible. I was about to pose the question: 'Are these situations realistic in Tanzania?' but my enquiry was pre-empted. One group paused and, turning knowingly towards me, asked: 'Have you been here before? That's exactly what happens here!'

'Walking where Mrs X walked' has subsequently become a popular educational aid among midwives and other health workers in many parts of the world. I have received positive feedback in recent years from countries as far apart and diverse as Ethiopia and Papua New Guinea and numerous other locations in between.

I visited Tanzania on several subsequent occasions, leading or participating in educational workshops or conferences. It was always a learning experience for me and hopefully for those I sought to serve there.

Moving mountains in Malawi

After I had completed several assignments in Malawi, colleagues there invited me to return and assist them to modify the Mrs X game and others that I had designed specifically to fit the Malawian context. This was a privilege and a challenge and I watched with interest as the games adopted indigenous names and designs. Working closely with these colleagues who had become friends, enabled me to encourage their natural creativity as well as appreciate their efforts in all too often adverse circumstances.

It was during a visit to Thailand that there had been a new opportunity for me to learn as well as to teach and share ideas. One stay in that area had introduced me to the concept of 'appreciative inquiry'. Reflecting with a colleague on the professional situation with regard to promoting safer childbirth, she had introduced me to appreciative inquiry and we had considered how this may be more widely used in maternity care. Discovering and appreciating what was successful and effective as opposed to using a problem-solving approach, instinctively appealed to me and I was aware that I had used the principle in my own consultancy practice. Along with Swedish colleagues I had arranged a workshop in Tanzania to explore the concepts of appreciative inquiry and we were assisted in this by three Pakistani doctors who were truly committed to as well as conversant with the approach. Now, in Malawi, there was an opportunity to build on what was successful, and appreciate one another in this intense and interesting environment where creativity thrived.

On a previous visit to this country known as the warm heart of Africa, I had attempted to utilise appreciative inquiry in my evaluation of an obstetric life-saving skills programme. It is easy to identify what is wrong, what is missing and what needs urgent attention, but there are always things that work, successes and achievements, and these are the discoveries that can form a good foundation upon which to build for the future. I remember asking midwives who had completed the life-saving skills programme to tell me about one case where the outcome was not good and what they had learned from it, and one where the outcome was good. Relating the former, the deeply saddened eyes of my respondents burned into my soul. The stories ranged from the terrible to the tragic; there were regrets and resolutions. Recalling the success stories brought a tangible pride and joy; unsurprisingly, such experiences renewed energy, commitment and purpose. I rather regretted asking them to review the negative side of the coin. However, this made a useful contribution to further learning and professional development.

Attempting to encourage rather than condemn, I was faced with a dilemma in one of the hospitals which cried out for an overhaul in its sanitation and safety features. A small army of cleaners leaned against the wall, supported by their mops and brushes, while the unhygienic environment in which puerperal sepsis existed abounded. 'Do these ladies know how important they are?' I asked within their hearing. I later discussed with my national counterpart the value of their realising the significant contribution they could make to reducing maternal mortality. My colleague told me of her experience in enlightening ambulance drivers about the importance of urgent transportation in cases of prolonged and obstructed labour, and how this had dramatically decreased mortality and morbidity. Previously, the vehicles had been diverted for other money-making ventures when apparently not needed, but now a maternity call constituted an emergency; it was given priority, and their altered response had made a difference. As illustrated in earlier chapters, indigenous solutions are always superior to imported remedies and there is a rich resource of the former awaiting discovery. However the cleaning issues were handled, I was to discover on a return visit to that same hospital that it was in a pristine condition with regard to cleanliness.

When maternal mortality looms large

Many a heartache has remained with me from my sojourns in Malawi. It is salutary to reflect that as visitors we only see the tip of the iceberg or should I say, the nose of the hippo.

Approaching the main referral hospital, my medical colleague pointed out what she had tried to discourage on numerous occasions; the presence of undertakers touting their wares. Here was the perfect place for their business. Inside I found a chilling reality. The labour ward had been recently upgraded and offered much better facilities; however, a mortuary was an integral part of the labour suite. My colleagues assured me of its usefulness and indeed its necessity. In spite of upgraded hospitals and enormous efforts to enhance clinical skills through life-saving skills courses and improved curricula, the problems which are well known to those of us who work on safer childbirth issues in different parts of the world, were blatantly evident here. Women all too often arrived at the hospital moribund, victims of distance, poor infrastructure, poverty and its inseparable companions – malnutrition and anaemia, traditional taboos and customs, and so much more.

Perhaps the saddest moment was shared with me after my return home from Malawi. One of the tutors with whom I had worked in adapting the educational material had given birth to twins. Heavily pregnant during our workshop she had contributed imaginatively with great enthusiasm, resting her feet and heavily pregnant body at every opportunity. We had teased her and helped her, she was one of us. News of the births did not reach me for a long time. I enquired about her several times and eventually another colleague wrote and told me the sad news. She had given birth to two beautiful healthy daughters, normally and without difficulty. She had returned home and was making good progress, but some days later she had been readmitted with severe puerperal sepsis and died before she could be treated. My colleague was distraught. 'You see, she didn't recognise the danger signs,' she told me later. The harsh reality made me sad. This little group of midwifery tutors had such potential, such commitment and now one of them was lost in the same way as many of her countrywomen.

It was members of this group, as we had been designing an educational game, that had chosen to acknowledge their own limitations in particular skills. We had been considering an activity to teach the use of the partograph, a comprehensive record used during labour. My colleagues acknowledged that part of the problem was that they, as tutors, were not confident themselves in the required skills. I had found it encouraging that we were now in a place where such issues could be confessed and addressed. It takes a lot of courage for any professional to admit that he or she is unskilled in a particular aspect of daily work, especially where losing face is a real issue, and within an institutional setting with a marked hierarchy. Hiding limitations ensures that they remain private, but once shared there is opportunity to expand knowledge and enhance practice.

In my experience the professional education system in many countries lays emphasis on theory to the detriment of practice. Not uncommonly, teaching is carried out by nurses and midwives who may never have had the opportunity to acquire skills themselves and so the disadvantage passes from one generation to the next. We were able to work on this particular issue together, learning to understand the approaches to detecting prolonged labour and preventing death and disaster from obstructed labour and its consequences. I recalled the story shared with me by African colleagues and seemingly told by women in some parts of Africa in preparing their children for another birth in the family (*Figure 5.2*). We must never turn away from the horror of maternal mortality until the event becomes as rare as it is in the privileged West.

In explaining to our children that we are going to give birth, this is what we say:

"I must go to the sea to fetch a new baby.
The journey is long and dangerous,
I may be some time . . .
. . . and I may not return"

Figure 5.2. An African tale (source unknown).

Once upon a journey

Travelling to the far south of Malawi to visit a rural hospital brought me close to the border with Mozambique. It constituted a 5am start and a late return that same night. I had arranged a packed breakfast from the hotel as I had perceived that the chances of finding food en route were not very high. Our little contingent set out in a four wheel drive heading due south. As we journeyed we were able to share the breakfast, thanks to the ample hotel provision. It was amazing how far that little package stretched and the driver was most impressed that he received a share too. On the return journey my colleagues located a local store where they were pleased to reciprocate my contribution, buying a huge slab of cake. This we shared together too. In Botswana, colleagues had told me of a traditional maxim stating that children of the same family share even the head of a fly. However, one cannot make assumptions and in some cultures motives may be misinterpreted, especially where gifts can be perceived as bribes, and taboos concerning food might exist. However, on this occasion our shared food drew us closer together as a team as we struggled with the more sinister challenges to survival confronting women and their families across this country.

In considering strategies for survival I am reminded of an influx of refugees trickling across the south Malawian border from Mozambique. Devastating floods had afflicted the area and people were escaping with their lives and just what they stood up in. I was to meet one such woman who arrived at the hospital with a small bundle of possessions which included a baby that she had given birth to on the roadside a few hours previously. The baby was covered with mud and gravel and still attached to the placenta. The woman needed some attention, but both mother and baby were well. It was her ninth child, the others were alive and she was clearly worn out, not just from the journey and the recent labour, but also from the repeated childbearing. The obvious postnatal care would have included offering some contraceptive advice, but here, I discovered, was a woman whose sole function was to produce children and who had no say in any matters to do with birth control or anything else. These would be her husband's decisions and he had chosen not to come into the hospital while she received the care she needed. I do not know what happened to her and her family, but it was evident that here was a woman, one among many, who had no rights and no control over her own body or even her life.

Mozambican initiatives

On one of the occasions that I visited Mozambique as part of a different evaluation exercise, I was impressed by the progress and ingenuity evident in a country that was no stranger to natural disaster. In attempting to promote survival of the newborn, men in village areas had been persuaded to take turns with their wives in providing 'kangaroo care' in order to ensure the warmth and safety of their vulnerable newborns. The proud fathers showed me how they could do everything their wives did – except breastfeed! They were ardent promoters of exclusive breastfeeding for the first six months, and the presence of numerous babies who had been reared this way convinced me of their place in its promotion. The men took a real interest in the welfare of their families and were important members on village committees to promote survival and safety of both mothers and babies.

Another initiative among Mozambican youth was sending health messages by SMS texts on their mobile phones. A committed army of healthcare workers firmly believed in using every possible means to reach a modern generation and this they did with enthusiasm. In the city, others were working on the social issues associated with health and were taking steps to enable women workers to lay claim to privileges considered as rights in the West. These included maternity leave and time to care for and feed their babies. It seemed that Mozambique was moving forwards. People at all levels, from the men at the Ministry to those in remote rural regions, were being mobilised and motivated. Across the generations people, from village elders with traditional values to modern youths, were being bombarded with messages about what saved the lives of women and babies. Clearly much remained to be done, since, as ever, a visitor can only see a small section of what is happening and an evaluation exercise often very naturally offers the best examples for examination. Nevertheless, I am convinced that appreciating what is working and building on it has much to commend it.

Examining the evidence

Education for practice

Since the launch of the Safe Motherhood Initiative (SMI, 1987) efforts to produce educational material suitable for midwives and others have accelerated. It is essential that materials focus on the important aspects of practice, particularly clinical skills, and promoting health messages incorporating outreach to the community. The World Health Organization (WHO) has since produced a second edition of the modules that I originally prepared (WHO, 1996, 2006). The later editions benefit from some additional updates, but the format remains the same. The educational materials have been widely used or adapted in many parts of the world where doctors, midwives and other healthcare workers are tackling the many threats to the survival of women and their newborn. The modules address five major causes of maternal mortality, namely, postpartum haemorrhage, obstructed labour, eclampsia, puerperal sepsis and abortion. These educational resources are directed at aspects of prevention and management of the obstetric conditions responsible for most fatalities. The first and foundation module focuses on issues in the community. Sessions in each module are outlined, incorporating guidance in clinical teaching and the essential theory that underlines practice as well as community visits and the learning games that have proved popular.

The American College of Nurse Midwives (ACNM) has produced 10 modules that have also proved useful in assisting learning life-saving skills (ACNM, 2008). These address various aspects of maternal and newborn care incorporating a problem-solving approach and advocating a caring attitude. They include procedures such as vacuum extraction, manual vacuum aspiration and symphysiotomy, and address neonatal resuscitation and infection in the newborn. The ACNM Home Based Life Saving Skills curriculum provides resources for midwives, childbearing women and communities and includes a manual, a set of large picture cards and other materials to support programme activities (ACNM, 2010).

Other educational materials address specific issues such as female genital mutilation or cutting (WHO, 2001a, b). This issue is of wide concern across Africa as well as parts of Asia and the Middle East and is currently being addressed with renewed enthusiasm. An additional 2000 communities have been reported to have abandoned the practice in 2011. This brings the total number of communities renouncing female genital mutilation or cutting to 8000 since the launch of the accelerated project to end the practice globally by UNFPA and UNICEF in 2008 (UNFPA, 2012). This is in line with the original joint statement on the issue a decade earlier (WHO, 1997).

Whatever materials are used, it is essential that they facilitate learning of essential skills based on the available evidence, backed by fundamental and relevant knowledge. In addition they should promote an attitude that commends and promotes confidence in the carer. Without the latter, the uptake of care is limited with devastating effects. Pettersson et al (2004) report that midwives' abilities to provide quality care in low income and post-war affected countries is restricted by numerous factors including attitudinal issues. They maintain that women's care-seeking behaviour is directly related to the reactions of midwives. Staff attitudes and the quality of their interpersonal skills have been widely reported as influencing uptake of care (Jewkes et al, 1998; Koblinsky et al, 2006; Iliyasu et al, 2010).

Evidence-based practice is of considerable importance in all aspects of education. The Africa Midwives Research Network (AMRN), in partnership with the Karolinska Institute in Stockholm, achieved much in introducing research as a critical component of midwifery care in several countries in the region (Forss and Maclean, 2007) and further details of such activities are discussed in *Chapter 8*. 'Kangaroo care' (Whitelaw et al, 1988), apparent in the Mozambican villages, provides an example of its usefulness and acceptability. Training of trainers forms an essential component of any education programme too as my experience in Malawi cited above illustrates. This is usually a first and critical step in the process, allowing senior personnel to enhance or even learn for the first time skills that they had not had opportunity to learn earlier in their professional lives.

Communicating by every possible means

Utilising or adapting available educational material can be a vital resource in promoting safe practice or any other educational message. However, in Africa there are age old methods of communication that get the message across effectively. Bray et al (2000) recognise that there is not a single African approach to indigenous education and that generalisations lead to inadequate or problematic conclusions amid a dynamic fusion of historical, social and ethnic factors. From his study of traditional communication methods in the old Calabar province of Nigeria, Wilson (1987) identifies 11 broad categories used to communicate information. Methods range from the use of drums and other musical instruments, singing, symbolic writing, sign language, colour schemes and symbolic displays. Emphasising the importance of traditional communication systems as a source of enlightenment in cultural, political, educational, health and other matters he stresses that:

> *It is becoming clearer to scholars on both sides of the socioeconomic divide (the First and Third Worlds) that a clear understanding of the*

structures, patterns, processes and uses of such media could enhance the multiple application of such channels for human and national growth.
(Wilson, 1987: 90)

Osho (2011) claims that the success of the 2011 Egyptian revolution within 18 days could be attributed to the use of oral media; numerous traditional means of communication being used in order to mobilise millions of people into action. This was undoubtedly enhanced by increasing access to the internet. One can but reflect on the possible outcome of the use of such traditional methods to mobilise professions, politicians and communities across the world into promoting safe motherhood.

Zulu (2006) emphasises the strengths of African education before the introduction of Christianity or Islam or of Western schooling across the continent. He emphasises that indigenous education incorporates a plethora of approaches including story telling, games, puzzles, music, dance and participation in ritual, to mention but a few. Omolewa (2007) highlights the point that the pursuit of excellence and a quest for quality has always assumed importance in indigenous African education. He urges the use of these traditional and holistic methods to improve quality in modern education. It is little wonder therefore that the story of Mrs X and the associated educational game cited above (WHO, 2006) found acceptance on the African continent. Such innovative methods are useful starting points in modern professional education, not only across Africa but also in other parts of the world.

Nussbaum (2000) has identified several contrasting values between the West and Africa in respect of wisdom (*Table 5.1*). He asks why the case for African wisdom, made so long ago by so many has been accepted by so few. He concludes that the Western paradigm, in common with all others, while revealing some issues, obscures others (Nussbaum, 2000: 39).

In Africa, illustration and communication take precedence over Western abstract thought, and oral maxims are preferable to written treatises. Effective communication therefore, whether through parable, folk legend,

Table 5.1. Contrasting values in African and Western societies	
African societies	*Western societies*
Ethics	Epistemology, metaphysics
Intuition	Deduction
Illustration and communication	Abstract thought
Oral maxim	Written treatise
Wisdom that is common, old and is derived from the group	Wisdom that is elite, new and derived from the individual
	Derived from Nussbaum (2000:39-43)

story or proverb is perceived and received in very different ways across the great African continent. No doubt this was in the mind of the original Egyptian storyteller, in relating the story of Mrs X to raise the profile of maternal mortality. The story probes into a maternal death. It reveals not only the direct obstetric cause, but traces back the issues that predisposed to the disaster, uncovering numerous injustices and inequities including social, economic and gender issues. The story has been utilised in promoting awareness and action ever since (WHO, 2006: Module 1).

Appreciative inquiry

The use of story telling and dialogue are approaches that are active in implementing appreciative inquiry. This approach holds that image and action are linked and that an organisation will move in the direction precisely related to the questions it asks. It also holds that organisational realities are not fixed, that change is constant and that valuing the best of the past can contribute to continuity in times of transition and change (Cooperrider and Whitney, 2000; Webb and Rockey, 2005). The concept of appreciative inquiry relates to an approach that can be used in numerous situations including management, education and capacity building and has been widely advocated (Cooperrider and Srivastva, 1987; Barrett, 1995; Johnson and Ludema, 1997; Cooperrider and Whitney, 1998). Appreciative inquiry seeks the best of 'what is' to stimulate the collective imagination of 'what might be'. The process aims to generate new knowledge and understanding, helping people to both envision and work towards a desired future. It is a way of being, a philosophy or set of principles, and a process for working through change with individuals, families, groups, organisations and communities. It has been proffered that appreciation relates to the discovery of factors that give life to an organisation and starts by identifying what is best in the current situation and valuing this (Barrett, 1995). It is reasoned that because appreciative inquiry is grounded in actual experience and focuses on the positive, participants will acquire 'a sense of commitment, confidence and affirmation that they have been successful' and will know how to achieve further successes (Hammond, 1996: 7).

The theory of appreciative inquiry is realised in the '4-D cycle' involving four distinct phases (see *Figure 5.3*):

- *Discovery*: determining what gives life to an organisation, through asking questions about the best of what already exists.
- *Dream*: calling for imagination, identifying an ideal future and creating a positive vision of what might be.
- *Design*: involving decision about ways to turn the vision into a reality.
- *Destiny*: regarding implementation of actions that strive towards the ideal.

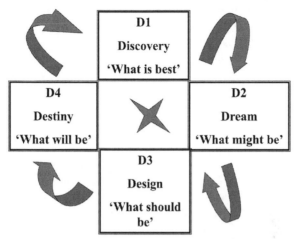

Figure 5.3. The 4-D cycle of appreciative inquiry. Sources: Cooperrider and Srivastva, 1987; Barrett, 1995; Cooperrider and Whitney, 1998.

The concept that is fundamental to appreciative inquiry finds resonance in the Makalu Model (*Box 5.1*) that presents one goal, two laws and three principles (Odell, 1998). Such an approach could be critical in some situations, turning the tide from depression and despair to hope, expectation and realisation.

Utilisation of appreciative inquiry has been reported with enthusiasm from various parts of the world (Sena and Booy, 1997; Odell, 1998; Abbatt, 1999; Moore and Charvat, 2007) and holds potential for use in addressing issues from a constructive rather than a negative and critical approach that can emanate from problem solving. A criticism of appreciative inquiry has been that the approach turns a blind eye to problems. However, its proponents argue

---

Box 5.1. The Makalu Model

- One goal
  - Seeing the root cause of success not the root cause of failure
- Two laws
  - What you are looking for is what you find. The questions you ask determine the answers you get
  - Where you think you are going is where you will end up
- Three principles
  - If you look for problems you will find more problems
  - If you look for success you will find more success
  - If you have faith in your dreams you can accomplish miracles

Derived from Odell, 1998

that problems are not merely used as a basis for analysis or action (Whitney and Trosten-Bloom, 2003), rather that AI finds other ways of tackling them. Indeed as Odell (1998) emphasises, what is looked for is what is found and if successes rather than failures are brought into focus, encouragement is generated and hope is born from which dreams can be realised.

Refugees and health issues

At the beginning of the new millennium a severe cyclone devastated many parts of southern Africa. The worst floods in living memory left a million people destitute in Mozambique. Not surprisingly some of these trickled over the border into Malawi. Refugees across Africa have been on the increase rather than decrease as various countries are hit by natural disasters, civil wars and violence. Women and children are often the worst victims in such situations. In a comprehensive analysis of the effects of natural disaster on vulnerable groups of people in 141 countries over two decades, Neumayer and Plümper (2007) identify that women and girls are much more disadvantaged. The usual life expectancy of females by comparison with males is reversed and more women and girls die in such disasters or in their aftermath. These disadvantages are associated with the socially constructed gender-specific vulnerability of females that is built into the socio-economic patterns of life.

'Environmental refugees' who have been displaced within or from their homeland because of natural disaster have been recognised as a mounting dilemma in the 21st century. In 1995 there were 25 million such refugees globally alongside 27 million persons displaced as a result of conflict and manmade disasters. The former were predicted to double over the ensuing 15 years (Myers, 2002). Prata (2009) points out that within low resource settings, it is the poorest couples that have the highest fertility and the greatest unmet need for contraception. These are the people that are also most vulnerable to maternal and child mortality. Refugees certainly fall into this category, as many countries, already with very limited resources, try to accommodate those who have had to seek refuge from their homes. UNHCR (2009) reports that African nations hosted 10.5 million refugees and displaced persons at the end of 2007, a million more than the previous year and a third of those for whom UNHCR have a concern worldwide.

A question of value

Values may be perceived very differently and it can be helpful to consider two main aspects. These are the value placed on individuals within a community, and the system of values enshrined within that civilization.

The value placed on individuals will be reflected to some extent by their own perception of self-worth and significance. Short (1971: 81) claims that 'dignity and esteem are the birthright of every child', yet the poor, and especially women and children, seem to be sold short of such a heritage; their place and value in many societies is challenged and threatened by conditions beyond their control. Refugees and asylum seekers are at risk of losing any sense of dignity, esteem and personal value and they are often perceived as threats and burdens to nations overwhelmed by their needs. The value of human life lies in the balance in many situations in the modern world, as those holding the power, position or possessions have the final word on what and who matters. It has been claimed that values held by individuals are strongly influenced by the society and the culture in which they have been nurtured (Erez and Earley, 1993).

Values have been perceived as those matters that give meaning to action and are defined as:

...enduring beliefs that a specific mode of conduct is personally or socially preferable to an opposite or converse mode of conduct or end-state of existence.

(Rokeach, 1973:5)

It has long been held that traditional religious values shape institutions within a society and that their influence is both profound and enduring (Weber, 1958). Hofstede (1991) declares that values form the core of a culture, while Inglehart and Baker (2000) maintain that a society's culture reflects its total historical heritage. Huntington (1993, 1996) perceives the world to be divided into eight major civilizations. These are derived from centuries of religious traditions that have moulded their cultural trends and persist into the modern day. The eight civilisations comprise those of Western Christianity, Orthodoxy, Islam, Hinduism, Confucianism, as well as the civilisations of Japan, Africa and Latin America. Yet, having undertaken an extensive study across Latin America, Lenartowicz and Johnson (2003) contend that to perceive the region as culturally homogenous and stereotypical is erroneous, and they point to a considerable divergence in the importance of values across the area. It would seem that to view any region of the 21st century world as homogenous will inevitably lead to flawed conclusions. Rokeach (1973) concluded that, in reality, values are often in competition with one another and that when they are in conflict individuals are forced to choose between them. Many value systems are currently being challenged in the modern world. As illustrated in *Chapter 4*, a cross-cultural visitor needs to be aware that the values and philosophies upon which ethical principles are based will undoubtedly influence a society's norms. Yet an assumption that a whole community will necessarily be in unison can lead to miscalculations and these issues need serious consideration before recommendations are made or changes proposed.

Personal reflections on practice

- Relevance is a quality worth seeking in any situation and is most valuable if it can be found when crossing cultures.
- There is always a considerable resource of indigenous creativity that can be tapped.
- Appreciating what is good and what works is inevitably more fruitful than criticism. No-one thrives on criticism, but encouragement can engender the energy needed to effect further progress.
- Maternal death is always abhorrent, more so when it is close at hand. Every mother who dies was close to someone, and the pain we share in such circumstances motivates me to continue striving towards relegating these untimely deaths to the history books.

Some lessons learned and shared

- Encouraging local creativity at every opportunity is beneficial since a home-made solution is invariably preferable to an imported one.
- Discovering the communication strategies that are popular within the culture being visited is informative. Check them out with a national colleague before utilising them where appropriate.
- It is useful to try to find out about some local proverbs and folklore and consider how these may impact on thinking, values and decisions. Imagine how they might influence the way in which a message can most effectively be conveyed in such a culture, especially if it is a difficult one.

Reflective exercises

- Considering the view expressed by Nussbaum (2000) and cited above (*Table 5.1*), reflect on how your value perspective causes you to come to conclusions.
- Examine some of the proverbs and childhood stories with which you grew up and consider the moral they are conveying. Then explore and consider some African stories and proverbs:
    - What messages do they convey?
    - Do the messages vary between the different cultures?
    - Are there similarities?

- Take a look at an aspect of your daily work. Using the appreciative inquiry approach, explore the 4-D cycle (*Figure 5.3*) and consider how you might use this to introduce change. As you do so, bear in mind the Makalu Model (*Box 5.1*). If practicable, invite some colleagues to consider this with you or to give you feedback on your ideas.

Resources

Educational resources can be downloaded in pdf form from the following sites:
- ACNM Life Saving Skills: http://www.midwife.org.
- WHO midwifery education modules: http://www.who.int/maternal_ child_adolescent/documents/9241546662/en/

See also the following websites to download full resources for the educational games:
- Walking where Mrs X walked (Note: the board is not included in the downloaded Module 1): http://www.who.int/maternal_child_adolescent/ multimedia/game/game1/en/index.html
- Do you know? A game to teach and revise facts and promote good practice relating to PPH: http://www.who.int/maternal_child_ adolescent/multimedia/game/game2/en/index.html

Other useful websites include:
- United Nations Population Fund (UNFPA) http://www.unfpa.org/
- United Nations Children's Fund (UNICEF) http://www.unicef.org/

References

Abbatt J (1999) *Challenging 'Ke Garne'. Experiences of the Nepal Safer Motherhood Initiative.* Options Consultancy Agency. 176/96/DFID

Africa.com (2012) *Tanzania facts and figures.* Available from: http://www.africa.com/tanzania/ facts [last accessed 10/02/2012]

American College of Nurse Midwives (2008) *Life saving skills manual for midwives* (4th edn). American College of Nurse Midwives, Silver Spring MD

American College of Nurse Midwives (2010) *Home based life saving skills* (2nd edn). American College of Nurse Midwives, Silver Spring MD

Barrett FJ (1995) Creating appreciative learning cultures. *Organizational Dynamics* **24**(1): 36–49

Bray M, Peter C, Stephens D (2000) Indigenous forms of education: The individual and society. In Brock-Unte B (Ed). *Whose education for all: Recolonization of the African mind.* Falmer Press, New York

Cooperrider DL, Srivastva S (1987) Appreciative inquiry in organizational life. In: Passmore W, Woodman R (eds.) *Research on organizational change and development* (Vol 1: 129–69). JAI Press, Greenwich, CT

Cooperrider DL, Whitney D (1998) When stories have wings: How 'Relational responsibility' opens new options for action. In: McNamee S, Gergen K (eds) *Relational responsibility.* Sage Publications, Thousand Oaks, CA

Cooperrider DL, Whitney D (2000) A positive revolution in change: Appreciative inquiry. In: Cooperrider D, Sorensen PF, Whitney D, Yaeger TF (eds) *Appreciative inquiry: Rethinking human organization toward a positive theory of change.* Stipes Publishing, Champaign, Ill

Erez M, Earley PC (1993) *Culture, self-identity and work.* Oxford University Press, New York.

Forss K, Maclean G (2007) *The Africa Midwives Research Network, Sida Evaluation 07/16.* Department for Democracy and Social Development, Swedish Department for International Development, Stockholm

Hammond SA (1996) *The thin book of appreciative inquiry.* Thin Book Publishing Co, Bend OR

Hofstede G (1991) *Cultures and organizations: Software of the mind.* McGraw-Hill, New York

Huntington SP (1993) The clash of civilizations? *Foreign Affairs* **72**(3): 22–49.

Huntington SP (1996) *The clash of civilizations and the remaking of world order.* Simon and Schuster, New York

Iliyasu Z, Abubakar IS, Galadanci HS, Aliyu MH (2010) Birth preparedness, complication, readiness and father's participation in maternity care in a north Nigerian community. *African Journal of Reproductive Health* **14**(1): 21–32

Index Mundi (2012) *Country comparison > population.* Available from: http://www.indexmundi.com/g/r.aspx [last accessed 28.09.2012]

Inglehart R, Baker WE (2000) Modernization, cultural change and persistence of tradidional values. Looking forward, looking back. Continuity at the change of the millennium. *American Sociological Review* **65**(1): 19–51

Jewkes R, Abrahams N, Mvo Z (1998) Why do nurses abuse patients? Reflections from South African obstetric services. *Social Sciences and Medicine* **38**:1069–73

Johnson S, Ludema JD (1997) *Partnering to build and measure organizational capacity. Chapter 5: Using Appreciative Inquiry to build capacity.* Christian Reformed World Relief Committee, Grand Rapids, MI

Koblinsky M, Mathews Z, Hussein J et al (2006) Going to scale with skilled care. *The Lancet.* Available from: www.thelancet.com DOI:10.1016/S0140-6736(06)69382-3

Lenartowicz T, Johnson JP (2003) A cross-national assessment of the values of Latin American managers: Contrasting hues or shades of gray? *Journal of International Business Studies* **34**: 266–81

Moore S, Charvat J (2007) Promoting health behavior change using appreciative inquiry: Moving from deficit models to affirmation models of care. *Family and Community Health* **30**(S1): S64–74

Myers N (2002) Environmental refugees: A growing phenomenon of the twenty first century. *Philosophical Transactions of the Royal Society* **357**(1420): 609–13

Neumayer E, Plümper T (2007) The gendered nature of natural disasters: The impact of catastrophic events on gender and life expectancy, 1982–2002. *Annals of American Geographers* **97**(3): 551–6

Nussbaum S (2000) Profundity with panache. The unappreciated proverbial wisdom of sub-Saharan Africa. In: Brown WS (ed) *Understanding wisdom: Sources, science and society* (pp. 35–55). Templeton Foundation Press, Philadelphia

Odell M (1998) Appreciative planning and action: Experience from the field. Evaluating a new strategy for empowering communities in Nepal. In: Hammond SA, Royal C (eds) *Lessons from the field: Applying appreciative inquiry*. Practical Press Inc, Plano, TX

Omolewa M (2007) Traditional modes of African education, their relevance in the modern world. *International Review of Education* **53**(5–6): 593–612

Osho SA (2011) *The uniqueness of African means of communication in a contemporary World.* Paper presented at a seminar organised by the Institute for Cultural Diplomacy (ICD), Kurfurstendamm, Berlin, Germany July 11 – 17, 2011. Available from: http://www.culturaldiplomacy.org/culturaldiplomacynews/participant-papers/africa/osho [last accessed 06.10.2012]

Pettersson KO, Christensson K, Freitas E da G, Johansson E (2004) Adaptation of health care seeking behaviour during childbirth. Focus group discussions with women living in the suburban areas of Luanda, Angola. *Health Care for Women International* **25**(3): 255–80

Prata N (2009) Making family planning accessible in resource poor settings. Philosophical *Transactions of the Royal Society* **364**(1532): 3093–9

Rokeach M (1973) *The nature of human values.* Free Press, New York

Safe Motherhood Initiative (1987) *Preventing the tragedy of maternal deaths.* A report of the international Safe Motherhood conference, Nairobi, Kenya. WHO, Geneva

Save the Children (2012) *State of the World's mothers 2012. The 2012 Mothers' Index.* Save the Children. Available from: http://www.savethechildren.org/ [last accessed 13/07/2012]

Sena SO, Booy DO (1997) Appreciative inquiry approach to community development: The World vision Tanzania experience. Global Social Innovations. *Journal of the Global Excellence in Management Initiative* **1**(2): 7–12

Short E (1971) *Education in a changing world.* Alden Mowbray Ltd, Oxford

United Nations Development Programme (2011) *International Human Development Indicators.* United Nations Development Programme. Available from: http://hdr.undp.org/en/statistics/ [Last accessed 13.02.2012]

UNFPA (2012) *2,000 More African communities end female genital mutilation/cutting in 2011*. Available from: http://www.unfpa.org/public/ [Last accessed 07/02/2012]

UNHCR (2009) *Global appeal 2009 update. Part II UNHCR Operations*. Available from: http://www.unhcr.org/ [Last accessed 07/02/2012]

UNICEF (2012) *State of the world's children 2012*. UNICEF, New York

Webb L, Rockey S (2005) *Organizational change inside and out. The impact of an appreciative inquiry. Journal for Non-Profit Management*. Available from: http://appreciativeinquiry.case.edu/practice/ [Last accessed 10/01/2012]

Weber M (1958) *The Protestant ethic and the spirit of capitalism*. 1904 version translated by Parsons T (Reprint) Charles Scribner's Sons, New York

Whitelaw A, Heisterkamp G, Sleath K, Acolet D, Richards M (1988) Skin to skin contact for very low birthweight infants and their mothers. *Archives of Disease in Childhood* **63**: 1377–81

Whitney D, Trosten-Bloom A (2003) *The power of appreciative inquiry*. Berrett-Koehler, San Francisco

WHO (1996) *Midwifery education modules. Education for safe motherhood. Educational material for teachers of midwifery*. WHO, Geneva

WHO (1997) *Female genital mutilation. A joint WHO/UNICEF/UNFPA Statement*. WHO, Geneva

WHO (2001a) *Female genital mutilation: Integrating the prevention and the management of the health complications into the curricula of nursing and midwifery*. A teacher's guide. Department of Gender and Women's Health, Department of Reproductive Health and Research, World Health Organization, Geneva

WHO (2001b) *Female genital mutilation: Integrating the prevention and the management of the health complications into the curricula of nursing and midwifery*. A student's manual. Department of Gender and Women's Health, Department of Reproductive Health and Research, World Health Organization, Geneva

WHO (2006) *Midwifery education modules. Education for safe motherhood. Educational material for teachers of midwifery* (2nd edn). World Health Organization, Geneva

WHO (2012) *Trends in maternal mortality 1990–2010*. WHO, UNICEF, UNFPA and World Bank. WHO, Geneva

Wilson D (1987) Traditional systems of communication in modern African development: An analytical viewpoint. *Africa Media Review* **1**(2): 87–104

World Factbook (2012) *World factbook*. Available from: https://www.cia.gov/library/publications/the-world-factbook/ [last accessed 09.07.2012]

Zulu IM (2006) Critical indigenous African education and knowledge. *Journal of Pan-African Studies* **1**(3): 32–49

Chapter 6

The highs and lows of the Himalayas

Never lose an opportunity of seeing anything beautiful, for beauty is God's handwriting.

(Ralph Waldo Emerson)

Perceptions of colonial rule will be very different, depending on which side of the colonial highway one was raised

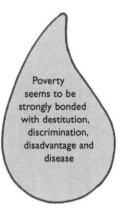

Poverty seems to be strongly bonded with destitution, discrimination, disadvantage and disease

Subject strands introduced

- Colonialism
- Modernisation and development
- Poverty
- The importance of traditions, values and societal norms
- Glimpses into anthropological perspectives
- Skilled attendance during childbirth

Practice points

- Adapting and enhancing one's skills
- Minimising jet lag
- Bridging an 'epoch gap'
- Considering an enabling environment
- Coping with a 'quality gap'
- Setting up helpful contacts for an overseas elective or assignment

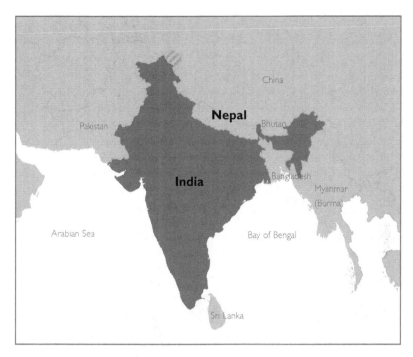

Figure 6.1. India and Nepal.

India: Background

India

India is the largest country in South Asia and the seventh largest in the world. It is bordered by Bangladesh, Bhutan, Myanmar (Burma), China, Nepal and Pakistan. The name is thought to mean 'Land of the Indus River' ultimately derived from 'Sindhu', the Sanskrit name for the river. Seven thousand kilometres of coastline meet the Arabian Sea on the western side and the Bay of Bengal in the east. India stretches for $3\,287\,363$ km^2 and Kanchenjunga in the Himalayan region close to the border with Nepal is the third highest mountain in the world. The capital of India is New Delhi, although Mumbai is the city with the largest population. A federal republic, India gained independence from Britain in 1947 and also partition from Pakistan. India has the second highest national population in the world with 1.2 billion people (estimated 2012) with 28% living in urban areas. The religion is predominantly Hindu (80%) with Islam being the largest of the minority religions practised. The legislative system is based on English common law with separate personal law codes that apply to Hindus, Christians and Muslims. The official national languages are Hindi and English with a further 22 official scheduled languages and a total of 438 reported 'living languages'. Exports include textiles, chemicals, jewellery, engineering goods, chemicals and leather.

Nepal

Nepal is a landlocked country extending partly across the Himalayas, being home to Mount Everest, and reaching to the plains known as the 'tarai' which are part of the basin of the river Ganges. The name is thought to derive from the Tibetan-Burman languages indicating those who domesticate cattle, but the Sanskrit *'nipalaya'* implies an abode at the foot of the mountains. It is bordered by China and India and extends for 147181 km². The capital city is Kathmandu. Nepal is one of the few countries that has never been colonised by a foreign power. It became a federal democratic republic in 2008, the king vacated the throne and the first president was elected. Nepal has a population of almost 30 million (estimated 2012) with 15% living in the urban areas. The country is recognised as a secular state with the predominant religion being Hinduism. The legal system is based on English common law and Hindu legal concepts. The official national languages are Nepali and English with a further 124 reported 'living languages'. Nepal is one of the world's poorest countries and natural hazards also challenge the country in the form of severe thunder storms, floods, droughts and famine. Natural resources include quartz, timber and natural beauty so that tourism has been an important industry in the area. Agriculture is the mainstay of the economy providing a livelihood for 75% of the population. Exports include textiles, clothing, carpets, pashima, pulses and jute.

India and Nepal: Data

India	Nepal
HDI*: medium (134)	HDI*: low 157
MMR: 200 (2010)	MMR: 170 (2010)
Lifetime risk of maternal death: 1 in 170	Lifetime risk of maternal death: 1 in 190
Mothers index ranking (2012)**: 76(Tier II)	Mothers index ranking(2012)**: 12(Tier III)
Births attended by skilled personnel: 53%	Births attended by skilled personnel: 19%

HDI: Human Development Index, MMR: Maternal Mortality Ratio
*Assessed according to life expectancy, educational and economic factors
**Ranked globally (within 3 tiers: I = more developed, II = less developed, III = least developed) according to health, education, economic and political status of women

Background and data sources: Ethnologue, 2012; Index Mundi, 2012, Infoplease, 2012; Nationmaster, 2012; Save the Children, 2012; United Nations Development Programme, 2010; UNICEF, 2012; World Facts, 2012; WHO, 2012

Exploring experience

Climb every mountain

My first ascent into the foothills of the Himalayas was during my early experiences of serving in India. The North Indian Missionary Language Board had a language school based near Mussoorie and the approach and style of learning I experienced there were far beyond most available at the time. My experiences at the school taught me a lot about language learning, as some of the most superb teachers worked tirelessly to perfect our pronunciation and handwriting in the Deva Nagri script. The latter had to be penned with a quill, no ballpoint or pencil would suffice, as the broad and fine marks had to be made with ink and had to be immaculate.

The climb into the mountains started soon after leaving Dehradun, the state capital, which nestled in the foothills. A series of hairpin bends and steep ascents soon left the heat of the Indian plains behind. Crossing the boundary into the region in the late afternoon on my first visit meant that night had fallen long before we reached our destination. The last lap of the journey had to be completed on foot and coolies assisting with baggage advised that it was best to keep to the left. I was to discover later, in the light of day, that there were steep drops to the right of the narrow moutain path. It was for the same reason that the experienced 'mountaineers' advised that one should always insist on taking the inner side of the path when coming face to face with a cow on a mountain trail. I was also to discover that the area was inhabited by black panthers. Although I did not have the dubious privilege of meeting them, no doubt they eyed me from time to time from a safe distance.

The rarefied air slowed down every newcomer, who could easily be recognised, not only by their rate of climbing but also by their clothing. This subtropical region was perceived as very warm by those arriving from a temperate climate, but after a short while, layers of warmer clothing indicated some adaptation to the environment.

It was years before I was able to view the snows that capped those mighty mountains, only visible at certain times of the year and in clear weather conditions from particular vantage points in the foothills. However, my first visit to Nepal posed no such challenge as the impressive snows of the Himalayas formed a massive backdrop seemingly at the end of every street of the capital city, Kathmandu.

I welcomed the first advice I received on arriving for an assignment with the World Health Organization (WHO). As well as briefing me on the situation and the challenges to providing healthcare that were faced in that mountainous country, my medical colleague added: 'And don't forget to nourish your soul too, there are such beautiful parts of this country!' It was my final visit that enabled me to view the mighty Mount Everest or, as it is called locally, '*Sagarmatha*', meaning head or forehead of the sky. I saw it not by climbing, but by flying near it, and it was without doubt such a breathtaking sight that it did indeed help to nourish the soul.

Prescribing and providing

My first encounter with an Indian village was in the northwest of the country. Fully prepared to provide any assistance within my professional scope of practice I faced a small queue of ailing individuals. However, the first and most urgent case was a boy with a dental abscess. I had worked for a time as a dental nurse before embarking on my professional education, but on this occasion I wished that I was a dentist. The tooth had been extracted, I never discovered how or by whom, but I had seen local tinkers at the job armed with pliers in a nearby town. The only antibiotic available was an intramuscular preparation of penicillin. I was informed that the schoolteacher's wife could give injections, what was needed was a prescription and I was required to write it. I very quickly learned that in such situations, referral may not be an option and even if it were, the cost to the village people can be prohibitive or at least has to be balanced with the benefit of what is obtained. It was perceived that I could provide them with a free consultation and prescription, so problem solved.

On the other side of that vast subcontinent on one of my visits to the poorest state in the east of India, I was presented with a baby. Small enough to be considered within my sphere of practice it would seem, but this tiny child was nine months old and suffering a severe chest infection. Again a prescription was required. I was in the area long enough to see the baby pull through and respond to the treatment. However, she would need to be nourished in order to survive a village life of poverty that claims many children before their first and certainly before their fifth birthday.

In a Nepali village, I was presented with a child with an insect in his ear. Not an everyday event for a midwife, but who cared about that? I had learned on many occasions that it is not so much what one would choose to do but always what needs to be done that requires attention, and visitors are expected to bring some relief to such situations. The fact that one is not a specialist in the field is of no consequence. Some help is better than no help. No doubt had I been a teacher or an engineer I would still have been asked to solve the problem. Offering simple instructions that were translated into the local language, I could only hope that my efforts would suffice in allowing the exit of this invading insect from the ear of the child. For those with more complicated problems, there would not always be a solution in such a situation. At times the dilemmas faced by these rural residents would defy all reasonable hopes of being resolved.

Overcoming the obstacles

It was the remoteness as well as the lack of infrastructure in parts of this country that prompted a medical colleague to offer me some strange advice. I had arrived in Nepal to plan and undertake training in obstetric life saving skills with auxiliary nurse-midwives (ANMs). Given the remoteness of some of the villages and hamlets and that the distance from any kind of health facility could be measured in days rather than hours, he advised, 'You know, sometimes the best thing you can teach these ANMs is how to enable a woman to die with dignity.' This was a difficult concept to absorb into a life saving skills curriculum. Had we been considering victims of incurable disease, it might have been easier to accept, but here were young women, some very young, who were doing no more than fulfilling a basic biological function which should have brought joy and hope. However, these young people all too often confronted a terminal condition in the process of giving birth. Experiencing the harshness of the terrain and the remoteness of so many little hamlets from any kind of medical help I could understand the advice of my medical colleague. Clearly, there were many obstacles to be overcome.

Along with a colleague I pursued every effort to teach the skills that could save lives. We decided to organise the course in three sections, returning to the country on each occasion in order to teach and review. The final weeks required each ANM to report back on her experiences and we also visited the health posts to see what each one had been able to implement. This process caused great excitement. The ANMs were not accorded much status in society. The fact that consultants from another country had come to visit their village helped their self-esteem, but nothing equalled the thrill of those who shared how they had saved lives because of what they had learned.

One participant arrived late every morning. Her delayed appearance was unavoidable given her home commitments and the unreliability of the transport from her village, but her passion was second to none. She aspired to work in London's Great Ormond Street Hospital. Her language limitation and lack of education did not deter her persistent enquiries, but it was the successful resuscitation of a newborn that fired her enthusiasm and the admiration of her colleagues. 'I saved his life!' she exclaimed, 'I made him breathe!' In such an environment as this I learned to see the beauty in people as well as in the natural environment. Those who had been born in obscurity and raised in adversity were struggling and succeeding against the odds.

What health workers can achieve is determined of course not only by their skills and their geographical location, but also by the supplies and equipment that is at their disposal. I have met with those who are unskilled and have well-equipped clinics, but also with those possessing the necessary skills but no supplies. I shall long remember a young ANM placed in a village thousands of miles from her home, telling me with tears of frustration that she could do so little for these villagers. She showed me the inferior place that served as her clinic in a north Indian village, and lamented the fact that she did not even have two paracetamol to administer to her patients. This echoed a conversation I had had with an obstetrician at the headquarters of the World Health Organization in Geneva. We were deploring some of the situations in which our colleagues work and he had acknowledged with a mixture of frustration and fury that in many circumstances he could not save a life either. It is for this reason that the skilled attendance initiative looks beyond the skills and into the environment where such skills need to be used.

Moving back a few centuries

On entering Kathmandu one enters a different world. Street corners not only accommodate entrepreneurs peddling their wares, but a plethora of shrines to the revered deities. Aromas of incense mingle with the appetising odours of Nepali cuisine and all aspects of life seem to be evident at the roadside. Crossing from one side of the busy streets to another needs an acute sense of timing. There are pushcarts and animal carts, cows that wander at will, and scooters, buses and other motor vehicles. Crossing such a thoroughfare presented me with a dilemma in my early days in the city and I eventually learned the timing from joining a group of locals well rehearsed in the art.

Visiting the city of Patan, sometimes known as *Lalitpur* ('place of beauty'), is like travelling back in time. Along with Kathmandu and Bhaktapur, Patan is one of the three legendary royal cities of Nepal situated in the Kathmandu Valley. Patan, believed to have been established in the third century BC, seems little changed since the Middle Ages. Temples abound and artisans produce their wares by age-old methods. Water and electricity cannot be taken for granted even in the 21st century, and cuts to the electricity supplies can last for 12 to 14 hours. Visitors can find themselves living in what seems like a bygone age, and skills of adaptation are necessary if one is not only to survive, but also complete the scheduled assignment.

On assignment in India, I stayed in a guest house in Delhi that regularly experienced electricity cuts and water shortages during the summer season. In such circumstances there can be a rapid deterioration in the function of everything that is needed to support life. The supplied candle resisted ignition and efforts were additionally foiled by a damp box of matches. In such circumstances a good torch is an essential ally. I learned during the course of the years experiencing this kind of environment, not only to pack essential back up supplies, but also, having done what I could to make the situation tolerable, to take note of the things that do work and of what is good. Being negative will only result in further frustration.

Examining the evidence

Expanding our skills and addressing our own shortcomings

The 'multicultural protean individuals' described by Fry and Thurber (1989) and discussed in *Chapter 2* express something of the necessity for the travelling professional to be like a chameleon, able to change and utilise a variety of specialist skills according to need. Although one can aspire to become a good all-rounder, no-one can be expert in every field and recognising one's limitations is an important part of being a professional. However, given the demands that are inevitably thrust upon the visitor, whether student or consultant, it is worth being forearmed. The Hesperian Health Guides, which can be downloaded from http://store.hesperian.org/ or obtained in hard copies, are invaluable in assisting in medical, dental and midwifery emergencies, in promoting health and providing basic care at the community level (Klein et al, 2009; Burns et al, 2010; Dickson, 2010; Werman et al, 2011). A comprehensive resource for public health practitioners, policy makers, programme officers and agencies has also been produced by those experienced in the field addressing issues associated with maternal and perinatal mortality in low resource settings (Hussein et al, 2012) and could prove a useful reference for consultants advising in these areas. Some professionals will take the opportunity to acquire further skills through short-term programmes especially designed for the purpose, such as those offered by the London School of Hygiene and Tropical Medicine or the Liverpool School of Tropical Medicine. Details of these organisations are provided at the end of this chapter.

The importance of adequate preparation for overseas assignments has long been recognised and adopting appropriate attitudes is of equal importance to adopting appropriate behaviour (Mendenhall and Oddau, 1985; Tung, 1987; Black and Mendenhall, 1990; Caligiuri, 2000; van Vianen et al, 2004, Shin et al, 2007; Maclean, 2011a,b,c). In my research, it was inappropriate attitudes and cultural offences that rated highest on the unacceptability scale and these were often rated as unforgivable sins (Maclean, 1998). Unacceptability of the visiting expert is summarised thus:

> *There are many things that make a consultant unacceptable. It is mainly their attitude, especially if they have a superiority complex and approach us as if they know more. Also, if they remind us of our colonial past and that they were the ruling powers; this does not go down well. If they are judgemental, negative and talk down to us. If they make comparisons with our worst standards and make us feel small.*
>
> *(Maclean, 1998: 285)*

Considering colonialism

Unlike India, colonialism did not form part of the history of Nepal, although it is claimed that the colonial presence in the rest of South Asia influenced Nepal's political economy and her society (Mikesell, 1988; Des Chene, 1991, 1994). Colonialism can be viewed from differing perspectives. Pels

(1997) perceives the subject from the anthropological viewpoint claiming that in this discipline, colonialism is viewed in one of three ways or in a combination of the three, namely:

> *...as the universal, evolutionary progress of modernization; as a particular strategy or experiment in domination and exploitation; and as the unfinished business of struggle and negotiation.*
>
> *(Pels, 1997: 164)*

Pels claims that the third of these views attained greatest emphasis in the final quarter of the 20th century. Little wonder then that palpable resistance to foreign intervention can be sensed in the course of some encounters within countries previously colonised, especially if the visitor originates from the land of the relevant colonial power.

In considering the opposing perspectives on colonialism and its effects in India, Yang (2007) considers how rebellion had been viewed from within the society during the latter part of the 18th century by contrast with opinions expressed by proponents of the Raj. Of the former group he writes:

> *Their resistance was celebrated and lionised, not criminalised, as it had been by the colonial authorities and in the narratives they created. Kings and bandits, after all, can have similar roots and routes, and their interplay in all its different manifestations forms a key plot point in the historical drama that unfolded in early colonial India.*
>
> *(Yang, 2007: 895)*

Reflecting on the dilemma of establishing historical issues in the Indian sub-continent, Bose (2003:146) proposes an innovative approach:

> *A new departure towards comparative and connective histories might be the best way to bid the defensiveness engendered by European colonialism in post-colonial histories of South Asia its final adieu. The shackles placed on historical writing by the post-colonial state, religious majoritarianism and a hyper-real Europe will then finally have been broken.*

One must consider that these post-colonial shackles may also inhibit relationships and limit progress in areas far beyond history writing. For example, in attempting to assist national efforts to improve healthcare, the visiting consultant, often in common with national colleagues, may well be confronted by various restraints. Every sense and sensitivity needs to be used in order to penetrate these obstacles, not to dominate but to provide the best resource for the development that is desired from within the country.

Just as the attitude of those whose ancestors have been colonised needs to abandon the concept, so does the mindset of the visitor whose ancestors colonised much of the world in past centuries. We are, undeniably, products of our history, from whichever side of the ocean we originate and however limited our knowledge of that history may be. Many injustices have been perpetrated in the name of progress; professionals in the 21st century have an opportunity to offer something better. Visitors to such regions are required to step away from a history that may have contaminated concepts of the nation they currently represent, but remember that it is also liable to influence their perception of the country now requesting their support.

Differing perceptions of modernisation and development

Some of the concepts with which we grapple on a day-to-day basis can resist precise definition. People originating from different disciplines will offer their own perspectives on such issues and in considering these, some light can be shed for the edification of others. For example, Gereffi and Fonda (1992) perceive development as a multidimensional phenomenon but acknowledge the difficulty in defining or measuring it, proposing rather to identify its ideal, namely that:

> *The essence of development is to improve the quality of life.*
> *(Gereffi and Fonda, 1992: 420)*

Such a principle will find resonance with healthcare professionals and must be the aspiration of most students in these disciplines too. Nevertheless, attempts have been made not only to define, but also to classify countries along the developmental highway. A World Systems Theory that classified nations in three tiers had been utilised during the latter part of the 20th century, identifying the least developed countries at the periphery and the most developed at the core. Other countries that comprise the semiperiphery region are perceived as maintaining the stability of the theory since they serve as a buffer between the two extremes (Wallerstein, 1974; Arrighi and Drangel, 1986; Arrighi, 1990).

This has been dubbed a highly political classification created by intellectuals attempting to account for the inability of countries in the semiperipheral sector to catch up with those at the core (Chirot and Hall, 1982). The writers also purport that the World Systems Theory evolved in contradiction to an earlier prevailing modernisation theory propounded by Rostow (1960) but acknowledge that despite the debatable ideology of Rostow's theory it contributed greatly to thinking on the topic. Rostow recognised that modernisation progressed in stages from traditional economies through evolving levels of industrialisation to an age of high consumption. In considering this process, Chirot and Hall (1982) warn that perspectives on modernisation and development always need to be viewed historically, and from the standpoint of centuries rather than decades, even when considering contemporary issues. In this context they cite the World Systems Theory as worthy of note.

As indicated above, anthropological studies identify colonialism as representing 'the universal, evolutionary progress of modernisation' (Pels, 1997: 164). In examining its different aspects, Inkeles and Smith (1974) point out that from the sociopsychological point of view, modernisation can be seen as a process of change in the way in which things are perceived, expressed and valued. This might indeed not be in contradiction to the anthropological view, since colonialism too would certainly have influenced perception and expression and may well have infiltrated the pre-existing value system. However, the work of Inglehart and Baker (2000) would question any lasting impact on time-honoured values and this issue is further explored below. Whether modernisation and development relate to the same or fundamentally different issues could be debated at length. Shukla (1987) identifies development as being synonymous with growth, progress and modernisation, stating that:

> *The link between development and modernisation is complex and intricate because development can be both the precursor and follower of modernisation...*
>
> *(Shukla, 1987: 7)*

Does modernity inevitably challenge tradition?

While working on development issues, the possibility of sweeping away the traditions of a society in the wake of modernisation needs to be recognised as a very real threat that may not be acceptable to an indigenous population. It would seem that few countries have managed to overcome the challenge of modernity with ease. Nevertheless, Inglehart and Baker (2000), from their survey of values among 65 societies incorporating 75% of the global population, maintain that although economic development is accompanied by massive cultural change there is evidence that distinctive traditions persist. They propose an update of the modernisation theory suggesting that this is not a linear process and that:

> *The rise of the service sector and the transition to a knowledge society are linked with a different set of cultural changes from those that characterised industrialisation.*
>
> *(Inglehart and Baker, 2000: 49)*

They also maintain that the process of modernisation can be reversed in the face of economic collapse. Furthermore, although organised religion may assume less importance in some modernised societies, the search for meaning in life appears to increase, and the effects of the ideology that shaped the society tend to persist and influence future development, whether this is Confucianism, Protestantism or Islam.

Tracing the Japanese experience of modernisation and development it is possible to consider how traditional cultural values have been retained and even expanded in the wake of modern technological advances (Kobayashi, 1981) thus offering direction not only for development as a discipline but also for those who seek to serve its purposes across the globe. It was through the ability of Japan to protect herself from the influences of economic colonialism that explains Japan's swift development (Moulder, 1977). If colonialism is not perceived as a stumbling block, its absence is deemed to offer liberty to develop in a more appropriate manner.

Lags and gaps that may be encountered

The reality of culture shock can be distressing and this was discussed in *Chapter 4*. However, there are other issues that the cross-cultural traveller will encounter.

Jet lag has been extensively described and is frequently experienced by travellers crossing time zones. Similar symptoms may be experienced by shift workers and have been described as 'shift worker's malaise' (Waterhouse et al, 1992). Both these conditions can cause tiredness and confusion and can disrupt the sleep pattern (NHS, 2012). Circadian rhythms give rise to physical, mental and behavioural changes. Biological clocks drive circadian rhythms (National Institute of General Medical Sciences, 2008) and, as Waterhouse (1999) explains, the body clock adjusts each day to function in phase with solar time, having both endogenous and exogenous components that are normally synchronised. It is the latter that is influenced by lifestyle and environment and can therefore fall out of phase with the inner body clock or endogenous element.

Travelling to the Indian sub-continent from the UK involves a time difference of between four and a half and six hours depending on the exact location and the season. Sleep experts advise adjusting exposure to light by avoiding it during certain hours and then seeking it in order to synchronise more nearly to the new time zone. Adopting mealtimes in accordance with the new environment and taking exercise will also influence adaptation of the body clock (British Airways, 2012). Ensuring good hydration and taking the opportunity to sleep during the flight, avoiding taking daytime naps on arrival and spending time in the sunshine are all advocated to minimise the effects of jet lag (NHS, 2012). Of course, a short-term visitor may not have much control over the daily programme and sometimes work must start immediately on arrival. Waterhouse (1999) advises visitors only spending a few days in a different time zone to time appointments to coincide with the daytime hours at home. This can be a useful tip for the short-term consultant needing to plan an important meeting; however, the ideal is not always attainable.

It was in the context of identifying the various stages of modernisation and development evident in today's world that I identified an 'epoch gap'. This gap occurs when a person traverses not only geographical and cultural barriers but steps back in history into a place that is at a different stage of modernisation and development (Maclean, 1998). The benefits of modern living and 21st century technology are not available in what is sometimes termed 'the developing

---

Box 6.1. A cross-cultural visitor's 'If'

If you can recognise, yet bridge the 'epoch gap', then travelling home, can bridge it in reverse,

If you can adjust your 'epoch clock' to match the moment, yet still consider time of no import,

If you can know instinctively what may not happen and not waste energy willing it to change,

If you can cope with frustration, disappointment, and not increase the burden others bear,

If you will wear a 'warning label' which states 'imported answers may not work!'

And with a smile, nod at your hazard warning, still game to offer what only you can give,

If you can devolve all expectation to those who have a right to call such hopes their own,

If you can blanch the stains imprinted by colonialism, and not leave marks of yet another coup,

If you can trace the footprints of development and not obscure them with modernity's murky marks,

If you can offer routes through 'modernisation minefields' and own the menaces that you have wrought and shared,

If you'll explode the myth that 'West is best', but not imply perfection lies anywhere,

If you can share wisdom before technology, sparing expense which cannot be justified

If you will learn that ideas cannot be transplanted,

But seeds of innovation nurtured,

When fertile minds both challenge and unite,

And if from time to time you see the wrinkles, the flaws besetting your post-modern world,

And try to point your clients from the pitfalls,

In spite of all, you have done your utmost,

To be someone worth importing,

And hear the words of those who hired you:

'We have achieved what *we* knew *we* needed

And *we* have done what *we* set out to do'

Adapted from Maclean 1998:404 (and acknowledging the inspiration of Rudyard Kipling)

---

world'. If we originate from the industrialised world we are part of a society that expects instant results, at the flick of a switch or press of a button. It can be demanding living in a country where the infrastructure does not facilitate ease of communication and transport or even reliable sanitation, electricity or water supplies. It can be particularly frustrating for those who are unaccustomed to the inevitable modification of pace of life and the lack of certainty in planning or proposing any initiatives. Bridging such a gap calls for numerous skills, as well as patience and determination. Bridging the epoch gap and bringing the assistance that is required without dominating or dictating, demands a fundamentally different approach to life and I have tried to summarise some of the issues in *Box 6.1*. The task of the visitor at any level is in enabling progress towards that which is desired by those who will implement the initiatives and will remain to see the task through.

Students and visiting consultants will also encounter a 'quality gap' in hospitals and clinics that will cause the working environment to differ greatly from that to which they are accustomed (Maclean, 1998). Supplies and equipment may not be available, staffing shortages may be acute, and the demand for services can incur waits of hours, even days, as patients attempt to be seen by a doctor or other healthcare professional. Patient expectations are often low and the human rights record in some countries may only serve to reinforce the limited prospects perceived by those in need of care (*Figure 6.2*).

Figure 6.2. The quality gap between countries at different levels of modernisation and development.

Skills, settings and scarcities

It is in tackling aspects of the quality gap that exists in countries where maternal mortality rates remain unacceptably high that emphasis has been placed on creating an enabling environment. The endeavour to enable every woman to obtain access to skilled care during childbirth embraces more than the skills of healthcare providers, it also addresses the situation in which these professionals need to function (WHO, 2004). As acknowledged earlier in this chapter, a highly skilled professional can do precious little to save life in many situations in the absence of essential supplies and equipment. The infrastructure needs to facilitate prompt referral of those who need further life saving treatment, and care needs not only to be accessible, but also acceptable and affordable. Regarding the latter, imposing patient fees has been a barrier to attaining healthcare in many countries, adding to the existing burden that women in poverty already experience in trying to access skilled care (Pettersson et al, 2007).

Poverty is a curse in any society and has been implicated as the chief culprit in limiting life expectancy and predisposing to untimely and avoidable deaths. It is by design and not accident that the first Millennium Development Goal (MDG) relates to eradicating extreme poverty and hunger (UN, 2000). It is salutary to consider that 1.4 billion people were estimated to live on less than $1.25 a day in 2008 (World Bank, 2008). The general trend is reported to indicate a decline percentage-wise in the proportion of the world's people in abject poverty during the preceding two decades.

The attendance of skilled healthcare professionals at birth has been identified as one of the indicators in achieving MDG5 (UN, 2000). It is not unreasonable to argue that MDG5 is pivotal in achieving these goals, since destitution, discrimination, disadvantage and disease dog the pathway to achieving a safe childbirth experience for millions of women across the world (Maclean, 2010). Global efforts to achieve safer childbirth have accelerated at the beginning of the 21st century and a slow decline was reported in the annual number of maternal deaths from the stated 576 000 in 1990 to 536 000 in 2005. Of the 87 countries that had a maternal mortality ratio of ≥100 in 1990, just 10 were considered to be 'on track' in improving maternal health (UNDP, 2010; WHO, 2010). By 2010, the global maternal mortality ratio had been reduced to 210 with an estimated 287 000 maternal deaths, and in addition to the 10 countries that had achieved MDG5, nine more were stated to be 'on track'. It is notable that Nepal was one of the countries that achieved MDG5 during this period. Fifty one countries were said to have been 'making progress', although 14 had made 'insufficient progress' and a further 11 had made 'no progress' (WHO, 2012).

The skills issue remains a major one and for this reason, obstetric life saving skills programmes have been offered in many countries. A legal framework controlling the practice of healthcare professionals is also an essential ally in protecting the public. This was discussed in *Chapter 3* where access to suitable resources for establishing a regulatory mechanism for midwives is offered. Information regarding the control of medical and other healthcare professions can be accessed through the relevant professional organisations. Multidimensional problems need to be tackled from every possible perspective. Skills offer an important contribution, but their utilisation can be limited by adverse settings and the devastating scarcities that beset so many societies.

Personal reflections on practice

- The expectations and the confidence that village people place in me is humbling and can be challenging. Whilst recognising my limitations, it behoves me to be as well prepared as I can, since, whatever the situation, sometimes there is an expectation that I should be able to do something about it.
- One begins to expect the unexpected and in so doing it seems the task becomes more manageable.
- Destitution, discrimination, disadvantage and disease – these are the enemies that confront so many of the people that I meet and they challenge me too. The resilience and the determination I see, I admire and need to emulate. Such attributes need to be harnessed. These are the weapons with which we work.
- The beauty of the most magnificent environment is eclipsed only by the beauty in people, the real champions who achieve wonders in spite of adversities.

Some lessons learned and shared

- Being as prepared as possible for the professional situations that will inevitably challenge the visitor, whether experienced professional or student, is fundamental. For the less experienced and for the unexpected, the internet can be useful for advice, information or merely the encouragement that helps one survive. Personal lifelines can be valuable for even the most experienced, for we all, inevitably, discover our weaknesses, it is part of being human.
- In adverse circumstances when one encounters a struggle for survival, it is encouraging to make a habit of establishing what works, what is good and what can be done. The converse sports negativity.

- Asking for local advice and taking it is fundamental. 'Keeping to the left' may not seem to be very important at night, but sometimes only the local people know what will be revealed in the light of day.

Reflective exercises

- Consider your working and/or living environment. Exclude from it anything that is dependant on modern utilities or resources (reliable electricity, water, sanitation, etc.). How would this compromise the quality of professional care you might be able to offer and your usual lifestyle? Itemise some alternatives that you might use.
- Identify any short courses that could help to prepare you for what lies ahead in your elective or your assignment.
- Make a list of resources that you will take with you. Include sources of information and contacts for advice or support that you anticipate needing. Programmes worth exploring in preparation for overseas assignments may include those offered at:
  - The London School of Hygiene and Tropical Medicine: http://www.lshtm.ac.uk/
  - Liverpool School of Tropical Medicine: http://www.lstmliverpool.ac.uk/

References

Arrighi G (1990) The developmentalist illusion: A reconceptualization of the semi-periphery In: Martin W (ed) *Semiperipheral states in the world-economy* (pp. 11–42). Greenwood, Westport, Conn

Arrighi G, Drangel J (1986) The stratification of the world-economy: An exploration of the semiperipheral zone. *Review* **10**: 9–74

Black JS, Mendenhall ME (1990) Cross-cultural training effectiveness: a review and a theoretical framework for future research. *Academy of Management Review* **15**(1): 113–36

Bose S (2003) Post colonial histories of South Asia: Some reflections. *Journal of Contemporary History* **38**(1): 133–46

British Airways (2012) *Jet lag calculator*. Available from: http://www.britishairways.com/travel/drsleep/public/en [last accessed 19.06.2012]

Burns A, Maxwell R, Lovich J, Shapiro K (2010) *Where women have no doctor*. (4th revised printing) Hesperian Health Guides. Available from: http://store.hesperian.org/ [last accessed 06.10.2012]

Caligiuri PM (2000) The big five personality characteristics as predictors of expatriate's desire to terminate the assignment and supervisor-rated performance. *Personnel Psychology* **53**(1): 67–88

Chirot D, Hall TD (1982) World-system theory. *Annual Review of Sociology* **8**: 81–106

Des Chene M (1991) *Relics of Empire: A cultural history of the Gurkhas*. Ph.D. dissertation, Stanford University

Des Chene M (1994) Soldiers, sovereignty and silences: Gorkhas as diplomatic currency. *South Asia Bulletin* **8**(1–2): 67–80

Dickson M (2010) *Where there is no dentist. A book of methods, aids and ideas for instructors at the village level*. Hesperian Health Guides. Available from: http://store. hesperian.org/ [last accessed 06.10.2012]

Ethnologue (2012) *Ethnologue Languages of the World*. Available from: http://www. ethnologue.com/ [last accessed 17.02.12]

Fry GW, Thurber CE (1989) *The international education of the development consultant: Communicating with peasants and princes*. Pergamon Press, Oxford

Gereffi G, Fonda S (1992) Regional paths of development. *Annual Reviews of Sociology* **18**: 419–48

Hussein J, McCaw Binns AM, Webber R (ed) (2012) *Maternal and perinatal health in developing countries*. CABI Books

Index Mundi (2012) *Country comparison > population*. Index Mundi. Available from: http://www.indexmundi.com/g/r.aspx [last accessed 28.09.2012]

Infoplease (2012) *Countries of the world. Country profiles*. Infoplease. Available from: http://www.infoplease.com/ [last accessed 20.06.2012]

Inglehart R, Baker WE (2000) Modernization, cultural change, and the persistence of traditional values. *American Sociological Reviews* **65**: 19–51

Inkeles A, Smith DH (1974) *Becoming modern: Individual change in six developing countries*. Heinemann, London

Klein S, Miller S, Thomson F (2009) *A book for midwives: Care for pregnancy, birth and women's health*. Hesperian Health Guides. Available from: http://store.hesperian.org/ [last accessed 06.10.2012]

Kobayashi V (1981) *The sage in the child, tradition, modernization, education: The case of Japan*. Paper presented at the annual meeting of the Comparative and International Education Society, Tallahassee, Florida, 18–21 March

Maclean GD (1998) *An examination of the characteristics of short term international midwifery consultants*. Thesis for the degree of Doctor of Philosophy. University of Surrey, Guildford, England

Maclean GD (2010) An historical overview of the first two decades of striving towards safe motherhood. *Sex and Reproductive Health, Journal of the Swedish Midwives Association* **1**(1): 7–14

Maclean GD (2011a) Short term international consultancy: Discussing the need. *British Journal of Midwifery* **19**(6): 387–93

Maclean GD (2011b) Short term international consultancy: Preparing and promising. *British Journal of Midwifery* **19**(9): 594–9

Maclean GD (2011c) Short term international consultancy: Evaluating practice. *British Journal of Midwifery* **19**(12): 814–9

Mendenhall ME, Oddou G (1985) The dimensions of expatriate acculturation: a review. *Academy of Management Review* **10**(1): 39–47

Mikesell S (1988) *Cotton on the Silk Road: The subjection of labor to the global economy in the shadow of empire.* PhD dissertation, University of Wisconsin, Madison

Moulder FV (1977) *Japan, China and the Modern World economy: Toward a reinterpretation of East Asian development ca. 1600 to ca. 1918.* Cambridge University Press, Cambridge

National Institute of General Medical Sciences (2008) *Circadian rhythms fact sheet.* National Institute of General Medical Sciences. Available from: http://www.nigms.nih.gov/Education/Factsheet_CircadianRhythms.htm [last accessed 19.06.2012]

Nationmaster (2012) *Facts and figures.* Nationmaster.com. Available from: http://www.nationmaster.com/ [last accessed 17.02.12]

NHS (2012) *Jet lag. NHS Choices.* Available from: http://www.nhs.uk/conditions/Jet-lag/ [last accessed 19.06.2012]

Pels P (1997) The anthropology of colonialism: Culture, history and the emergence of Western governmentality. *Annual Review of Anthropology* **26**: 163–83

Pettersson KO, Christensson K, Freitas E da G, Johansson E (2007) Strategies applied by women in coping with ad-hoc demands for unauthorised user fees during pregnancy and childbirth: A Focus Group study from Angola. *Health Care for Women International* **28**(3): 224–46

Rostow WW (1960) *The stages of economic growth: A non-Communist manifesto.* Cambridge University, Cambridge

Save the Children (2012) *State of the world's mothers 2012, The 2012 Mothers' Index.* Save the Children. Available from: http://www.savethechildren.org/ [last accessed 13/07/2012]

Shin JS, Morgeson FP, Campion MA (2007) What you do depends on where you are: understanding how domestic and expatriate work requirements depend on the cultural context. *Journal of International Business Studies* **38**: 64–83

Shukla AS (1987) *The other side of development: Social-psychological implications.* Sage Publications, India Pvt Ltd, New Delhi

Tung RL (1987) Expatriate assignments: enhancing success and minimizing failure. *Academy of Management Review* **1**(2): 117–26

UN (2000) *UN Millennium Declaration, September 2000.* United Nations, New York

UN Development Programme (2010) *What will it take to achieve the Millennium Development Goals? An International Assessment.* UNDP, New York

UNICEF (2012) *State of the World's children 2011*. UNICEF, New York

van Vianen AEM, De Pater IE, Kristof-Brown AL, Johnson EC (2004) Fitting in: surface- and deep-level cultural differences and expatriates' adjustment. *Academy of Management Journal* **47**(5): 697–709

Wallerstein I (1974) *The modern world-system, I: Capitalist agriculture and the origins of the European world-economy in the Sixteenth century*. Academic Press, New York

Waterhouse J (1999) Jet lag and shift work: (1) Circadian rhythms. *Journal of the Royal Society of Medicine* **92**: 398–401

Waterhouse J, Folkard S, Minors D (1992) *Shifting, health and safety. An overview of the scientific literature 1978–1990*. HMSO, London

Werman D, Thuman C, Maxwell J (2011) *Where there is no doctor.* (12th revised printing). Hesperian Health Guides. Available from: http://store.hesperian.org/ [last accessed 06.10.2012]

WHO (2004) *Making pregnancy safer: The critical role of the skilled attendant*. Joint Statement by WHO, ICM and FIGO. WHO, Geneva

WHO (2010) *Trends in Maternal Mortality 1990–2008*. WHO/UNICEF/UNFPA/World Bank. WHO, Geneva

WHO (2012) *Trends in maternal mortality 1990 to 2010*. WHO, UNICEF, UNFPA and World Bank. WHO, Geneva

World Bank (2008) *New data show 1.4 billion live on less than US$1.25 a day, but progress against poverty remains stong*. Press rlease 16 September 2008. Available from: http://www.worldbank.org/en/news/2008/09/16/new-data-show-14-billion-live-less-us125-day-progress-against-poverty-remains-strong [last accessed 21.10. 2013]

World Facts (2012) *World Facts and Figures*. Available from: http://www.worldfactsandfigures.com/ [last accessed 05.07.12]

Yang A (2007) Bandits and kings, moral authority and resistance in early colonial India. *Journal of Asian Studies* **66**(4): 881–96

Chapter 7

A South American diversion

If you plan for one year, plant rice. If you plan for ten years, plant trees.
If you plan for one hundred years, educate mankind.

(Chinese proverb)

The Brazilian population originates from at least four continents and comprises people of numerous ethnic groups, blending to contribute to a unique Brazilian identity

Crime still threatens lives! While tens of thousands of lives are saved as infant mortality declines, almost four times as many die violent deaths in adolescence

Subject strands introduced

- Educational approaches
- Teenage dilemmas
- Unintended pregnancy
- Unsafe abortion
- Gender issues

- Humanised evidence-based maternity care
- Capacity development
- Sustainable development

Practice points

- The importance of personal continuing education
- Producing one's own resources

- Travelling and working alone
- Promoting personal safety

Figure 7.1. Brazil.

Brazil: Background

Brazil

Brazil shares borders with every other South American country except Ecuador and Chile while the eastern coast meets the Atlantic Ocean. The name of the country is thought to derive from brazilwood, literally red-wood originating from the Latin (*brasa*) describing the similarity of the wood to red hot embers. It is Latin America's largest country covering 8511965 km². The capital is the modern city of Brasilia while Sao Paulo is the business hub of the country. Brazil gained independence from Portugal in 1822, became a republic in 1889 and the leading Latin American economic power in the 1970s. Ethnic groups comprise those of white European origin who form more than half of the population, whilst others originate from black African races, mixed races and a smaller percentage of Japanese, Arabs and Amerindians. The fifth most populous country in the world, Brazil has a population around 200 million people (estimated 2012) with 83% residing in urban areas. Eighty percent of the population are stated to be nominally Roman Catholic with a smaller number of Protestants and other religions including Spiritualist and Bantu/Voodoo. The official language is Portuguese but some English, French and Spanish are also spoken, The country has many natural resources including gold, platinum, petroleum, hydropower, uranium and timber. Exports include automobiles, transport equipment, footwear, iron ore and agricultural products such as coffee, beef and soya beans.

Exploring experience

Different dimensions

My sojourns in South America introduced me to a very different international assignment, as well as a variety of natural environments and manmade habitats. A request came to my sister to teach English in Brazil and my assistance was requested. My only virtue in the linguistic field was to have had experience in learning languages, but teaching them was another matter. Sheila, by contrast, had experience of teaching children English, but not adults and not as a foreign or second language. However, between us we decided we would respond to the request, our main qualification being native speakers of the English language.

Our journey took us to a language school set up as part of a Christian mission enterprise to enable pastors, professionals, business men and women as well as students and other interested persons to benefit from fluency in the English language. Since Portuguese, the *lingua franca* of Brazil, is spoken in just a handful of countries, learning English is an essential rather than a luxury for those who desire to progress in business, and for those who wish to travel. We undertook short assignments over six consecutive years based in various locations with conditions varying from torrid January heat of Foz do Iguaçu to the cool, damp environment of Curitiba, reminiscent of a British summer.

In seeking to establish what behaviour was acceptable and what was unacceptable before our first visit, we were assured of a warm and heartfelt Brazilian welcome. We were not disappointed. Whereas in some parts of the world touching another person is taboo and even a handshake is not appropriate, especially between opposite sexes, our Brazilian brothers and sisters greeted us with outstretched arms and warm hugs. It seemed there were no barriers to be overcome, save any shyness which just did not seem to fit naturally into the culture.

Culture, crime and the delights of creation

Brazil enjoys a diversity of cultures and traditions acquired from seemingly all corners of the earth. The population of this vast country originates from Africa, Asia, Europe and other regions of the Americas, all contributing to a rich medley of individuals and a unique Brazilian identity that has to be experienced to be appreciated. The overall impression is of a carefree people, indeed some of our students told us that there is always a reason for a party in Brazil. Of course, there are inevitably challenges and no shortage of problems. As we got closer to some of our students and fellow teachers we were privileged to share some of their problems too and, through living alongside them and travelling across that vast land, gain a little insight into some of the difficulties with which they wrestled.

Brazil is not devoid of economic and other internal problems. In a country where business is booming and there is palpable progress in achieving poverty reduction, slum dwelling in the notorious favelas still dogs the lives of many. Cities wrestle with some of the predicaments of modernisation, where unacceptably high crime rates cost lives and safety. The beautiful beaches of Rio de Janeiro were only a stone's throw from battle grounds of armed gangs and drugs dealers. Friends showed us the bullet marks of a recent feud fought near their home. Yet this country has a range of wonderful natural features including waterfalls, beautiful beaches, magnificent rainforests, and exotic flora and fauna. Forays into neighbouring countries took us briefly into the Spanish speaking countries of Argentina and Paraguay, but the focus of our work was in Brazil.

A country of contrasts

Inevitably, such a vast country as Brazil displays considerable contrasts. The urban metropolises of cities such as Sao Paulo find no similarities in regions such as the Amazon. Our students were representative of such contrasts and contradictions too. We taught businessmen from Sao Paulo and conservationists from the Amazon rainforest, pastors from large city churches and those preparing to serve in various other parts of the world, students and teachers, parents and teenagers. Some students were from European, others from African or Asian ethnic origins and yet others represented the indigenous peoples of the region. They were a medley of individuals, as different from each other as were their racial roots or professional backgrounds. Our experience was enriched by what we learned from them and after our first visit Sheila and I committed to studying the more intricate skills of teaching English as a foreign language (TEFL), enrolling in a distance learning programme ourselves in order to improve our own ability.

Since our responsibility was to teach the more advanced students, most of the time our inability to speak all but 'emergency Portuguese' posed no problem. In fact the director of the school firmly and repeatedly asserted to students that speaking Portuguese was strictly forbidden since the school philosophy was to offer the students total immersion in English. Some students made rapid progress while inevitably others struggled, but all participated with considerable commitment and certainly deserved to succeed. Unsurprisingly when children were enrolled in the sessions, they often overtook their parents and other more mature students in being able to communicate with surprising fluency as they graduated from the beginners' class at the end of the two weeks. Youth certainly has advantages in language learning, but commitment often allows many to achieve incredible progress. Our advanced class students would take the opportunity to speak publicly to the rest of the class or the whole school. Business people would give a talk on their particular subjects, pastors would preach and other students would gain experience in translating what they heard into Portuguese.

Distance, determination and dedication

As I had discovered in other parts of the world, the thirst for knowledge was intense and the determination to learn English insatiable. The school attracted people from diverse areas of Brazil, from the tropical north to the more temperate south. Some students travelled for three days and nights by coach to reach the language school, such was their determination to learn. One of the leaders, intent on instilling the right attitude into the students from the start, insisted that they repeat over and over again, 'I am *determinated* to speak English!' My desire not to belittle someone in authority was in conflict with my new role as a language teacher. I quietly pointed out the error to the person concerned. To my relief she was highly amused and insisted that I immediately get the assembled students chanting the correct statement. Dedication to learning resulted in long hours of classes throughout the day and late into the evening.

We used a variety of learning strategies, and, as with other students of various disciplines, the educational games that we had prepared were very popular. Interactive learning was appreciated and there was no shortage of volunteers to participate in discussions, debates or role play. Brazil has reached a high level of development and modern technology has taken hold in many parts of the country. However, when planning an educational programme we learned that taking all we needed, or the resources to produce what we needed, was the simplest approach. Producing our own resources meant that expense as well as inconvenience could be spared an organisation working with very limited assets. It was with this in mind that we were asked after several visits to produce educational materials for the mission to use in their various language schools. This we proceeded to do and eventually we were able to offer a set of learning and teaching manuals as well as a pack containing the educational games we used. Our efforts were welcomed as they provided the organisation with a resource that was specifically designed for their use, acknowledging their ethical and religious stance. It was in order to facilitate further study in English that I was asked during one visit to contribute a module on cultural anthropology and adaptation, which would form part of a degree programme offered by the same institution.

Wings of Mercy

One excursion took us to Annapolis near to the capital city of Brasilia to contribute to another English language school that students whom we had previously taught were setting up for their mission. This mission provided flights of mercy into remote regions of Brazil and some of the surrounding countries. Again we encountered a very busy programme and, in addition to the language classes, we were asked to lead focus groups during the afternoon. For the morning and evening sessions, students were divided into the usual language ability groups ranging from beginners to advanced level. However, each afternoon the students were arranged in professional interest groups and these included pilots, aeroplane mechanics, pastors and healthcare workers. Sheila focused on theology with the pastors and I was allotted the healthcare group and met with a variety of professionals including veterinary specialists, dentists and physiotherapists. Professional midwives do not feature greatly in Brazil since midwifery is not widely practised; care during childbirth usually being designated to obstetricians and nurses. However, there were interesting sessions as we discussed issues that these workers met in responding to calls across vast areas including the Amazon basin and sometimes crossing borders into other regions, such as Columbia.

The need for emergency skills was underlined during a visit to one of the schools on the outskirts of Sao Paulo. An accident, which fatally injured a workman on the campus, emphasised the need for well-trained and well-equipped paramedics. I was called to the scene, but the trapped man could not be released and, seriously injured, he urgently needed assistance. The ambulance which eventually arrived was ill equipped to treat the crushed patient who could not for some time be released from beneath his overturned vehicle. The students and staff of our language school gathered around and did the only thing they could do in the crisis, namely to pray with considerable fervour, crying out loudly on behalf of the victim. My concern, beyond that for the patient who was fast losing his hold on life, was for the safety of the crowd, assembled dangerously close to the vehicle that had overturned on a steep incline and was threatening to roll down. However, the man was eventually released without further incident, but too late to survive. The accident brought a cloud over the whole campus for many days. Some of the staff and students of the language school joined the young grieving family in their home and during the wake which preceded the funeral.

Selfless objectives and obligation

One young woman we were privileged to teach aspired to learn enough English to study in Canada to become a paramedic, with the objective of returning to Brazil to set up an effective service for her own people. Many of the students we met held selfless ambitions to educate themselves in order to serve their country or other nations; others aspired to do well in business or to acquire a fluency in English that would enable them to translate for visiting speakers to their institutions or churches.

The pilots in the mission aviation service, like their contemporaries in passenger or freight airlines, needed English for their work, but they desired to do much more than acquire the bare essentials of the language. They too were committed to personal and professional development through as much education as they could access. The mechanics, working alongside the pilots and healthcare workers, were adept at mending things and I was grateful for an 'operation' performed on the locks of my brief case. Years later the case still functions admirably. I have great respect for these young men and women who fix planes in all sorts of environments and in places where drug syndicates and smugglers threatened their own safety and survival. They persevered through natural and manmade disasters, committing themselves to an arduous existence so that lives could be saved and hope brought into desperate situations.

Examining the evidence

Enthusiasm for education

Most countries in the industrialised world enjoy relatively easy access to primary and secondary education, but across the globe this is by no means the norm. Attitudes to education appear to differ where it is harder to attain, expensive, or where the quality of that locally accessible is deemed inferior. Quite often it seems that the more difficult it is to access, the more appreciated it may be. Duarte (2007), in studying attitudes to learning among Portuguese university students, concluded that where there is a high personal desire to learn, regarded as 'intrinsic motivation', learning is described as deep rather than superficial and is usually successful. This issue was raised in *Chapter 4*. Further evidence suggests that where there is increased personal and situational interest, more learning occurs and there are higher levels of achievement (Schiefele et al, 1992; Eccles et al, 1998; Pintrich and Schunk, 2002). While individuals inevitably differ in their linguistic aptitude and ability, the motivation to learn English was most certainly evident in our Brazilian students. At considerable personal cost and often making substantial sacrifices they attended the language schools and completed long hours of study, often during their only vacation period, in order to acquire as much of the language as possible.

Brazil passed legislation in 2009 to extend compulsory education from 9 to 14 years (Poirier, 2009) establishing a major national milestone in that area. There is evidence that education produces numerous positive outcomes and the education of girls offers a more secure and even a healthier future. A girl in the developing world with seven or more years of education tends to marry four years later; and a girl who has had an extra year at primary school will eventually boost her wages by between 10 and 20%. There is evidence too that better infant and child health correlate with higher levels of schooling (UNICEF, 2011) and, conversely, illiteracy has been associated with higher incidences of maternal mortality and morbidity (Hafez, 1998; McAlister and Baskett, 2006). Girls who marry early are more likely to be undernourished and suffer problems associated with impaired early childhood development (UNICEF, 2009a).

Educational approaches

Language teaching calls for specialised educational skills and numerous courses can be accessed by distance learning even when existing work or study commitments deny opportunity for access to other forms of study. Texts that offer explanation concerning some of the intricacies of the English language can be a useful adjunct for elective and gap year students too who may find that whatever their original intention they become an easily accessible resource for enhancing the English language skills of local people. Ability to speak a language is one thing, being able to explain the nuances of grammar quite another. We were challenged on our first visit by the need of students to understand such phenomena as phrasal verbs and the precise and appropriate uses of the present perfect and past perfect tenses. These issues may not be easily explained by those without specialist language teaching skills unless some appropriate grammatical reference is at hand. In a consultancy capacity I have experienced the need to offer advice on language learning in areas of countries where access to study English is not easy or affordable yet professional studies demand an understanding of the language. For those likely to encounter this need, some resources are listed at the end of this chapter. However, as indicated in other chapters, speaking and writing clear, unambiguous language is undoubtedly appreciated and in many situations it is necessary to avoid the use of jargon, euphemism and colloquialism when communicating with all but those most conversant in the language.

Unquestionably, whatever the subject being taught, there are advantages in utilising a variety of educational approaches, although introducing change into the usual teaching style may not always be easy. The challenges encountered in education across some cultures were discussed in *Chapter 4*, although innovations can also be welcomed as illustrated in *Chapters 2, 5 and 9*. Education can be a powerful tool in effecting change. Waghid (2002), in his exploration as to whether higher education in a post-apartheid South Africa could be transformed into something more relevant, maintains that:

> *Given the extent of world-wide moral, economic and social problems, there is increasing pressure on universities to bridge the gap between higher education and society.*
>
> *(Waghid, 2002: 457)*

Furthermore, Waghid proposes that within higher education, change can be perceived when the level of knowledge acquired, produced and implemented by both teachers and learners involves questioning and reflection. As indicated in earlier chapters, encouraging questioning in some cultures may not initially be an acceptable approach. The art of reflection in education and practice has been advocated increasingly in recent decades and despite being advocated by some, such as Freire (1972a, b), Jarvis (1995) maintains that it is not inevitably innovative. However, Giddens (1990) purports that reflexivity in modern society embraces perpetual examination and re-examination of social practices in the light of incoming information. Interestingly, education can be a significant preceding factor in initiating change if it is approached in a manner appropriate to the current situation and cultural context. However, care must be taken to consider the latter, as Bude (1983) realised long ago:

> *The question whether it is pedagogically reasonable to transfer educational ideas and methods from one culture to another without alterations is*

always a point of debate if the results fail to meet the expectations.
(Bude, 1983: 341)

Duarte (2007), in his analysis of conceptions of learning, associated the occurrence of personal change with intrinsic motivation. The latter he links with positive emotional experiences associated with learning, epitomised in the words of one respondent: 'the study of certain subjects is really fascinating' (Duarte, 2007: 790). Issues surrounding intrinsic and extrinsic motivation to learn are well documented, extending across decades, for example from the work of Torrance (1963) up to that of Chong and Michael (2000). It therefore behoves anyone involved in adult education, whatever the level or subject, to strive towards nurturing and maintaining that intrinsic motivation to study. Yair (2008), in a careful consideration of excellence in university teaching amidst the age old debate as to whether good teachers are born or made, maintains that 'good teaching practices can be taught, shared and learned' (Yair, 2008: 447).

Further aspects of development

Both sustainable development and capacity development have become popular concepts across the globe. Sustainable development has been defined as 'development that meets the needs of the present without compromising the ability of future generations to meet their own needs' (UN, 1987). Global summits held in Rio de Janeiro in 1992 and 10 years later in Johannesburg have led to the concept extending beyond ecological and environmental issues to encompass 'all sectoral agencies and key private sector stakeholders' (UN, 2007). The UN commitment to sustainable development was renewed in 2012 following the Rio+20 summit with the pledge 'to achieve sustainable development in all its dimensions' (UN, 2012: 1). Consultants undertaking project evaluation are frequently asked whether or not appropriate types of development are in evidence, namely, are the investments promoting capacity development and are they sustainable? Capacity development was considered briefly in *Chapter 2*, and in the Brazilian context our aim was to develop the capacity of local teachers. However, in language learning, native speakers are inevitably sought in order to facilitate accurate pronunciation.

In this situation our challenge focused on responding to the need to provide an educational resource that was both suitable and acceptable in a Christian establishment. It needed to enable the mission to proceed independently if desired, providing language teachers and learners with the essential tools to achieve their aims. The educational resources which we produced in cooperation with the mission were well received (Maclean and Maclean, 2008) and provided a resource that was specific to their needs.

In general, with respect to an assignment, a visiting expert needs to promote capacity development. The greatest compliment to consultants is that they are no longer needed when their task is done because national colleagues are able to continue in a way that is inevitably more appropriate in the situation. Before introducing any change, it is wise to consider whether such approaches or attitudes are likely to be sustainable. This needs to be considered in the light of available national resources and checked out with indigenous colleagues. Such considerations need to be made by elective students as well as professional consultants if any meaningful change is to be sustained.

Triumph and tragedy

While increasing educational opportunities in Brazil offer hope for the future, this nation like any other faces enormous challenges too. Whereas achievements deserve acknowledgment and appreciation, even with a touch of optimism, making progress can seem like taking two steps forward and one back. For instance, in the decade preceding 2008, Brazil had successfully reduced infant mortality, saving 26000 lives, yet during the same period 81000 adolescents were murdered (UNICEF, 2011). Certainly the country faces enormous challenges in reducing crime and promoting the safety of the most vulnerable.

Crime is a constant threat in many parts of Brazil and efforts to reduce violence, drug smuggling and civil unrest relentlessly confront the authorities. Foreigners, especially those who do not speak Portuguese, are considered at high risk for targeted street crime in some cities (Overseas Security Advisory Council, 2011). Websites offering advice are included at the end of this chapter. One report indicates a marked decline in homicides since 1998 in Sao Paulo and Rio de Janeiro. This is attributed to economic growth and better policing, although it is claimed that the overall incidence of such violence remains high, merely being transferred to other areas. The reduction of extreme poverty has been hinted at as an advocate in tackling these issues of criminal violence (Economist, 2011). Contrary to popular opinion it is a minority of young people that falls into drug abuse, violence and criminality (UNICEF, 2011) although adolescents suffering the disadvantages of poverty are more likely to be drawn into crime (Weatherburn and Lind, 1998), and social disadvantage has been shown to increase the homicide risk even in countries with low crime rates (Nieuwbeerta et al, 2008). Some countries are involving young people in programmes to develop poverty reduction strategies (UNICEF, 2009b), and in Brazil initiatives have encouraged adolescents to become actively involved as partners in social budgeting, undertaking research and becoming effective advocates (UNICEF, 2011).

Adolescent dilemma or distinction?

Teenage pregnancy is a challenging predicament in many countries, and Brazil is one of seven countries in the world that account for more than half of all adolescent births (UNICEF, 2011). The negative consequences of teenage pregnancy on mental and physical health and the limitation it places on educational opportunities and consequently on economic welfare are well documented (Department for Education and Skills, 2006). Daughters whose mothers were teenagers have a higher incidence of becoming pregnant as teenagers too (Berrington et al, 2005) and, overall, children born in such circumstances tend in later life to be inferior socially and to have a poorer health status than their peers (Swann et al, 2003). In many parts of the world, child marriage and malnutrition predispose to the higher incidences of death and disability associated with adolescent pregnancy. With the exception of China, one third of girls across the developing world are married before the age of 18 years and almost one third of those before their 15th birthday (UNICEF, 2011). A study undertaken in an Ecuadorian region of the Amazon basin revealed that 40% of girls aged between 15 and 19 years either had been or were currently pregnant. Such pregnancies were unlikely to be associated with choices made by the girls but rather emanated from poverty, sexual abuse or parental absence (Goicolea et al, 2009). In a major population study across three capital cities, Heilborn and Cabral (2011) report that contrary to popular opinion, becoming a parent, particularly in the poorer segments of Brazilian society, is not inevitably the result of promiscuity. Rather, parenthood carries the kudos that otherwise eludes young people lacking the professional prospects of their more affluent peers. The latter regard parenting as something to be achieved after consolidation of professional and financial stability. Unsurprisingly therefore, there is evidence that the incidence of pregnancy in women aged less than 20 years demonstrates an inverse relationship to the number of years spent in education across every stratum of society (Almeida et al, 2006; Almeida and Aquino, 2009). While teenage mothers inevitably experience a radical change in their lives with limitations in their social activities, those of lower socioeconomic status report being affected more severely and were more likely to experience feelings of loneliness and isolation (Heilborn and Cabral, 2006).

Community education fosters healthier attitudes in society and a specific agenda designated 'Program H' has been particularly successful in Brazil in generating gender-equitable behaviour in young men. The programme has been established in four Latin American countries with the aim of raising awareness among boys and men about the disadvantages of traditional gender roles and the associated unhealthy behaviour that it fosters (UNICEF, 2011).

Unintended, unwanted and unsafe

Abortion is illegal in Brazil except when pregnancy occurs as a result of rape or if the mother's life is endangered. In other countries in Central America such as Nicaragua and El Salvador the practice is totally outlawed (Guttmacher, 2012). Making abortion illegal does not reduce its occurrence and illegal abortion is usually unsafe. The global incidence of abortion declined between 1995 and 2003 but figures have subsequently stalled. Almost half of all abortions are estimated as unsafe and 98% of these occur in the developing world (Sedgh et al, 2012). Unsafe abortion is estimated at 32 and 29 per 1000 respectively in Latin America and Africa. These incidences compare with 19 per 1000 in North America, 12 per 1000 in Western Europe and 43 per 1000 in Eastern Europe. The discrepancy between the two European regions is related to lower or unreliable use of contraception in the latter. Almost 100% of abortions in Central and South America are classified as unsafe. Complications from abortion account annually for 47000 deaths, 13% of the total maternal deaths worldwide (WHO, 2011).

Estimates in 2005 identified that across the world 8.5 million women suffered post-abortion complications requiring medical attention but that at least three million did not receive such care (Singh, 2006). In the developing world it is the poorest women who have the least access to contraceptive information and supplies, and these are the most likely to submit to unsafe abortion (Guttmacher, 2012). A total of 215 million women from developing countries are reckoned to have an unmet need in respect of contraceptives, and unsurprisingly 82% of unwanted pregnancies worldwide occur among these women (Singh et al 2009). Issues surrounding unsafe abortion have long been described as a clandestine epidemic across Latin America (Paxman et al, 1993).

Harden et al (2009) report from an evidence base that is described as small but reliable, that programmes in early childhood and adolescence designed to reduce unintended teenage pregnancies are both effective and appropriate in providing a sound evidence base to inform public policy. In this respect, Brazil has been active in facilitating adolescent-created media where teenagers can discuss sensitive issues such as pregnancy. Even though the majority of teenage mothers were neither working nor in education, multi-media digital products were used to start debate on critical issues of concern with the aim of dispelling both the guilty and the romantic notion of pregnancy (UNICEF, 2011). However, considering the size of the global problem relating to unintended and unwanted pregnancy, the unmet needs in contraception and the prevalence of unsafe abortion, much remains to be done across many regions of the world.

The finer facets of maternity care

Accessing affordable maternity care is important, but aspects of acceptability that hinge on the finer facets of care provision can be critical in any part of the world. There is universal free access to healthcare across Brazil with around 97% of births taking place in hospital (Leal, 2008). Brazil managed to decrease the maternal mortality ratio annually by 3.9% between 1990 and 2008 (Hogan et al, 2010). Yet a lack of equitable access to care of a high quality as well as over-reliance by medical practitioners on technology and unnecessary operative delivery have been implicated in what is still an unacceptably high level of maternal mortality. This plight lingers amid reports of neglect and verbal abuse by healthcare workers (Center for Reproductive Rights, 2010).

Such abuse is by no means peculiar to this region and has been implicated across the globe. It may interfere with a woman's desire to seek maternity care, ignore her autonomy, discriminate against some individuals or result in abandonment or detention in health facilities. It has been claimed that such concerns have been shrouded in 'a veil of silence' (White Ribbon Alliance, 2012).

In a general consideration of the issue, Bowser and Hill (2010) identify a continuum comprising various categories of interpersonal issues ranging from subtle disrespect to overt violence. Acknowledgement of this universal problem has led to the development of a charter featuring the declarations that affirm a woman's rights to respectful maternity care with the intention of promoting the concept that every woman should experience this as a matter of right (White Ribbon Alliance, 2011). Seven issues perceived as the rights of women during childbirth have been identified and these are summarised in *Box 7.1*. Lifting this 'veil of silence' and promoting such rights wherever women give birth is likely not only to improve the uptake but also the quality of care.

Box 7.1. Seven rights of childbearing women

Every woman has the right to

• Dignity	• Liberty
• Privacy	• Information
• Confidentiality	• Freedom from harm
• Equality	

Derived from White Ribbon Alliance, 2011

Efforts to humanise childbirth are being made in Brazil incorporating respect for and promotion of the right to evidence-based care for women and children. This includes aspects of safety, satisfaction and effectiveness (Diniz and Chacham, 2004). Electronic forums and websites assist women who want to obtain humanised evidence-based care (see Xôepisio, 2009). Cecatti et al (2007), considering severe maternal morbidities from their studies across the city of Campinas, Brazil, report that preliminary findings indicate that some women experience considerable obstacles and difficulties in accessing adequate care. These encompass problems in the quality of care at primary level, lack of resources, and delays in the referral process.

Poverty and social disadvantages are also implicated. They stress that the incidence of complications in pregnancy are likely to be similar across countries at different levels of human development, but it is the way in which they are diagnosed and managed that is likely to determine the outcome and account for the vast statistical differences in terms of maternal mortality and morbidity. They find resonance with the conclusions of Paxton et al (2005) who maintain that where low maternal mortality is evident, obstetric complications are both identified and treated swiftly in the context of functional health systems.

Clearly, the finer facets of maternity care will determine not only whether a woman can access the care she needs, but also whether she will do so. It is essential for her to know that when she needs it she can acquire a prompt diagnosis along with timely assistance and that only essential interventions will be made. If care is to be acceptable, it also needs to be encompassed by the dignity and respect that characterise any woman's fundamental human right.

Personal reflections on practice

- Being equipped to do the job is essential, whatever the challenge. I must make every effort to learn what I can, it is always possible to enhance one's knowledge and skills.
- The commitment of others to learn and to utilise new skills to serve others, often at considerable personal cost, challenges me never to tire of giving of myself and my skills wherever I can. Any sacrifice I may make diminishes in the shadow of their achievement.
- Building local capacity is essential if the work is to continue.
- There are commonsense issues that I can implement to take responsibility for my own personal safety, but local colleagues are best placed to advise me specifically about potential dangers.

Some lessons learned and shared

- Continuing education is a life-long process, always pursue it, never forsake it.
- Being able to produce one's own resources can save time and money where local supplies are limited, but finding a local source is essential in the long term if the project is to be sustainable.
- Respecting the prevailing religious and moral stance is very important. Unless this can be done it is necessary to decline an assignment.
- Personal safety must always be a priority, taking unjustifiable risks can prove costly not only personally but also to local colleagues who usually take visitors' security very seriously.

Reflective exercises

- Consider the seven rights of childbearing women presented in *Box 7.1*:
    - Note how many of these rights were observed during a recent day that you have spent in a clinical area. Were there any that were overlooked or neglected?
    - If you were a role model for a colleague or another student, how do you think your practice or presence may have demonstrated these rights?
    - Select one of the rights that you want to improve in your own practice and identify targets to work towards. Discuss these targets and the outcomes you have achieved during your efforts with a trusted colleague, supervisor or fellow student.
- Think about an initiative that you would like to introduce in the area where you have been working. What issues do you need to take care of if such an initiative is to be sustainable?
- Reflect on the matter of 'capacity development', either
    - Discuss with colleagues in positions of responsibility how they perceive their needs in this respect, or
    - Make a personal action plan for yourself if you were to be appointed to a post of responsibility in an area where you are now working. Consider what would enable you to develop your capacity to do such a job well.

Resources

- For Teaching English as a Foreign Language (TEFL) or for Teachers of English to Speakers of Other Languages (TESOL):
  - http://www.mes-english.com/
  - http://www.eslbase.com/resources/
- Textbook that can help to give explanations for the correct usage of English:
  - Swann M (2005) *Practical English usage* (3rd edn) Oxford University Press, Oxford or available as a free download at http://www.firstload.com/
- Useful websites when considering personal safety:
  - http://www.safetravel.co.uk/
    This website provides travel safety tips and advice from experts, including issues facing elective and gap year students and those travelling alone.
  - http://www.bbc.co.uk/health/treatments/travel/safe_personal.shtml
    Website providing information regarding aspects of health and safety.

References

Almeida MC, Aquino EML (2009) The role of education level in the intergenerational pattern of adolescent pregnancy in Brazil. *International Perspectives on Sex and Reproductive Health* **35**(3): 139–46

Almeida MC, Aquino EML, De Barros AP (2006) School trajectory and teenage pregnancy in three Brazilian state capitals. *Cadernos de Saúde Pública* **22**(7): 1397–409

Avery L, Lazdane G (2008) What do we know about sexual and reproductive health of adolescents in Europe? *European Journal of Contraception and Reproductive Health Care* **13**(1): 58–70

BBC (2012) *Brazil: Key facts and figures*. Available from: http://news.bbc.co.uk/1/hi/world/americas/8702891.stm [last accessed 28.06.2012]

Berrington A, Diamond I, Ingham R et al (2005) *Consequences of teenage motherhood: pathways which minimise the long term negative impacts of teenage childbearing.* University of Southampton, Southampton

Bowser D, Hill K (2010) *Exploring evidence for disrespect and abuse in facility-based childbirth: Report of a landscape analysis.* Bethesda, MD: USAID TRAction Project, University Research Corporation, LLC, and Harvard School of Public Health

Bude U (1983) The adaptation concept in British colonial education. *Comparative Education* **19**(3): 341–55

Business Travel Report (2012) *Brazil facts and figures.* Available from: http://www.thebtr. com/pages/countryfactfiles/brazilfactfile.htm [last accessed 28.06.2012]

Cecatti JG, Souza JP, Parpinelli MA, deSousa MH, Amaral E (2007) Research on severe maternal morbidities and near misses in Brazil. What we have learned. *Reproductive Health Matters* **15**(30): 125–33

Center for Reproductive Rights (2010) *Statement to the ECOSOC: Maternal mortality and the MDGs.* Available from: http://reproductiverights.org/en/press-room/statement-to-ecosoc-maternal-mortality-and-the-mdgs [last accessed 18.04.2012]

Chong S, Michael WB (2000) A construct validity study of scores on a Korean version of an academic self-concept scale for secondary school students. *Education and Psychology Measurement* **60**: 17–30

Department for Education and Skills (2006) T*eenage pregnancies next steps: Guidance for Local Authorities and Primary Care Trusts on effective delivery of local strategies.* Department for Education and Skills, London

Diniz SG, Chacham AS (2004) 'The cut above' and 'the cut below': Abuse of caesareans and episiotomy in São Paulo, Brazil. *Reproductive Health Matters* **12**(23): 100–10

Duarte AM (2007) Conceptions of learning and approaches to learning in Portuguese students. *Higher Education* **54**(6): 781–94

Eccles J, Wigfield A, Schiefele U (1998) Motivation to succeed. In: Damon W (Series ed) and Eisenberg N (Vol. ed), *Handbook of child psychology: Vol. 3. Social, emotional, and personality development* (5th edn, pp. 1017–95). Wiley, New York

Economist (2011) *Murder in Brazil: Always with us.* June 9. Available from: http://www. economist.com/node/18805840 [Last accessed 17.04.12]

Freire P (1972a) *Pedagogy of the oppressed.* (Translated by Ramer MB) Penguin, Hammondsworth

Freire P (1972b) *Cultural action for freedom.* Penguin, Hammondsworth

Giddens A (1990) *The consequences of modernity.* Polity Press, Cambridge

Goicolea I, Wulff M, Ohman A, Sebastian MS (2009) Risk factors for pregnancy among adolescent girls in Ecuador's Amazon Basin: A case-control study. *Revista Panamericana de Salud Public* **26**(3): 221–8

Guttmacher (2012) *Facts on induced abortion worldwide: Worldwide incidence and trends. Fact Sheet.* Guttmacher Institute, New York

Hafez G (1998) Maternal mortality: a neglected and socially unjustifiable tragedy. *European Mediterranean Health Journal* **4**(1): 7–10

Harden A, Brunton G, Fletcher A, Oakley A (2009) Teenage pregnancy and social disadvantage: Systematic review integrating controlled trials and qualitative studies. *British Medical Journal*: doi: 10.1136/bmj.b4254 http://www.ncbi.nlm.nih.gov/pmc/articles/PMC2776931/ [last accessed 06.10.2012]

Heilborn ML, Cabral CS (2006) Parentalidade juvenil: transição condensada para a vida adulta. In: Camarano AA (org) *Transição para a vida adulta ou vida adulta em transição?* (pp. 225–54), IPEA, Rio de Janeiro

Heilborn ML, Cabral CS (2011) A new look at teenage pregnancy in Brazil. *Obstetrics and Gynaecology.* doi: 10.5402/2011/975234 http://www.ncbi.nlm.nih.gov/pmc/articles/ PMC3170800/ [last accessed 06.10.2012]

Hogan MC, Foreman KJ, Naghavi M et al (2010) Maternal mortality for 181 countries 1980 – 2008. A systematic analysis of progress towards Millennium Development Goal 5. *The Lancet.* DOI:10.1016/S0140-6736 (10) 60518-1 http://cdrwww.who.int/pmnch/ topics/maternal/20100402_ihmearticle.pdf [last accessed 06.10.2012]

Index Mundi (2012) *Country comparison > population.* Available from: http://www. indexmundi.com/g/r.aspx [last accessed 28.09.2012]

Jarvis P (1995) *Adult and continuing education, theory and practice* (2nd edn). Routledge, London and New York

Leal M do C (2008) The challenge of the millennium: maternal mortality in Brazil. *Saúde Pública, Rio de Janeiro* **24**(8): 1724–5

Maclean SD, Maclean GD (2008) *Enjoying English, a resource pack for upper intermediate and advanced level, containing teacher's handbook, student handbook and learning games.* Transcultural Mission, Belo Horizonte Brazil

McAlister C, Baskett TF (2006) Female education and maternal mortality: A worldwide survey. *Journal of Obstetrics and Gynaecology Canada* Novembre: 983–90

Nieuwbeerta P, McCall PL, Elffers H, Wittebrood K (2008) Neighborhood characteristics and individual homicide risks: Effects of social cohesion, confidence in the police and socioeconomic disadvantage. *Homicide Studies* **12**(1) 90–116

Overseas Security Advisory Council (2011) *Brazil 2011. Crime and safety report: Brasilia.* US Dept of State, Bureau of Diplomatic Security

Paxman JM, Rizo A, Brown L, Benson J (1993) The clandestine epidemic: The practice of unsafe abortion in Latin America. *Studies in Family Planning* **24**(4): 205–26

Paxton A, Maine D, Freedman L, Fry D, Lobis S (2005) The evidence for emergency obstetric care. *International Journal of Gynaecology and Obstetrics* **88**: 181–93

Pintrich PR, Schunk DH (2002) *Motivation in education: Theory, research, and applications* (2nd edn) Prentice Hall, Upper Saddle River, NJ

Poirier M-P (2009) Brazil ranks amongst countries taking responsibility for longer mandatory education. *Panorama* **96**: (11 November)

Save the Children (2012) *State of the World's mothers 2012. The 2012 Mothers' Index.* Save the Children. Available from: http://www.savethechildren.org/ [last accessed 13/07/2012]

Schiefele U, Krapp A, Winteler A (1992) Interest as a predictor of academic achievement: A meta-analysis of research. In Renninger KA, Hidi S, Krapp A (eds) *The role of interest in learning and development* (183–212) Erlbaum: Hillsdale, NJ

Sedgh G, Singh S, Shah IH, Ahman E, Henshaw SK, Bankole A (2012) Induced abortion: incidence and trends worldwide from 1995 to 2008. *The Lancet*. DOI:10.1016/S0140-6736(11)61786-8 [Last accessed 06.10.2012]

Singh S (2006) Hospital admissions resulting from unsafe abortion: estimates from 13 developing countries. *The Lancet* **368**(9550):1887–92

Singh S, Darroch JE, Ashford LS, Vlassoff M (2009) *Adding it up: The costs and benefits of investing in family planning and maternal and newborn health*. Guttmacher Institute, New York

Swann C, Bowe K, McCormik, Kosmin M (2003) *Teenage pregnancy and parenthood: A review of reviews. Evidence Briefing*. Health Development Agency, London

Torrance EP (1963) *Education and the creative potential*. University of Minnesota Press, Minneapolis

UN (1987) *Report of the Brundtland Commission: Our common future*. Oxford University Press, Oxford

UN (2007) *Framing sustainable development: The Brundtland Report 20 years on. Sustainable development in Action*. UN Commission on Sustainable Development, Backgrounder, April 2007

UN (2012) T*he future we want. Resolution adopted by the General Assembly, 66th session*, 11 September 2012

UN Development Programme (2011) *International Human Development Indicators*. United Nations Development Programme. Available from: http://hdr.undp.org/en/statistics/ [Last accessed 13.02.2012]

UNICEF (2009a) *Tracking progress on child and maternal nutrition: A survival and development priority*, UNICEF, New York

UNICEF (2009b) *Youth participation in poverty reduction strategies and national development plans: A desk study*. Adolescent Development and Participation Unit, ADAP Learning Series 4. UNICEF, New York

UNICEF (2011) *State of the World's children 2011*. UNICEF, New York

UNICEF (2012) *State of the World's children 2012*. UNICEF, New York

Waghid Y (2002) Knowledge production and higher education transformation in South Africa: Towards reflexivity in university teaching, research and community service. *Higher Education* **43**: 457–88

Weatherburn D, Lind B (1998) *Poverty, parenting, peers and crime-prone neighbourhoods: Trends and issues in crime and criminal justice. Paper 85*. Australian Institute of Criminology, Canberra. Available from: http://www.aic.gov.au [last accessed 18.04.12]

White Ribbon Alliance (2011) *Respectful maternity care: The universal rights of childbearing women*. White Ribbon Alliance for Safe Motherhood. Available from: http://www.whiteribbonalliance.org/WRA/assets/File/Final_RMC_Charter.pdf [Last accessed 20.04.2012]

White Ribbon Alliance (2012) *Respectful maternity care: Every woman's right*. White Ribbon Alliance for Safe Motherhood. Available from: http://www.whiteribbonalliance. org/index.cfm/the-issues/respectful-maternity-care/ [Last accessed 20.04.2012]

WHO (2011) *Unsafe abortion: Global and regional estimates of the incidence of unsafe abortion and associated mortality in 2008* (6th edn). WHO, Geneva

WHO (2012) *Trends in maternal mortality 1990 to 2010*. WHO, UNICEF, UNFPA and World Bank. World Health Organization, Geneva. Available from: http://www.who. int/reproductivehealth/publications/monitoring/9789241503631/en/ [last accessed 13.09.2012]

World Facts (2012) *World Facts and Figures: Brazil*. Available from: http://www. worldfactsandfigures.com/countries/brazil.php [last accessed 06.07.2012]

Xôepisio (2009) *Xôepisio! Episiotomia? Não!* Available from: http://www.xoepisio. blogger. com.br [last accessed 05.05.2012]

Yair G (2008) Can we administer the scholarship of teaching? Lessons from outstanding professors in higher education. *Higher Education* **55**(4): 447–59

Chapter 8

Insight, innovation and initiative across Africa

No man can whistle a symphony. It takes a whole orchestra to play it.
(H E Luccock)

Interdisciplinary and multidisciplinary teams can bring a wide range of expertise and experience to an assignment. Team effectiveness can vary greatly. Recognising one's own strengths and limitations and respecting those of others is essential

Teenage girls desperate to escape poverty lose their lives through the only way they know of earning an income

Subject strands introduced

- Millennium Development Goals
- Poverty
- Gender inequity and social injustice
- HIV/AIDS

- Malaria and other tropical diseases
- Human resources for health
- Rights-based approaches
- Female genital mutilation

Practice points

- Team work
- Protecting personal health
- Advocacy

- Appreciating indigenous wisdom and respecting local culture

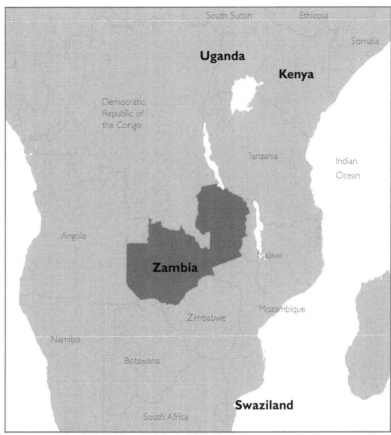

Figure 8.1. Kenya, Swaziland, Uganda and Zambia.

Kenya: Background

Kenya

Kenya was named after Mount Kenya from the Kikuyu word meaning 'mountain of whiteness'. In East Africa it is bordered by Ethiopia, Somalia, South Sudan, Tanzania and Uganda and covers an area of 580367 km^2. Nairobi is the capital which has also been dubbed 'the safari capital of the world' since the 'Big Five' animals: lion, leopard, buffalo, rhinoceros and elephant can be found in the country. Mombasa is another large city and a major port on the eastern coast bordered by the Indian Ocean. Kenya obtained independence from the UK in 1963 and is a semi-presidential republic using a mixed legal system comprising Islamic, common and customary law with judiciary review in the High Court. The population is in excess of 43 million (estimated 2012) with 39% living in urban areas. The religions include Christianity and Hinduism. There are 11 languages spoken, including Swahili and English. The main exports include tea, coffee, and petroleum products.

Swaziland, Uganda and Zambia: Background

Swaziland

Swaziland takes its name from the dominant ethnic group in the country being derived from the name of a former monarch, King Mswati I. It is a landlocked country in Southern Africa bordered by Mozambique and South Africa. Swaziland covers an area of 17364 km². The capital city is Lobamba; Mbabane and Manzini are among the other large cities. Swaziland is an absolute monarchy. It was a protectorate of the UK and obtained independence in 1968. Swaziland has a mixed legal system comprising civil, common and customary law. The population exceeds 1.3 million (estimated 2012) with 24% living in the urban areas. Swaziland is among the African countries with the highest HIV/AIDS incidence. The religion is predominantly Christian with a small percentage of Hindus, Muslims and those of the Bahai faith. English and SiSwati are the spoken languages. The economy is dominated by the service industry, manufacturing and agriculture. The main exports are sugar, citrus fruits and forest products.

Uganda

Uganda takes its name from the Buganda Kingdom which encompassed part of the south of the country including the capital city, Kampala. It is a landlocked country in East Africa bordered by Kenya, South Sudan, DR Congo, Rwanda and Tanzania. Uganda extends for 236040 km² with a large portion of the mighty Lake Victoria lying within its borders. The country gained independence from the UK in 1962 and has a mixed legal system comprising English common and customary law. The population exceeds 34 million (estimated 2012) with12% living in the urban areas. Uganda has experienced a large influx of refugees and asylum seekers from DR Congo, Rwanda, Somalia and Burundi. More than 80% of Ugandans profess to be Christian, with a small percentage of Muslims. The official languages are Swahili and English, although a number of other languages are also spoken. Uganda has rich natural resources including cobalt and copper and untapped sources of crude oil and natural gas. The main exports are coffee, tea, cotton and tobacco.

Zambia

Zambia takes its name from the River Zambezi which flows through the east of the country. It is a landlocked country in southern Africa bordered by DR Congo, Tanzania, Malawi, Mozambique, Zimbabwe, Botswana, Namibia and Angola and covers 752618 km². The capital city is Lusaka. The country was captured in the 19th century and became the British Protectorate of Northern Rhodesia, gaining independence from the UK in 1964. Zambian politics are in the form of a presidential representative democratic republic. Zambia has a mixed legal system comprising English common law and customary law, with judicial review of legislative acts by an ad hoc constitutional council. The population is around 14 million (estimated 2012) with 36% living in the urban areas. Up to 75% profess to be Christian although traditional religious thought blends with Christian beliefs in many syncretic churches. The official languages are English, Nyanja, Bemba, Lunga and Tonga. The main exports are copper, cobalt, electricity, cotton, tobacco and flowers.

Kenya, Swaziland, Uganda and Zambia: Data	
Kenya HDI*: Low (143) MMR: 360 (2010) MMR: proportion related to HIV/AIDS: 20.2% Lifetime risk of maternal death: 1 in 55 Mothers index ranking (2012)**: 72(Tier II) Births attended by skilled personnel: 44%	**Swaziland** HDI*: Medium (140) MMR: 320 (2010) MMR: proportion related to HIV/AIDS: 67.3% Lifetime risk of maternal death: 1 in 95 Mothers index ranking (2012)**: 64(Tier II) Births attended by skilled personnel: 82%
Uganda HDI*: Low (161) MMR: 310 (2010) MMR: proportion related to HIV/AIDS: 25% Lifetime risk of maternal death: 1 in 49 Mothers index ranking (2012)**: 5(Tier III) Births attended by skilled personnel: 42%	**Zambia** HDI*: Low (164) MMR: 440 (2010) MMR: proportion related to HIV/AIDS: 30.7% Lifetime risk of maternal death: 1 in 37 Mothers index ranking (2012)**: 27(Tier III) Births attended by skilled personnel: 47%
HDI: Human Development Index, MMR: Maternal Mortality Ratio *Assessed according to life expectancy, educational and economic factors **Ranked globally (within 3 tiers: I = more developed, II = less developed, III = least developed) according to health, education, economic and political status of women	
Background and data sources: Index Mundi, 2012; Africa.com, 2012a, b, c, d; Save the Children, 2012; UN Development Programme, 2011; UNICEF 2012b; World Factbook, 2012; WHO 2012c	

Exploring experience

All creatures great and small

My experiences of working in Africa have been numerous. My initial encounter with this vast continent was during an assignment in Botswana, which offered insights that were by no means typical of Africa, and which taught me that generalisation can be misleading. Indeed, as I moved between countries, the peoples, cultures and languages seemed at times to bear more differences than similarities. On one occasion I was working with a colleague from a different African country who suffered more culture shock than I ever had when assigned to another part of that continent. 'What strange people!' she had exclaimed in pure astonishment, as she experienced great difficulty in trying to understand them.

Accommodation across Africa offered all sorts of experiences too. I love wildlife and have been privileged to spend short periods in the bush, marvelling at the wonders of creation. However, I have had the questionable privilege of sharing a room with bats and rats, and at one hotel there were crocodiles within a stone's throw of the guests' dining tables. I was assured of safety in that the creatures were not allowed to stay on hotel property once they had grown to a certain length. Then 'the crocodile man' would come and remove them to a conservation area, unless of course, they were to end up on someone's dinner plate. At another hotel, we were warned to keep off the grass because a green mamba had been seen there earlier.

The Swedish connection

I have had experiences of working with international interdisciplinary teams in many parts of the world. However, it was through attending conferences in Africa that I made a Swedish connection. Funding by the Swedish government had enabled midwives from many parts of Africa to further their studies, undertake research and implement evidence-based practice. It was the need to evaluate some of these programmes that enabled me to benefit from participating in interdisciplinary teamwork.

I had become accustomed to reviewing numerous aspects of a project single-handed, stretching my skills and imagination considerably, as previous chapters have indicated. Two major evaluations on behalf of the Swedish authorities took me to several parts of Africa and on these assignments I was able to benefit from the valuable skills of an economist and a nutritionist. Whilst forays to the labour ward made my economist colleague decidedly uncomfortable, I no longer needed to sweat over budgets and consider expenditure. Teamwork certainly has its advantages. I was grateful on each occasion that these teams worked well together; had I had a choice, these colleagues whom I had never met before the assignments would have been my 'A' team. There were no frictions or vying for dominance; we respected each other's areas of expertise and acknowledged our own limitations.

In our evaluations we used a variety of approaches, including interviews, focus groups, non-participant observation and, on one occasion, an electronic questionnaire distributed by email to 80 respondents in 29 countries. The latter elucidated some useful information but the response rate was low, indicative of the limited access to the internet in the countries studied. Although evaluation frequently consists of searching through quantitative data from which to draw conclusions, examples of initiatives that involve qualitative evaluation will stay with me long after the statistics fade from my consciousness. Whatever the evaluation in which I am involved, I always plan observational visits to the clinical areas in as many and as varied settings as possible. It is during such visits that one begins to touch the grassroots of the society within which one is working and about which one is attempting to gain insights. No amount of reading or talking could, for me, ever replace the reality of such experiences.

Initiative and enterprise

In every country where I have worked I have met people who epitomise life's successes and struggles. They represent for me the peaks and troughs of the challenges that are faced within the topic area to which I am expected to contribute or evaluate. I recall midwives across several countries for whom further educational opportunities had offered new insights and had engendered enormous motivation in their professional practice. One Ugandan midwife in private practice had become increasingly aware of the multifaceted issues that predispose to maternal mortality and morbidity. She had set up numerous initiatives in her small urban clinic, working long hours in difficult conditions to improve the lot of women and girls born into poverty. Since she became aware that the lives of illiterate women are more often at risk, she had set up literacy classes for young girls so poor that they needed to work instead of attend school. Her awareness of poverty as another predisposing factor to maternal death had motivated her to invite women with business expertise to advise on micro-finance schemes for women from the surrounding community dogged by disadvantage and devoid of financial assets. No-one was barred from this little clinic which offered glimmers of hope to the struggling neighbourhood.

In a rural area of Zambia, I met a midwife in a senior position who had totally changed her attitude to practice since her opportunity to acquire critical thinking skills.

'I used to come on duty and things were not right...' she explained, *'... and I would think: well, that's how it is. I never thought I could do anything to change it!'* Then, with considerable enthusiasm, she declared *'...since doing the research course, I come on duty and think: What's happening here? What is wrong? What can we do about it?'*, concluding with determination, *'There's always something we can do to improve the situation!'*

Considering the conditions in which she worked, I admired her stance and reflected on the difference she was making to so many lives.

In visiting Swaziland I learned that this kingdom of just over a million people was among a handful of African countries that had developed men's groups and youth groups to promote optimum infant and young child feeding. They were moving away from the concept of this being an exclusively female area of responsibility. In Swaziland, too, radio programmes, drama and poetry were used to promote 100% breastfeeding and correct approaches to infant and young child feeding, whilst children's written work on the subject was being published in the national newspapers.

Pressures of poverty and injuries of injustice

In several countries that we visited to evaluate the effectiveness of the midwives' research programme we had the opportunity to discuss some personal research that the midwives had undertaken. Poverty loomed large in most situations. The plight of teenage girls forced into prostitution was the focus for several investigations. Girls found themselves in such circumstances, sometimes simply by their own admirable desire to be able to afford an education which would offer hope of finding a way out of the abject poverty experienced by generations of their families. Having little notion of the reality of the reproductive process they all too frequently found themselves pregnant. Some girls, dreading bringing shame on their families, resorted to back street abortions and many of these succumbed to the inevitable consequences of haemorrhage and infection. Such complications ended the lives of too many youngsters, little more than children themselves. Those who survived were sometimes destined to lifelong secondary infertility. The price of their desperate youthful actions condemned them to become childless and possibly rejected and ridiculed by their future husbands and communities. I saw the infants of some girls, who had carried their pregnancies to term and given birth in adverse places, such as a pit latrine, rescued and cared for in a special care baby unit. Other challenges were HIV/AIDS, malaria, endemic in many parts of this vast continent, and numerous other life-threatening yet often preventable infections.

Another issue of concern to health workers is the deeply ingrained cultural practice of female genital mutilation. Previously known as female circumcision, the injustice of this procedure has led to its recognition as a form of mutilation. Doctors, nurses and midwives practising in much of Africa and increasingly among immigrants in Western countries are challenged by the pathologies that complicate this procedure and the problems that it presents during childbirth. It is perhaps the most unjust injury inflicted on a human being. However, changing cultural practice demands not only good technical knowledge but also courage, diplomacy, dedication and insight into local cultural beliefs and practices.

Scarcity of skills

The issue of scarcity in respect to providing skilled attendance during childbirth was explored in *Chapter 6*. Africa is experiencing the realities of the brain drain where health professionals emigrate in search of better conditions, pay and prospects for themselves and their families. Such migratory movement is totally understandable, but it is saddening that colleagues who are key professionals in their own country aspire to abandon their own land in search of better things. Conversely, I have the utmost admiration for highly qualified colleagues who could easily redeploy themselves and their families into a more affluent situation, but choose to remain in adversity for the benefit of those less fortunate than themselves. Providing a more secure future for their offspring than they could anticipate in the land of their birth may, for many of these individuals, outweigh the morality of serving their fellow countrymen. My responsibility is never to judge the ethics or appropriateness of such decisions, rather, wherever possible, to attempt to work with colleagues and their governments to promote better conditions that will attract the most skilled individuals to remain where they are so badly needed. The acceptability of national expertise is always likely to surpass that of imported professionals. An elective student can learn much from such individuals and, no less, visiting consultants will find their specialist knowledge enhanced when enveloped within an indigenous framework. Indeed it is essential too to check out any proposed recommendations with national colleagues to verify their viability in the situation as well as their acceptability to those likely to be charged with implementing them.

In my international experience, staff shortages are acute in most government health institutions. An elective student is likely to be thrust into the midst of such an environment and will need considerable wisdom and maturity. Discussion beforehand with one experienced in the dilemma can be valuable, whether this be a professional practised in this kind of environment or a returned elective student. I remember in one African hospital, a major referral centre, there was a crowded postnatal ward, with dozens of women recovering from caesarean section. The ward was served by one nurse-midwife who doggedly ploughed through a process of removing wound sutures. Long queues of patients stretched along the corridor awaiting the procedure and others requiring her attention were inevitably 'put on hold'. To add to her dilemma, she had no access to clean water with which to wash her hands and a limited number of instruments with which to work. I watched with horror as she removed sutures from a highly infected wound and prepared to use the same unwashed instruments on the next patient.

Idealism is admirable, but improvisation is essential given inadequate supplies. It was no wonder that sepsis contributed to a high mortality rate in the region. It would be good to think that such a situation was scarce, but experience has shown that all too often the lack of human resources compounded by the lack of even the most basic clinical resources, beleaguer attempts to carry out the simplest procedures safely. In a rural health centre there was a similar situation. There was clearly no running water available throughout the clinical area. In commenting, I talked empathically to the local doctor about this problem. She assured me that there was no excuse for the lack of hygiene in that centre because there was a well at the bottom of the garden with plenty of water. Sometimes there are solutions to such dilemmas, although the visitor may not readily identify them.

In another African capital city, during an evaluation visit to a university hospital, the water supply had been cut off for the previous two days. In an area afflicted by HIV, among other infections that take hold rapidly in the tropical climate, labouring women and the staff attending them faced risks to their lives and health. Women in labour were desperately thirsty, but there was no drinking water available. One lady confided that she was praying for a safe birth and a quick deliverance from the situation, resigned to the fact that there was nothing else she could do.

In situations of desperate human need, being unable to respond appropriately, I have sometimes faced unenviable dilemmas. When watching wildlife programmes I am aware that the cameramen and commentators are under an agreement not to interfere with the natural order of events. Their temptation to save a young animal from its predator must be considerable. I am not under any such agreement when I find myself part of an equivalent human scenario, except when undertaking 'non-participant observation' research, and even then I have at times still made a life-saving intervention. The long-term answer inevitably lies with higher authorities, and part of a consultant's task usually involves courtesy visits to a number of institutions, such as local ministries of health and education, other departments holding the purse strings as well as non-governmental organisations and international funding agencies. It is critical in such situations to ascertain from within the country not only the real needs but also the internal obstacles to achieving the most desirable outcome. International experts can but seek to become advocates for those wrestling with the problems.

Examining the evidence

Team tactics

Multidisciplinary teams have been described as those that work side by side, in contrast with interdisciplinary teams that seek to integrate their work (Leibler, 1994). In my experience of evaluating projects, most teams are interdisciplinary. However, it is the efficiency and effectiveness with which a team can work together that will dictate the quality of its efforts. Team effectiveness has long been associated with two important elements of a team's structure, namely, interdependency and autonomy (Cummings, 1978; Campion et al, 1993; Cohen and Bailey, 1997). Building upon previous work by Emery and Trist (1969) and Campion et al (1993), Stewart and Barrick (2000: 137) define interdependence in this context as:

...the extent to which team members cooperate and work interactively to complete tasks. Further, they assert that: *...high interdependence occurs when team members interact co-operatively and depend on each other for information, materials, and reciprocal inputs.*

There is evidence to suggest that individuals or groups with a high level of interdependence tend to operate more effectively than those with a moderate interdependency (Gladstein, 1984; Saavedra et al, 1993; Wageman, 1995). Autonomy within a team has been found to be useful in enabling teams to resolve conflict on the premise that an external leader can sometimes inhibit trust between team members (Eisenstat, 1990). However, Stewart and Barrick (2000) observed that this tends to depend on the nature of the work. They found that teams displaying moderate levels of interdependence and more external leadership were more effective when performing behavioural tasks that tend to be routine and practical than when they were undertaking conceptual tasks that incorporate planning, decision making and negotiation.

In a technical report, Leibler (1994) offers guidance in the development of interdisciplinary teams, recognising that complicated situations can become stressful and it is easy to end up confusing priorities. In order to avoid this, it is urged that the team leader is responsible for promoting strategies that help decide between possible options. There is evidence, as well as my personal experience, that priorities frequently need reviewing as a project proceeds. Leibler (1994) cites an example of choosing between producing a polished report or running a workshop to present findings and develop recommendations. The latter, in my experience, pays dividends in facilitating an appropriate outcome with recommendations more likely to be implemented.

Challenges to health

UNICEF has highlighted the fact that around eight million families across the developing world are as devastated by deaths from preventable and treatable diseases as they would be if an earthquake had struck. Every four seconds a mother in the developing world loses her child and each day 22 000 children aged under five years die, mostly as a result of pneumonia, malaria or diarrhoea. An equivalent number die during the first month of life, with preterm birth, asphyxia and sepsis being leading causes during the neonatal period (Save the Children, 2011). Urban poverty curses the lives of many across the globe. Nairobi, the capital city of Kenya, reports an extremely high under-five child mortality rate which has been attributed to two-thirds of the population living in overcrowded conditions deprived of adequate water supplies and sanitation. Additionally, the use of hazardous cooking fuels in badly ventilated spaces beleaguer the lives of the poor who also cannot afford to access healthcare (UNICEF, 2012a). Malnutrition contributes to more than a third of child deaths worldwide and almost half of these deaths occur in five countries, namely, the Democratic Republic of Congo, Nigeria, India, Pakistan and China (Black et al, 2010; Save the Children, 2011).

Malaria infects up to 500 million people each year, kills a child somewhere in the world every 30 seconds, and 90% of these deaths occur in Africa. Malaria also contributes to anaemia in children and is a major cause of poor growth and development. In pregnancy, malaria causes severe anaemia and predisposes to low infant birth weight. In addition, the disease has been implicated in contributing to economic decline and perpetuating poverty across Africa. It is estimated that the use of insecticide-treated nets at night can reduce child mortality by 20%; however, usage of these nets is rated around 5% in Africa. Evidence suggests that co-existent malaria and HIV interact, with malaria seemingly accelerating progression to AIDS, and HIV worsening the effects of malaria (UNICEF, 2012b).

Across Africa, 92 million girls aged 10 or more years have undergone female genital mutilation and worldwide 140 million women and girls are estimated to be suffering the effects of this injury, which has become accepted as a violation of human rights (WHO, 2012a). It behoves international visitors to be prepared to encounter this issue and elective students working in maternity units in relevant areas would do well to consider in advance the pathology of the problem and approaches in providing care both during and after birth. The practice is most widely used in parts of northern, eastern and western Africa and of the 29 countries where the incidence of female genital mutilation is greater than 1%, Yemen is the only country implicated outside of the African continent (UNICEF, 2011). Manuals on this topic have been published by the WHO (2001a, b) and this resource is listed at the end of the chapter.

Facing the foes

Numerous and serious challenges to health need to be confronted on a global and also on a personal basis. The Millennium Development Goals (MDGs) *(Table 8.1)* endeavour to address many health issues, including malaria, HIV/AIDS and the underlying scourge of poverty which is believed to contribute to so many problems across the world.

It has been estimated that six out of the eight MDGs could be achieved if effective control of malaria was in place (Roll Back Malaria, 2005). Major efforts are under way and are surely set to continue long beyond the target date of 2015 as the world tries to address some of these scourges of society. The Abuja Declaration was agreed by heads of African States

Table 8.1. The Millennium Development Goals	
Goal	*Specified targets between 1990 and 2015 (unless otherwise stated)*
1. Eradicate extreme poverty and hunger	• Halve the proportion of people whose income is less than $1/day • Achieve full and productive employment and decent work for all, including women and young people • Halve the proportion of people who suffer from hunger
2. Achieve universal primary education	• Ensure that children everywhere, both boys and girls, will be able to complete a full course of primary education
3. Promote gender equality and empower women	• Eliminate gender disparity in primary education (by 2005) and in all levels of education (no later than 2015)
4. Reduce child mortality	• Reduce the under-5 mortality rate by two-thirds
5. Improve maternal health	• Reduce the maternal mortality ratio by three-quarters • Achieve universal access to reproductive health
6. Combat HIV/AIDS, malaria and other diseases	• Halt and begin to reverse the spread of HIV/AIDS • Achieve universal access to treatment for HIV/AIDS for those who need it (by 2010) • Halt and begin to reverse the incidence of malaria and other major diseases
7. Ensure environmental sustainability	• Integrate the process of sustainable development into country policies and programmes and reverse the loss of environmental resources • Reverse biodiversity loss, achieving significant reduction in the rate of loss (by 2010) • Halve the proportion of the population without access to safe drinking water and basic sanitation • Achieve a significant improvement in the lives of 100 million slum dwellers (by 2020)
8. Develop a global partnership for development	• Address the special needs of the least developed countries, landlocked countries and small island developing states • Develop further an open rule-based, predictable non-discriminatory trading and financial system • Deal comprehensively with developing countries' debt • In cooperation with the private sector, make available the benefits of new technologies, especially information and communications
	Source: UN, 2011

as part of a Roll Back Malaria effort at the turn of the millennium. The pronouncement called on the United Nations to identify the first decade of the 21st century as a decade for malaria, and nominate 25 April each year as Africa Malaria Day (World Health Organization, 2003). Malaria, as well as other infections that threaten the lives of young children, also poses a threat to overseas visitors who will not have had the opportunity to build up a natural immunity to such assaults. Short-term workers and elective students therefore need to take appropriate precautions in terms of malaria prophylaxis and immunisations, and observe careful food hygiene, especially in respect of drinking water. Water is, of course, essential for life, but can be one of the most dangerous substances on earth when contaminated, causing debilitating and even life-threatening gastrointestinal infections. The WHO provides regular and updated information to reduce the health risks encountered during an estimated 900 million annual international journeys. WHO maintains that many such health risks can be minimised by observing precautions before, during and after travel (WHO, 2012b). Consultants who regularly undertake international assignments should maintain their immune status so that they are available to travel at short notice. Elective students need to plan an immunisation programme well in advance so that it can be completed without undue interference with study and examinations.

Rights-based approaches to development

Human rights issues in the context of health had gained increasing global prominence by the end of the 20th century. Nevertheless, the matter can be controversial. Alston (2005) challenges the international communities that focus on development on the one hand and human rights on the other. He contends that although the MDGs have a great deal in common with the human rights agenda, this has not been embraced with sufficient enthusiasm. However, Nelson (2007), drawing on documentary evidence and a review of 40 non-governmental and social movement organisations, argues that the MDGs and rights-based approaches have less in common than first appears. He maintains that the Goals are designed to mobilise support from donors. Luttrell and Quiroz (2009) raise the issue of cultural imperialism in this context and cite the common query raised among human rights advocates as to whether or not rights-based approaches seek to impose Western values. Uvin (2002) perceives human rights approaches attracting aid from countries and organisations wishing to gain credibility for a high moral stance. Whatever the motivation, Sweden and Britain are among the donor countries that have adopted a rights-based approach to development (Piron and Watkins, 2004; Ministry of Foreign Affairs Sweden, 2006).

In line with this sentiment our evaluations in Africa during the early years of the 21st century needed to include a consideration of rights-based approaches to development and to reproductive health. Therefore we explored the matter of advocacy both from rights-based and evidence-based perspectives.

WHO claims that numerous national and international declarations and treaties relating to human rights that can be used in respect of promoting maternal health have been underutilised. These include the International Covenant on Social, Economic and Cultural Rights, the Women's Convention, and the African Charter on Human and People's Rights (WHO, 1998). Such documents may need to be highlighted when advocating issues that protect the health and lives of women. Cook et al (2001) underline the importance of identifying those bound by legal duty in respect of human rights. These include individuals carrying out government responsibilities or working under the authority of government or government agencies. They point out that if human rights are not backed by legally enforceable duties they remain in the realm of moral rights, although agencies, officers and others can be made morally accountable for observing them. Representation at all levels can be strengthened by approaching matters with evidence-based advocacy. Nanda et al (2005) suggest that this approach can be used to enhance political commitment and can promote an enabling policy environment. The effectiveness of consultants attempting to promote maternal health, for example by recommending small business investment for women in the poorer sections of society, could be enhanced by producing appropriate evidence. For instance, it has been shown that when women and girls earn, they reinvest 90% of this into their families whereas men and boys contribute just 30–40% (UNICEF, 2011).

Luttrell et al (2005) claim that there is no single 'correct' understanding of rights-based approaches, but a common theme emerges that the intention is to realise the rights of people as specified in the Universal Declaration of Human Rights (UN, 1948). In considering rights-based approaches it is important to identify the relationship between groups and individuals with valid claims on the one hand and the State, as well as others with relevant obligations, on the other. The former are known as 'rights holders' and the latter as 'duty bearers'. A rights-based approach in development therefore aims to strengthen the capacity of the rights holders to claim their rights as well as the ability of the duty bearers to meet their obligations (UNICEF, 2004).

When carrying out an evaluation, a consultant inevitably needs to establish the stance on human rights approaches held by the donor country sponsoring the assignment. In addition, in offering advice on or input into projects, it is helpful to bear these issues in mind. Both consultants and elective students would do well to take into consideration how any approaches used or proposed are likely to comply or possibly conflict with human rights issues. When the most appropriate way forward involves recommending change, the risk of imposing Western values in a very different cultural context demands due consideration.

However rights are perceived, the poor across much of the developing world are entangled in a web of injustice. It has been widely acknowledged that disparities exist not only between countries at different levels of development but also between groups of different socioeconomic status within a country (Braveman et al, 2001; Kunst and Houweling, 2001; Murray, 2001). Furthermore, it has been claimed that narrowing the existing disparities in health between social groups can form part of an ongoing battle against social injustice (Peter and Evans, 2001). Development work therefore inevitably demands consideration of those in situations of desperate need. Undoubtedly there is an increasing risk to life and health in the face of mounting poverty, and gender analysis has revealed that imbalances of power that are enforced through culturally sanctioned concepts can have deeply devastating effects on women in such circumstances (Hawkins et al, 2005). This side of the cultural coin provides an unenviable alternative to that which imposes Western culture or values. Such a coin denotes the 'bad penny' in cultural currency and impacts development in an inappropriate manner (*Figure 8.2*). Contrasting cultures are not necessarily good or bad, but different – and they can be very different. In tossing the cultural coin it is indeed unenviable if both sides prove to be undesirable.

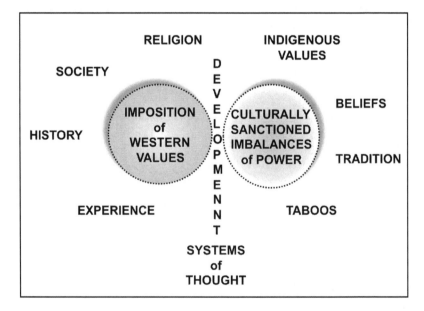

Figure 8.2. The 'bad penny' in cultural currency and some of the factors that contribute to cultural norms. Derived from Maclean (1998), Hawkins et al (2005), and Luttrell and Quiroz (2009).

Human resources for health

Numerous issues contribute to the lack of human resources in the health services of countries attempting to tackle unacceptably high mortality and morbidity rates. In respect of maternal mortality this has been attributed to:

> *...an overall lack of qualified staff, inequitable distribution of providers, high levels of absenteeism and increasing attrition of skilled workers due to the impact of HIV/AIDS and regional/international migration.*
> *(Macdonagh, 2005: 17)*

In the second decade of the 21st century large gaps still persist in many countries between the numbers of skilled attendants required and those available to meet government targets in the context of MDG5. It has been estimated that most countries need to double, triple or even quadruple their midwifery workforce in order to meet the need for coverage by skilled health professionals during childbirth (UNFPA, 2011). Therefore, where insufficient national experts are available, visiting consultants are frequently required to assist with curriculum planning, education or providing professional updating for doctors, midwives and others across the spectrum of health services. Elective students may find themselves in situations where staff shortages make working conditions highly pressurised. Being prepared for this is an important step, and learning how to balance a busy workload with adequate rest is a useful skill. Students may also assume a role in providing up-to-date information for local colleagues. Where access to journals and the internet is limited or inaccessible, updating is not easy and fresh input is almost always appreciated, providing it is offered appropriately. In one country I recall having extreme difficulty in trying to convince doctors that routine episiotomy for primiparae was not justifiable, in line with current evidence-based practice. However, adopting the active management of the third stage of labour was accepted readily and attributed to our input as visiting consultants. This followed our demonstration of the technique and our availability to supervise colleagues until they were confident.

It has been emphasised that appropriate workforce strategies must be country-led and country-based, but they usually require international backing and reinforcement (Chen, 2004). Many countries struggle not only with training but also with retainment of staff. Deficits in human resources have been attributed to numerous factors including the influence of poor remuneration. However, the lack of motivation, professional fulfilment and limited career opportunities lie alongside the more practical issues that deprive staff of adequate transport and housing and threaten personal safety (Vujicic et al, 2004; Mathauer and Imhoff, 2006). Such issues have certainly been on the agenda in my experience during discussions with colleagues and in evaluating programmes in countries plagued by a shortfall in human resources. Consultants may need to address such issues at government level on behalf of national colleagues. In this context, Thailand has made dramatic strides in healthcare and in reducing maternal mortality (Hogan et al, 2010). Following decades of experience in addressing these issues, the Thai government implemented a strategy to improve pay and conditions for doctors working in rural areas. Logistic, educational, administrative and financial strategies were used in order to facilitate more equitable deployment of skilled professionals. The Thai Rural Doctors Society has also been influential in medical education, raising morale and improving the distribution of doctors across the country (Wibulpolprasert and Pengpaibon, 2003).

While the matter of migration is outside the scope of, although perhaps not entirely beyond the influence of, the short-term visitor, university and professional exchange programmes provide benefits for participants both East and West. Goodwin and Nacht (1984) describe a businessman's differentiation between importing an expert and exporting students. The former has been dubbed, 'The King of Siam option', while sending students abroad, 'The Peter the Great approach'. Expertise imported to plan and conduct programmes in-country undoubtedly creates opportunities for a greater number of people at a lower cost than exporting them to a Western university or hospital, without the risk of feeding the brain drain and adding to the economic cost to a country. Clemens and Pettersson (2008) estimated that there were 65 000 African-born physicians and 70 000 nurses working in developed countries at the turn of the millennium. Pursuing the 'King of Siam option' is not therefore a minor consideration for those involved in development work.

Personal reflections on practice

- It is easy to see what is wrong and what is missing, my national counterparts know these things better than I. It is recognising the initiatives and the enterprises and offering sincere encouragement that is more likely to see them continue and even replicated than cataloguing the deficiencies.
- There are many problems that I cannot solve or even relieve, but that does not prevent me from using every avenue open to me to assist or represent my colleagues who continue in unequal struggles.
- Adopting change in actively managing the third stage of labour was much easier than preventing routine use of episiotomy. This may have been associated with the immediate rather than the long-term effects associated with the former by comparison with sequelae associated

with the latter. It may also have been because we diligently worked with colleagues in the clinical area on third stage management.

Some lessons learned and shared

- The importance of visiting clinical areas can never be overestimated. Attempting to do so in as wide a variety of settings as practicable will provide useful insights for elective students and for consultants evaluating or advising on programmes.
- The wisdom of national colleagues is essential in seeking to be an advocate for them at government level and no less so in determining what will work before finalising any recommendations. Rights-based and evidence-based approaches are worthy considerations in advocacy.
- A handful of encouragement given in earnest will outweigh a bucketful of criticism along the pathway of progress.
- It is never acceptable to denigrate spiritual norms and values or decry deity. If you originate from a secularised environment and cannot relate to the belief, it is appropriate at the least to show respect.

Reflective exercises

- Reflect on an approach that you plan to use in practice or a recommendation you have in mind. Is there any risk that this may impose Western values in a very different cultural context?
- Think about a team in which you work or have worked. What has contributed to or distracted from the team's efficiency and effectiveness? List the qualities that you consider contribute to positive teamwork experiences.
- Consider an aspect of your study or practice that needs addressing. If you were to represent your student or professional group on this issue at national or government level, what evidence-based and rights-based approaches may be appropriate to utilise?

Resources

- Female genital mutilation:
  - *Female Genital Mutilation: Integrating the prevention and the management of the health complications into the curricula of nursing and midwifery. A Teacher's Guide.* WHO. Available from: http://www.who.int/reproductivehealth/ publications/fgm/RHR_01_16/en/index.html

- *Female Genital Mutilation: Integrating the prevention and the management of the health complications into the curricula of nursing and midwifery. A student's manual.* WHO. Available from: http://www.who.int/gender/other_health/ Studentsmanual.pdf
- Prevention of malaria: http://www.patient.co.uk/health/Malaria-Prevention.htm

References

Africa.com (2012a) *Kenya facts and figures*. Available from: http://www.africa.com/kenya/ facts [last accessed 28.06.2012]

Africa.com (2012b) *Swaziland facts and figures*. Available from: http://www.africa.com/ swaziland/facts [last accessed 28.06.2012]

Africa.com (2012c) *Uganda facts and figures*. Available from: http://www.africa.com/uganda/ facts [last accessed 28.06.2012]

Africa.com (2012d) *Zambia facts and figures* http://www.africa.com/zambia/facts [last accessed 28.06.2012]

Alston P (2005) Ships that pass in the night: The current state of the human rights and development debate seen through the eyes of the Millennium Development Goals. *Human Rights Quarterly* **27**: 755–829

Black RE, Johnson SC, Cousins HL et al (2010) Global, regional and national causes of child mortality in 2008: A systematic analysis. *Lancet* **375**(9730): 1969–87. doi: 10.1016/S0140-6736(10)60549-1

Braveman P, Starfield B, Geiger H (2001) World Health Report 2000: How it removes equity from the agenda for public health monitoring and policy. *British Medical Journal* **323**: 678–81

Campion MA, Medsker GJ, Higgs AC (1993) Relations between work group characteristics and effectiveness: Implications for designing effective work groups. *Personnel Psychology* **46**: 823–50

Chen LC (2004) *Harnessing the power of human resources for achieving the MDGs*, High Level Forum on the Health MDGs, Session: Human Resources in Health, January 9, 2004. Co-sponsored by WHO and the World Bank, WHO, Geneva

Clemens MA, Pettersson G (2008) New data on African health professionals abroad. *Human Resources for Health* 6(1): 11. Available from: Biomed Central: http://www.human-resources-health.com/content/6/1/1 [last accessed 08.10.2012]

Cohen SG, Bailey DE (1997) What makes teams work? Group effectiveness research from the shop floor to the executive suite. *Journal of Management* **23**: 239–90

Cook RJ, Dickens BM, Wilson OAF (2001) *Advancing safe motherhood through human rights*. Occasional Paper WHO/RHR/01/05, World Health Organization, Geneva

Cummings T (1978) Self-regulated work groups: A socio-technical synthesis. *Academy of Management Review* **3**: 625–34

Eisenstat RA (1990) Fairfield coordinating group. In JR Hackman (ed) *Groups that work and those that don't: Creating conditions for effective team-work.* Jossey-Bass, San Francisco

Emery FL, Trist EL (1969) Socio-technical systems. In Emery FE (ed) *Systems thinking* (pp. 281–96). Penguin, London

Gladstein DL (1984) Groups in context: A model of task group effectiveness. *Administrative Science Quarterly* **29**: 499–517

Goodwin CD, Nacht M (1984) *Fondness and frustration: The impact of American higher education on foreign students with special reference to the case of Brazil.* Institute of International Education, New York, IIE Research Report 5

Hawkins K, Newman K, Thomas D, Carlson C (2005) *Developing a human rights-based approach to addressing maternal mortality. A Desk Review.* DFID Health Resource Centre, London

Hogan MC, Foreman KJ, Naghavi M et al (2010) Maternal mortality for 181 countries 1980–2008. A systematic analysis of progress towards Millennium Development Goal 5. *Lancet* DOI:10.1016/S0140-6736 (10) 60518-1

Index Mundi (2012) *Country comparison > population.* Available from: http://www.indexmundi.com/g/r.aspx [last accessed 28.09.2012]

Kunst AE, Houweling T (2001) A global picture of poor-rich differences in the utilisation of delivery care. *Studies in Health Services Organisation and Policy,* **17**: 297–315

Liebler C (1994) *Making interdisciplinary teams work: A guide for team leaders and technical assistance managers.* WASH Technical Reports 92, under WASH Task 381. USAID, Washington DC

Luttrell C, Piron LH, Thompson D (2005) *Operationalising Norwegian people's aids rights based approach.* Overseas Development Institute, London

Luttrell C, Quiroz S (2009) *Understanding and operationalising empowerment.* Working Paper 308. Overseas Development Institute, London

Macdonagh S (2005) *Achieving skilled attendance for all; a synthesis of current knowledge and recommended actions for scaling up.* Department for International Development, Health Resource Centre, London

Maclean GD (1998) *An examination of the characteristics of short term international midwifery consultants.* Thesis for the degree of Doctor of Philosophy. University of Surrey, Guildford, England

Mathauer I, Imhoff I (2006) Health worker motivation in Africa, the role of non-financial incentives and human resource management tools. *Human Resources for Health* **4**(24): 1–17

Ministry of Foreign Affairs, Sweden (2006) *Sweden's international policy on Sexual and Reproductive Health and Rights.* Regeringskansliet, Ministry of Foreign Affairs, Sweden

Murray C (2001) Commentary: comprehensive approaches are needed for full understanding. *British Medical Journal* **323**: 680–1

Nanda G, Swillick K, Lule E (2005) *Accelerating progress towards achieving the MDG to improve maternal health: A collection promising approaches.* Health, Nutrition and Population Discussion Paper, International Bank for Reconstruction and Development/ The World Bank, Washington, DC

Nelson PJ (2007) Human rights, the Millennium Development Goals and the future of development cooperation. *World Development* **35**(12): 2041–55

Peter F, Evans T (2001) Ethical dimensions of health equity, In: Evans T, Whitehead M, Dikerichsen F, Ihuiya A, Wirth M (eds) *Challenging inequities in health: from ethics to action* (pp. 24–33). Oxford University Press, New York

Piron LH, Watkins F (2004) *DFID Human Rights Review. A review of how DFID has integrated human rights approaches into its work.* Overseas Development Institute, London

Roll Back Malaria (2005) *Global Strategic Plan: Roll Back Malaria 2005–2015.* UNICEF/ UNDP/WHO/World Bank, RBM Partnership Secretariat, Geneva

Saavedra R, Earley PC, Van Dyne L (1993) Complex interdependence in task-performing groups. *Journal of Applied Psychology* **78**: 61–72

Save the Children (2011) *State of the World's mothers 2011.* Save the Children. Available from: http://www.savethechildren.org/ [last accessed 17/10/2012]

Save the Children (2012) *State of the World's mothers 2012.* The 2012 Mothers' Index. Save the Children. Available from: http://www.savethechildren.org/ [last accessed 13/07/2012]

Stewart GL, Barrick MR (2000) Team structure and performance: Assessing the mediating role of intrateam process and the mediating role of task type. *Academy of Management Journal* **43**(2): 135–48

UN (1948) T*he Universal Declaration of Human Rights.* The United Nations Organization, New York. Available from: http://www.un.org/en/documents/udhr/index.shtml [last accessed 14.05.2012]

UN (2011) *The Millennium Development Goals Report 2011.* UN, New York

UN Development Programme (2011) *International Human Development Indicators.* United Nations Development Programme. Available from: http://hdr.undp.org/en/statistics/ [Last accessed 13.02.2012]

UNFPA (2011) *The state of the World's midwifery 2011; Delivering health, saving lives.* UNFPA, New York. Available from: www.stateoftheworldsmidwifery.com [last accessed 28.06.2012]

UNICEF (2004) The human rights based approach: Statement of common understanding. In: *State of the World's Children 2004, Annexe B* (pp. 91–3). UNICEF, New York

UNICEF (2011) *State of the World's children 2011.* UNICEF, New York

UNICEF (2012a) *State of the World's children 2012.* UNICEF, New York

UNICEF (2012b) *Health: Malaria*. UNICEF, New York. Available from: http://www.unicef. org/health/index_malaria.html [last accessed 11.05.2012]

Uvin P (2002) On high moral ground: the incorporation of human rights by the development enterprise. *Praxis* **17**: 1–11

Vujicic M, Zurn P, Diallo K, Adams O, Dal Poz MR (2004) The role of wages in the migration of health care professionals from developing countries. *Human Resources for Health* 2(3). Available from: http://www.human-resources-health.com/content/pdf/1478-4491-2-3.pdf [last accessed 08.10.2012]

Wageman R (1995) Interdependence and group effective-ness. *Administrative Science Quarterly* **40**: 145–80

WHO (1998) *Safe Motherhood: a matter of human rights and social justice. World Health Day 7 April 1998*. WHD 98.03. Available from: http://www.who.int/docstore/world-health-day/en/pages1998/whd98_03.html [last accessed 18.05.2012]

WHO (2001a) *Female genital mutilation: Integrating the prevention and the management of the health complications into the curricula of nursing and midwifery. A teacher's guide*. WHO, Geneva

WHO (2001b) *Female Genital Mutilation: Integrating the prevention and the management of the health complications into the curricula of nursing and midwifery. A student's manual*. WHO, Geneva

WHO (2003) *The Abuja Declaration and the plan of action, an extract from the African summit on Roll Back Malaria, Abuja 25 April 2000*. WHO/CDS/RBM.46

WHO (2012a) *Female genital mutilation, Fact sheet number 241*. February 2012. WHO, Geneva. Available from: http://www.who.int/mediacentre/factsheets/fs241/en/ [last accessed 10.05.2012]

WHO (2012b) *International travel and health*. WHO, Geneva. Available from: http://www. who.int/ith/en/index.html [last accessed 08.10.2012]

WHO (2012c) *Trends in maternal mortality 1990 to 2010*. WHO, UNICEF, UNFPA and World Bank. WHO, Geneva

Wibulpolprasert S, Pengpaibon P (2003) Integrated strategies to tackle the inequitable distribution of doctors in Thailand: four decades of experience. *Human Resources for Health* **12**. Available from: www.human-resources-health.com/content/1/1/12

World Factbook (2012) *World Factbook*. Available from: https://www.cia.gov/library/publications/the-world-factbook/ [last accessed 09.07.2012]

Chapter 9

Priorities in Pakistan

Be kind, for everyone you meet is fighting a harder battle.

(Plato)

Personality and preferred learning styles vary considerably among individuals. Appreciating and respecting them can open the doors and windows of an educational process and increase a sense of esteem and personal value

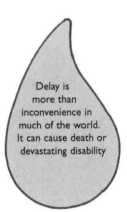

Delay is more than inconvenience in much of the world. It can cause death or devastating disability

Subject strands introduced

- Learning styles, personality and appreciative inquiry in education
- Clinical competence
- Clinical teaching

- Delay
- Obstetric fistulae
- Gender issues

Practice points

- Tailoring educational approaches to meet needs
- Demonstrating clinical skills
- Teaching by example

- Using evidence-based advocacy
- Appreciating gracious hospitality
- Personal security when living in danger zones

Figure 9.1. Pakistan.

Pakistan: Background

Pakistan

The Islamic Republic of Pakistan is bordered by China, India, Iran and Afghanistan and has a coastline of more than 1000 km where it meets the Arabian Sea. The name of the country is thought to have been derived from an acronym indicating the different regions comprising the state. The name Pakistan literally translates from the Persian word for pure '*pak*' as 'Land of the Pure'. Pakistan extends over 803 940 km^2. The capital city is Islamabad, although the largest city and business hub is the port of Karachi. Once under British rule, Pakistan became an independent country in 1947 when the act of partition separated India and Pakistan. The country was initially divided into East and West Pakistan. The former became Bangladesh and the latter Pakistan in a further separation following hostilities in 1971. This federal republic has become a nuclear power and uses a common law system with Islamic law influence. The population exceeds 190 million (estimated 2012) with 34% living in urban areas, and 40% were estimated to be living below the poverty line at the turn of the millennium. The country is vulnerable to natural disasters in the form of earthquakes and floods. Pakistan is estimated to be 97% Islamic; Sunni Muslims comprising the vast majority. Pakistan is home to several ethnic groups, Urdu is the official language and English is also spoken as well as several other languages including Punjabi, Pashtun and Sindhi. Exports include cotton, rice, petroleum, leather and fish products.

Pakistan: Data
Pakistan HDI*: low (145) MMR: 260 (2010) Lifetime risk of maternal death: 1 in 110 Mothers index ranking (2012)**: 78(Tier II) Births attended by skilled personnel: 39%
HDI: Human Development Index, MMR: Maternal Mortality Ratio *Assessed according to life expectancy, educational and economic factors **Ranked globally (within 3 tiers: I = more developed, II = less developed, III = least developed) according to health, education, economic and political status of women
Background and data sources: Index Mundi, 2012; Save the Children, 2012; UNICEF, 2012; World Facts and Figures, 2012; WHO, 2012

Exploring experience

Beyond the borders

My first glimpse of Pakistan had been many years previously when, residing in India, I travelled to the northwest with a friend who was returning to work on the other side of the border. The ceremony at sunset as the military guards took down the flags of both nations and closed the border for the night was impressive. However, there was a sense of uneasiness, as there can be across frontiers of lands that have experienced recent hostilities. It was such a situation that had prevented me landing in the port of Karachi some years earlier.

I had been heading for work in what was then East Pakistan, now known as Bangladesh. I had travelled by sea, and the intention was that I should disembark in Karachi and fly across to Dhaka. However, the ship on which I travelled had an Indian crew and at that time there was no way in which the crew could be permitted to sail into a Pakistani port. I was therefore advised to stay on board, disembark in Bombay (Mumbai) and travel overland to Calcutta (Kolkata) which was not too distant from the border. I never did get to Dhaka, leave alone to the hospital in the Chittagong Hill Tracts where I had been appointed. The political situation between India and Pakistan had worsened and, although my luggage travelled to Dhaka, I was not able to proceed to that country; instead I spent a number of years working in India, only being reunited with my baggage years later after returning home to the UK.

During those early years I had to learn to do without, and to manage to live with a minimum of possessions, since many things were not easily available in that part of the world at the time. Such an experience stood me in good stead on a much later assignment when I was asked to join a Pakistani and British team of experts undertaking an assignment in Islamabad. We were to be in Pakistan for just one week, but we were instructed that in order to avoid delays at the airport and be available for meetings immediately on arrival, we were to carry just hand luggage. It is surprising how one can manage with few possessions in such circumstances and our local Pakistani colleagues were all too willing to assist us with essential items should we have the need.

My first real encounter with Pakistan had come years after I had initially glimpsed it beyond the borders of India. I was invited to undertake some teaching in Karachi and this time flew in without hindrance. My students were professionals who taught midwifery; some were doctors, some were nursing and midwifery tutors and all were involved in teaching midwifery to pre-registration students. I had been asked to do some sessions on the art of clinical teaching. It was an interesting experience. I discovered that, as in many countries, clinical skills seemed to be low on the list of priorities of the tutors. Theoretical knowledge was considered important, but practical skills were not a popular option. We looked at the theory behind clinical teaching, supervision and assessment but also utilised as many opportunities as possible to undertake bedside teaching. I discovered at first that my colleagues were reluctant to go to the wards for teaching sessions. 'Why?' they had questioned. Perhaps the relevance was not very apparent. However, as I got to know them better I realised that they were handicapped by the same problem that faces many who have undergone training programmes in countries where clinical skills have received a low priority in their own pre-registration training, they were not confident in the skills themselves. My heart went out to them. I was therefore encouraged by the end of the programme that when I gave the group a choice of activity on the last day, they unanimously decided to go onto the wards. That was progress. They had moved through the pain barrier and were beginning to gain confidence.

Discussing this matter with my Pakistani medical colleague on another occasion some years later I had underlined the fact that unless those teaching the students were able to demonstrate clinical skills, we were not really going to be able to address significantly the need for skilled attendants during childbirth. If teaching concentrated mainly on the theory we were in trouble, and the handicap would be passed on from generation to generation of future midwives. Defending their lack of ability by acknowledging the deficit in their own training I pleaded their cause, whereupon my colleague replied, 'No, it is not their fault if they come on this course without clinical skills, but it will be their fault if they leave it without them!' He was prepared to make a way for these professionals to redress the balance in their own experience by offering them opportunities to make good their loss. Stepping beyond the borders of the classroom, out into clinical areas called for considerable confidence and courage, especially for those already in senior positions. However, I continue to hope that programmes that offer clinical updates as well as academic excellence will flourish in this country as in many others struggling with unacceptably high maternal and infant mortality rates.

The unenviable plight of women

Visiting the hospitals and clinics of Pakistan's cities and districts can paint a picture of gloom and despair. Overcrowded, understaffed and under-resourced just begins to tell some of the story. However, it is the women who do not make it as far as a hospital or health centre who can suffer horrific injuries as a result of childbirth. Of course, too many, too young, die without any hope or help, as the statistics readily reveal. For this reason, major efforts are being made to train midwives and allocate them to the more remote areas where many women have no access to healthcare and emergency services.

It was during one of my visits that I was asked, as the only midwife member of an expert team, to meet with one of the men from the Ministry to discuss a proposed midwifery programme. The issue surrounded the proposal to train girls straight from school as midwives. I believed that this could offer a useful professional resource to address the considerable shortage of skilled attendants across the country, especially in rural areas. However, the plan to train them adequately in three months was far from achievable and the notion filled all who knew the reality of midwifery and obstetric practice with horror and dismay. The programme would in effect have produced another type of traditional birth attendant that would not have addressed the high maternal mortality and morbidity levels. One seldom knows what effect one's own efforts may have had, sometimes it is just a link in the chain, other times it may be too soon, too late or just an unacceptable counter-proposal. In this case I could but act as an advocate armed with the best available evidence to try and dissuade the disastrous decision.

A later teaching assignment I undertook in Karachi was based at a private hospital that had been set up for the care and treatment of women with obstetric fistulae. This desperate but preventable injury is the plight of women who have no access to skilled care and suffer the inevitable consequences of a prolonged and traumatic labour. The focus of the Koohi Goth Hospital served to make the training of midwives and tutors on that site all the more poignant as the immense risks of giving birth without skilled assistance were all too evident. On one occasion I sent the students I was teaching onto the wards where women were recovering from surgery to repair the horrific injuries they had sustained. I had asked them to interview the patients, their relatives and the staff to explore what made giving birth so unsafe in the regions from which they had come and what might improve the situation.

Some had come from remote rural or desert areas and as the students shared their stories during a feedback session the reality of their plight was revealed. Distance, compounded by lack of communication and transport, and poverty, accentuated by cultural traditions and taboos had spelled the end of life for some, and untold misery for others. Such suffering had made them outcasts, shunned by friends and often rejected by family too. The medical team that visited these areas had carried out life-changing surgery in fistula camps, working under punishing conditions with a minimum of essentials in order to bring hope and healing to these women. Those who could not be treated in the camp were referred back to Karachi where better facilities enabled most to be restored and return home. Some of the women I met had suffered the indignity of these injuries for many years, others for just a few months, but all could have been prevented if only skilled midwives were available who could detect abnormalities early enough and refer the women to a place of safety to give birth.

Many of the women told stories that needed to be heard and assimilated into the preparation of midwives who would be working in such areas. Families spoke of the tradition of not seeking help when a woman is labouring until she has laboured for five days, and then the low priority placed on women's health and needs delaying the process for even longer. The journey to the nearest medical help from some of these villages was measured in days. Some had to cross mountain paths and treacherous byways. The only transport available may be in the form of camel carts or mules; it was never easy and never rapid.

Traditional birth attendants (*dais*) are the main providers of maternity care in many of these areas. I knew that my colleagues, both medical and midwifery, had a massive task in trying to penetrate the territory of these women who were practised in the traditional arts, but mostly unable to help women facing such desperate dilemmas. Even in the cities, delay could not inevitably be avoided. There were instances of women dying on the way to hospital, trapped in traffic jams or crowded streets where there is no priority for emergency vehicles and often there were no emergency vehicles to help rescue the situation. At times, civil unrest and violence contributed further to delays encountered by those even attempting to access antenatal clinics or a maternity hospital for birthing. Such is the plight of many in numerous big cities across the world, and the inferior place women hold in society only serves to accentuate the predicament. Discussing this unenviable situation with a young woman doctor, stressing the need for midwives to show respect to the women in their care, she had offered the opinion that sometimes women, including themselves, were their own worst enemies. It is my impression that in countries where women are frequently disadvantaged, the attitudes of nurses and midwives can often seem to accentuate the dilemma.

In an African country my colleagues had raised the question themselves during an obstetric life-saving skills programme. 'Why are we so unkind to the patients?' one midwife had asked. 'Why do we shout at them?' added another. There was considerable debate, but the overall consensus was that because they themselves were not respected they found it difficult to respect the women in their care. It was not surprising therefore that there was disbelief when I declared in Karachi that the patient was the most important person in the room. A village woman from a poor part of the outskirts of the city had willingly agreed to be available for us to demonstrate antenatal examination and I do not think that she had ever felt special in her life, but here we thought about who she was, what her needs were and how important it was for us to show her kindness and respect. These were new concepts to most of my students, even though many were experienced tutors themselves.

Breaking down barriers

Within hours of touching down in Karachi on my first visit, I had found myself in a local radio station. The information that 'we' were to be on a live radio programme took me not a little by surprise. My opportunity to learn Urdu whilst in India was now a valuable asset in listening to the questions that were phoned in to my medical colleagues whom I accompanied. I had not bargained for needing to recall the language from the remote recesses of my brain on air on Radio Karachi some 30 years later! However, my colleagues were helpful and encouraging.

The weekly programme invited people to ring in with their queries or comments. This was one of the many ways in which attempts were being made to break down barriers and enable women to have access to the expertise they needed. Later, in one of my assignments, having regained some confidence in using the language, I responded to a request from some of my students to teach in Urdu. Their limitation in English was proving a problem and so, with their hearty approval, I ventured across the linguistic divide. I somehow think that my limitations exceeded theirs, but the effort broke down barriers and drew us closer together as colleagues striving towards the same goals. Another approach I used with this group was to consider the importance of personality and preferred learning styles in education. Visible relief dawned on the faces of experienced tutors who had never had the opportunity to explore these dimensions of learning. Some doors were unlocked and limits surpassed as individuals learned for the first time to appreciate their own individuality and needs.

Another barrier was removed in one of the city hospitals by using an appreciative inquiry approach. This concept was discussed in *Chapter 5*, but here I was to witness how it had transformed attitudes and changed practice.

One of the outcomes of an exercise had been the establishment of a rapid reaction team to deal with obstetric emergencies. Here each member of the team from consultant to ancillary worker sat down together and discussed the issues with which they were all required to wrestle every day. Whereas admission had been a protracted process and even gaining entry to the hospital had been difficult, now the *chowkidar* (the security watchman at the gate) understood the need for urgent admission and was able to expedite access to life-saving assistance. However skilled and able the doctors may have been, lives were being lost as a result of delays within the hospital. Now people respected one another's role and responsibility, and recognised their interdependence within a team.

My first glimpse of Pakistan had been at the international border where soldiers vigilantly safeguarded their territory. On my most recent visit I was provided with a personal bodyguard. The threat of terrorism has hung over Pakistan for a number of years and foreigners can be targets. My colleagues, appreciating that I might have become a useful hostage, took no risks. An armed guard was appointed to avert any such danger, and I was assured that in the unlikely event of any such attempt, the sight of my bodyguard would convince any assailant to look elsewhere. I must admit I felt uneasy at first, but then strangely reassured by the young man who preceded me into the street each morning and each night, brandishing his gun, visibly scanning and then pointing the weapon in each direction, finally escorting me to the vehicle where he sat with the gun very visibly at the ready. One becomes accustomed to a very different environment on such assignments. It behoves foreigners to take the advice of their hosts who can themselves be placed at risk by thoughtless actions of those whom they seek to protect.

Taking care is a multifaceted phenomenon. Personal security is one facet, gracious hospitality another. During one assignment when several expatriates were working with national colleagues on planning strategies, we arrived in Islamabad during Ramadan. Our hosts, in the majority, were fasting from sunrise to sunset, but they were careful to ensure that we had sufficient refreshment throughout the long working days. This was kindness and selfless consideration and these attributes I experienced during each of my visits, whether staying with a family or being lavishly entertained. Hospital food in any country can rarely be described as lavish, but here my hosts took pains to provide food with which I was comfortable, by special request avoiding the chillies which inevitably send me into spasms of coughing. On one occasion, dining with a paediatrician, she painstakingly analysed every dish put before me to ensure the meal was free of the offending spices. Years previously in another part of the sub-continent I recall visits to village areas where poor people would provide a large meal for visitors. They would not eat themselves, but stand back and watch the food being consumed. That could be painful. It was a humbling experience to note the generosity and humility of the poor towards a guest from afar. To decline the hospitality or offer to share the food with them would have been very hurtful, even rude. One could only hope and pray that they would not go without for too long in payment for their selfless giving. I had learned that in this region it is courteous to eat all that has been put on one's plate, thus indicating appreciation. In other countries, for example in Indonesia, it is most appropriate to leave a little to show that one has been given more than enough. It is helpful if the visitor can get these things right! Western hospitality does not begin to touch the courtesies demonstrated in much of the orient.

Examining the evidence

Learning styles and personality in education

The education of adults has developed over the years and has emanated from the work of many experts. During the 20th century these have included the andragogical approach advocated by Knowles (1978, 1989), the transformation theory of Mezirow (1971), experiential learning as promoted by Kolb (1984) and Kolb et al (2001), action learning advanced by Revans (2011) and reflection advocated by Schön (1983). Perhaps the most meaningful discoveries I have made in the course of education and practice, encompass three concepts, namely appreciative inquiry (Barrett, 1995), the Myers-Briggs Type Indicator (MBTI) (Myers and Myers, 1980) and preferred learning styles (Lawrence, 1982).

Appreciative inquiry was discussed in *Chapter 5* and is mentioned above. The approach uses valuing and building on what the students know and can do, rather than highlighting their deficiencies. The latter tends to be a dominant trend in many countries where I have worked. Davis (2005) maintains that as an approach to learning and teaching appreciative inquiry is still in the early stages and acknowledges that it is up against centuries of tradition using critical and deficit-based educational philosophies. However, Hargis (2006) stresses that appreciative inquiry can be used as an effective communication tool in higher education, and Cockell and McArthur-Blair (2012) purport that fully integrating appreciative inquiry into higher education could have an exponential effect on the next generation of positive change agents across the globe.

The need to determine and respond to differing learning styles has been used extensively over the past few decades (Kolb et al, 2001). Capretz (2002) maintains that making adjustments in teaching to accommodate differing learning styles can increase achievement and also enhance the enjoyment of learning. Embracing the concept of dissimilar personalities he professes that:

The MBTI and its inferences provide a way to conceptualize a student as an organized dynamic personality, which predisposes each student to certain ways of behaving and gives the student a unique learning pattern.
(Capretz, 2002: 137)

From his study of learning styles among nursing students, Frankel (2009) stresses the importance of training programmes reflecting their individual preferences. He concludes that current programmes are not meeting the need and recommends more work-based rather than classroom-based learning. He further proposes that it is advantageous to enable students to acquire the essential skills for seeking, analysing and utilising information effectively and predicts that such an approach will better facilitate the integration of theory and practice. He also contends that a positive learning environment would improve the quality of care that nurses provide. The latter point is critical for all education for practice in the healthcare professions.

The importance of clinical skills

A skilled birth attendant has been defined as an accredited health professional, such as a midwife, doctor or nurse, who has been educated and trained to proficiency in the skills needed to manage normal or uncomplicated pregnancy, childbirth and the immediate postnatal period, and in the identification, management and referral of complications in women and newborns (WHO, 2004 and see *Box 1.3* in *Chapter 1*). Yet there is evidence that the combination of a lack of skills and a lack of knowledge impede the utilisation of the necessary interventions, and militate against the implementation of beneficial evidence-based practice in many resource poor countries (Siddiqui et al, 2011). It has become evident that 'trained' does not inevitably mean 'skilled' and the recognition of this fact has provided a landmark in efforts to address the skills issue (Graham et al, 2001).

In Pakistan the workforce shortage is estimated at 7030 for 95% coverage of skilled attendants to be achieved by 2015 (UNFPA, 2011). However, some experienced professionals within the country estimate that Pakistan needs at least 150000 midwives to work in the villages alone (Syed and Ishtiaq, 2012). In order to save lives and avert disaster, skilled attendants must be competent to implement appropriately a range of life-saving interventions. Competence has been defined in various ways, such as the possession of skills and knowledge sufficient to meet the predefined clinical standard (Kak et al, 2001) or again, a complex combination of knowledge, performance, skills, values and attitudes that enable a practitioner to practise to a defined level of proficiency (WHO, 2011a, b). In an assessment of the competency of care providers in four countries, Benin, Ecuador, Jamaica and Rwanda, Harvey et al (2004) conclude that a wide gap exists between current evidence-based standards and the level of competence of those identified as skilled attendants. The majority of the participants in their study could not demonstrate basic preventive and life-saving skills. For example, there was concern about an inability to conduct active third stage management, to control postpartum haemorrhage, to use good aseptic technique and to utilise the partograph. These findings giving rise to concerns as to whether or not the providers would be able to identify and treat or refer problems appropriately. However, the researchers reason that care providers cannot be expected to carry out procedures that they have never been taught. Acknowledging that no-one really knows how skilled 'skilled attendants' are, the researchers warn that until such deficits are rectified the number of births attended by skilled personnel may be a poor indicator for Millennium Development Goal 5.

The fact that a lack of clinical competence prevents the use of life-saving interventions in many countries struggling to reduce maternal and perinatal mortality has been a recurrent cause for concern (Islam et al, 2005; Pattinson, 2006; van den Broek and Hofman, 2010). In Pakistan, as in other parts of Asia, the appointment, especially in rural areas, of male medical officers who have no obstetric expertise has fostered cultural offence too, resulting in a marked limitation of the professional help that is available and acceptable to women in such circumstances (Ariff et al, 2010). A policy to include training in core obstetric skills for all final year medical students in Pakistan was approved in 2010 with the aim of addressing this vital issue (Siddiqui et al, 2011). Policies designed to address the numerical deficit of skilled attendants in some countries further threaten the quality of training where large numbers of students compete for clinical experience (Bell et al, 2003; Freedman et al, 2003; Bailey et al, 2006). This is a most relevant matter for consultants advising on policy and curriculum issues. Aspirations to provide a sufficient quantity of skilled attendants, although understandable, can be counter-productive when attempting to prepare quality practitioners, and reference was made to this dilemma in *Chapter 3*. Such healthcare providers need to have received adequate clinical teaching and supervision and have been skilfully assessed as competent and confident to practise.

The most appropriate tutor-to-student ratios in clinical practice may vary according to a number of factors. These include the level of the students, the competency to be learned, the amount of experience available and the teaching competency of the tutor. However, one tutor to two students in the labour room is suggested (UNFPA, 2011). The International Confederation of Midwives (ICM) recommends that the overall ratio of tutors, clinical teachers and preceptors to students should be determined by the midwifery programme and the requirement of the national regulatory authority (ICM, 2010), presupposing that midwifery education is appropriately regulated. WHO has developed a list of core competencies for the different cadres of healthcare providers concerned with sexual and reproductive health (WHO, 2011c) and these can be a useful resource in planning curricula and in updating programmes. There is also a series of documents designed to facilitate the strengthening of numerous aspects of midwifery and these are identified below (WHO, 2006, 2011d; ICM, 2010).

William Arthur Ward has been attributed with the dictum:

The mediocre teacher tells.
The good teacher explains.
The superior teacher demonstrates.
The great teacher inspires.

There would seem to be a crying need for teachers in medicine and midwifery as well as other health and related sciences who can both demonstrate and inspire, not only in Pakistan but across the globe.

It has been determined that 2281 obstetric and newborn complications can be anticipated each day in Pakistan, with more than half of these occurring in rural areas. Among those countries with high mortality rates in these age groups, the numbers are only exceeded in India and Nigeria, both more populous nations. Nevertheless, Pakistan has managed to reduce maternal mortality by 48% during the two decades since 1990, but the density of doctors, midwives and nurses per one thousand population is estimated at just 1.4, representing an urgent necessity to prepare more skilled attendants to meet national requirements. In countries with high maternal mortality a triple gap has been identified comprising not only competencies, but also coverage and access to skilled maternity care. Knowing that approximately 15% of births result in obstetric complications, across the world we know that, each day, around 35 000 women will experience such problems in giving birth and 900 will die (UNFPA, 2011), even though it has been estimated that most maternal deaths could have been prevented (WHO, 2012).

Devastating but avoidable

It is estimated that about two million women across the developing world suffer the indignity of obstetric fistulae, commonly vesico-vaginal fistulae, and a further 50 000 to 100 000 new cases occur each year (WHO, 2010). In the northern region of Nigeria alone 800 000 cases of obstetric fistulae are estimated to exist and the escalating number has been attributed to longstanding traditional and religious practices (Haberland et al, 2003). vesico-vaginal fistulae described as a devastating injury which is rare in developed countries, is a common complication of childbirth in the developing world (Wall, 2006). Fistulae occur where women experience prolonged obstructed labour and are more common where early marriage is customary, emergency obstetric care facilities are poorly staffed and ill-equipped, and user fees further hamper access to emergency obstetric care (UNFPA, 2001; Okonofua, 2005; Syed and Ishtiaq, 2012). From a small study undertaken in Liberia, Söderbäck et al (2012) describe the overwhelming experiences of loss that women afflicted with vesico-vaginal fistulae endure, comprising loss of control over a perceived traumatic birth, loss of status as a woman and as a wife and loss of social fellowship. These devastating injuries have been attributed to the lack of skilled help available to parturient women, particularly in rural and remote areas (Naidu, 2005). In Pakistan, where between 4000 and 6000 women develop fistulae each year, the injury has also been associated with poverty, belief that it is caused by possession with an evil spirit, and sometimes inflicted by the interference of unqualified doctors (Balloch, 2011). Vesico-vaginal fistulae has been dubbed the scandal of the century (Graham, 1998).

Although 90% of fistulae can be successfully repaired surgically it has been reported that since 2003 just 12 000 women have been treated in 45 countries (WHO, 2010). In seven centres across Pakistan the condition is being treated with a 95% success rate and in addition to providing medical care and accommodation, counselling is offered to help women recover both mentally and physically (Balloch, 2011). In Pakistan, emphasis has been laid on avoidance of obstetric fistulae, maintaining that the country has the infrastructure and medical skills available whereas many countries do not. Therefore it has been urged that:

Prevention is the only option left now, before more lives are wasted.
(Syed cited in Balloch, 2011)

It is evident that fistulae can be prevented by delaying the age of first pregnancy, avoiding harmful traditional practices and timely access to quality obstetric care (WHO, 2010). Consultants may well be involved in advising on this devastating but avoidable condition and elective students may encounter the condition in practice. It is clear that efforts to relegate obstetric fistulae to the medical history book involve tackling cultural and traditional attitudes and practices in addition to essential medical and surgical treatment. Promotion of skilled midwifery practice is critical in the role of prevention.

The desperation of delay

The problem of delay is epitomised in the plight of women who sustain the devastation of obstetric fistulae. Prolonged labour and other life-threatening

---

Box 9.1. The three phases of delay

- Phase 1:   Delay in the decision to seek care
- Phase 2:   Delay in arriving at a health facility
- Phase 3:   Delay in the provision of adequate care

Source: Thaddeus and Maine, 1994

---

complications of childbirth can be associated with a lack of ability on behalf of the attendant to identify deviations from normal and take timely and appropriate action. However, as Thaddeus and Maine (1994) poignantly highlight, delay can be multifactorial and may occur at various stages and in numerous places along the route of attempting to achieve safe motherhood (*Box 9.1*).

The matter of delay in all its guises encompasses issues of poverty, infrastructure, quality of care, education, cultural traditions and many other factors that need to be taken into consideration by consultants planning, teaching, evaluating and making recommendations. Students during elective periods are likely to encounter this obstacle to providing safe care and need to be prepared to observe or treat patients with conditions that are much more advanced than they are likely to meet in their home country. It is salutary to note that such conditions can and will occur anywhere in the world in the absence of skilled and timely interventions. Gabrysch and Campbell (2009), in an extensive literature review, identify 20 determinants that influence access to skilled care and classify these in four categories, namely socio-cultural factors, the perceived benefit of or need for skilled attendance, and economic and physical accessibility. They also examine the perceived quality of preventive and emergency care in this context.

Numerous factors influence the decision to seek care and, as observed in remote desert areas of Pakistan, these may be associated with distance but can be accentuated by cultural and traditional attitudes and beliefs. There is much evidence that highlights the influence of ethnicity, religion and tradition in avoiding the use of a health facility for birth or even of seeking help at all (Glei et al, 2003; Mesko et al, 2003; Gyimah et al, 2006; Mrisho et al, 2007). Gabrysch and Campbell (2009) report that the level of maternal education is a very strong factor influencing health-seeking behaviour and the use of skilled attendance during childbirth, and that educated husbands are more likely to be well disposed towards modern medicine. Women's autonomy and ability to move around independently can also affect the situation since, in some cultures, women may not have control over material resources, their mobility may be restricted, and they may have no access to transport, including the use of bicycles and animals (Stock, 1983; Gabrysch and Campbell, 2009). Furuta and Salway (2006) report gender inequality as a major constraining factor inhibiting women's access to healthcare in Nepal and this issue is discussed further below. Mumtaz and Salway (2005) present an integrated analysis of large-scale survey data along with detailed ethnography in their examination of the link between women's mobility and the uptake of reproductive healthcare in Pakistan. They confirm that women's mobility is circumscribed but that there is no evidence to suggest that the ability to move around independently predisposes to a better uptake of care. By contrast, accompanied women tend to make better use of antenatal services. Within the cultural context they warn against introducing Western concepts of freedom of movement. Acknowledging the wider impact of limited mobility on women's reproductive health they highlight the policy implications that need to be addressed. The issue of imposing Western values across cultures was discussed in *Chapter 8* and a visiting consultant always needs to consider this before making recommendations.

A matter of gender

The place and value of women in society, and their participation in decision making and addressing gender norms, have been repeatedly highlighted as important issues in promoting maternal health (Bloom et al, 2001; Rottach et al, 2009; Senarath and Gunawardena, 2009; Ying and Hui, 2011). UNICEF (2011) contends that although girls often face considerable obstacles in life, they also hold unique promise when a society embraces them and invests in them. This has been described as 'The Girl Effect' that can create ripples leading to significant economic and social change, benefiting family, community and country. Examples are cited, providing substantial evidence that the effect is real, and that its impact is far-reaching and profound. Global efforts to reduce maternal mortality and morbidity currently emphasise the shame and tragedy of our limited progress in this area of women's health. In the context of addressing the massive shortfall of midwives across the world, particularly in the 58 countries most acutely affected by maternal and perinatal deaths, Ban ki Moon, as Secretary General of the United Nations, states:

> *This is not a matter of statistics. The woman who perishes from hemorrhaging during childbirth or the infant who dies during a complicated birth each has a name and a family who love and cherish them. Beyond individual tragedy, these losses carry untold social and economic repercussions for society.*
>
> *(UNFPA, 2011)*

As poignantly illustrated above, too many women who survive face a life of misery, losing all sense of dignity and worth. In describing the plight of a 15-year-old, Syed and Ishtiaq (2012) describe the wailing of the mother who had brought her daughter for fistula repair surgery. Reporting the large number of girls dying in childbirth in her area she added, '...she was not even lucky enough to die'. Such is the cruel fate of many young girls who are not among those who lose their lives giving birth, in a country where one woman dies in so doing every 20 minutes. In some cultures women are not valued or even respected but viewed as replaceable when they can no longer function as wives and mothers. A dictum from the Sindh area of Pakistan illustrates this all too brutally:

If your cow dies, it is a tragedy. If your wife dies, you can always get another one.

(Kristof, 2009)

This attitude is by no means unique to Pakistan.

The influence of men in transforming attitudes towards gender in this context is underlined. In an extensive analysis of 58 evaluation studies Barker et al (2007) conclude that well-designed courses that work with men and boys provide compelling evidence that such involvement can and does lead to changes in both attitude and behaviour. The programmes that involve deliberate discussion of gender and masculinity among the male participants with definite efforts that seek to transform gender norms have been more effective than those that merely mention norms and roles. Boender et al (2004), drawing data from 400 reproductive health programmes, assert that integrating a gender component into these has a positive effect in achieving the health outcomes and in promoting gender equity. They reviewed programmes addressing maternal mortality and morbidity, sexually transmitted diseases including HIV, unintended pregnancy and the quality of care. The WHO Foundation Module includes education material for midwifery teachers that focuses on the place and value of women and also on promoting safe motherhood as a human right (WHO, 2006). Uses of these modules were discussed in *Chapter 5*. Details for accessing them are also given below.

Personal reflections on practice

- Although the ultimate goal should surely be to inspire, in the clinical field, the value of time spent demonstrating will always outweigh that spent in explanation.
- Unless the disastrous element of delay is challenged at every stage, needless suffering and loss of life will persist.

- Showing respect for women of all classes and creeds can be a powerful lesson, but it is those who have experienced respect that are best able to convey it to others.

Some lessons learned and shared

- Actions observed are more likely to be memorable, even if words are forgotten.
- Attitudes as well as actions may well speak louder than words.
- Demonstrating clinical skills is often a high priority. It is as well to share these without presuming on obtaining help from local counterparts who may be hoping for opportunities for some updating themselves.

Reflective exercises

- Identify your own preferred learning style and consider your personality type. Examine the characteristics of people with very different profiles from yourself. Think about a topic that you might debate. Outline the approach that other people might adopt and where there might be conflicts. Reflect on how you might lead such a discussion in order to enable various personalities to be heard.
- Reflect on the three phases of delay (*Box 9.1*). What situations and facilities enable you or your family to access essential healthcare without delay in your current situation? Consider what might interfere with this in a different cultural and geographical context.
- List the most essential items that you need to pack when asked to travel light. Justify each inclusion and see how compact your baggage could be.

Resources

- Documents relating to midwifery education and clinical competence can be downloaded from the following sites:
  - WHO: *Strengthening midwifery toolkit*. Available from: http://www.who.int/maternal_child_adolescent/documents/strenthening_midwifery_toolkit/en/index.html
  - International Confederation of Midwives: *Global Standards for Midwifery Education*. Available from: http://www.internationalmidwives.org/Whatwedo/Policyandpractice/ICMGlobalStandardsCompetenciesandTools/GlobalStandardsEnglish/
  - WHO: *Midwifery education modules*: http://www.who.int/maternal_child_adolescent/documents/9241546662/en/

References

Ariff S, Soofi SB, Sadiq K et al (2010) Evaluation of health workforce competence in maternal and neonatal issues in public health sector of Pakistan: an assessment of their training needs. *BMC Health Service Research* **10**: 319

Bailey P, Paxton A, Lobis S, Fry D (2006) Measuring progress towards the MDG for maternal health: Including a measure of the health services capacity to treat obstetric complications. Averting Death and Disability. *International Journal of Gynecology and Obstetrics* **93**: 292–9

Balloch S (2011) Obstetric fistula: Some call for exorcisms for this condition but doctors say they have the magic cure. *The Express Tribune with the International Herald Tribune, Karachi.* Available from: http://tribune.com.pk/story/127263/obstetric-fistula-some-call-for-exorcisms-for-this-condition-but-surgeons-say-they-have-the-magic-cure/ [last accessed 28.05.2012]

Barker G, Ricardo C an, Nascimento M (2007) *Engaging men and boys in changing gender based inequity in health. Evidence from programme interventions.* WHO, Geneva

Barrett FJ (1995) Creating appreciative learning cultures. *Organizational Dynamics* **24**(1): 36–49

Bell J, Curtis SL, Alayon S (2003) *Trends in delivery care in six countries, DHS Analytical Studies, No 7.* Operational Research Corporation, Macro and International Research Partnership for Skilled Attendance for Everyone (SAFE), Calverton Maryland

Bloom SS, Wypij D, Gupta DS (2001) Dimensions of women's autonomy and the influence on maternal health care utilization in a north Indian city. *Demography* **38**(1): 67–78

Boender C, Santana D, Santillan D, Hardee K, Greene ME, Schuler SR (2004) *The 'So What?' report. A look at whether introducing a gender focus into programs makes a difference to outcomes.* IGWG, Washington DC

Capretz LF (2002) Implications of MBTI in Software Engineering Education. Inroads *SIGCSE Bulletin* **34**(4): 134–7

Cockell J, McArthur-Blair J (2012) *Appreciative inquiry in higher education: A transformative force.* Jossey Bass, San Francisco

Davis CM (2005) *Appreciative inquiry as a tool for faculty and organizational development.* Selected Works. Available from: http://works.bepress.com/christopher_davis/3/ [last accessed 1.06.2012]

Frankel A (2009) Nurses' learning styles: promoting better integration of theory into practice. *Nursing Times* **105**(2): 24–7

Freedman L, Wirth M, Waldman R, Chowdhury M, Rosenfield A (2003) *Background paper of the Task Force on Maternal and Child Health.* The Millennium Project. UN Development Group, New York

Furuta M, Salway S (2006) Women's position within the household as a determinant of maternal health care use in Nepal. *International Family Planning Perspectives* **32**(1): 17–27

Gabrysch S, Cambell OM (2009) Still too far too walk. Literature review of the determinants of delivery service use. *BMC Pregnancy Childbirth* **9**(1): 34

Glei DA, Goldman N, Rodriguez G (2003) Utilization of care during pregnancy in rural Guatemala: does obstetrical need matter? *Social Sciences and Medicine* **57**: 2447–63

Graham W (1998) The scandal of the century. *British Journal of Obstetrics and Gynaecology* **105**(4): 373–4

Graham WJ, Bell JS, Bullough CHW (2001) Can skilled attendance at delivery reduce maternal mortality in developing countries? In: DeBrouwere V, Van Lerberghe W (eds) *Safe motherhood strategies: a review of the evidence* (pp. 97–130). Studies in Health Services Organization and Policy

Gyimah SO, Takyi BK, Addai I (2006) Challenges to the reproductive-health needs of African women: on religion and maternal health utilization in Ghana. *Social Science and Medicine* **62**: 2930–44

Haberland N, Chong E, Bracken H (2003) *Married adolescents*: An overview paper prepared for the WHO/UNFPA/Population Council Technical Consultation on Married Adolescents. WHO, Geneva

Hargis LC (2006) *Appreciative inquiry in higher education as an effective communication tool: A case study*. Weatherhead School of Management, Case Western University

Harvey SA, Ayabaca P, Bucagu M, Djibrin S, Edson WN, Gbangbade S, McCaw-Binns A, Burkhalter BR (2004) Skilled birth attendant competence: an initial assessment in four countries, and implications for the Safe Motherhood movement. *International Journal of Gynecology and Obstetrics* **87**: 203–10

Index Mundi (2012) *Country comparison > population*. Index Mundi. Available from: http://www.indexmundi.com/g/r.aspx [last accessed 28.09.2012]

International Confederation of Midwives (2010) *Global Standards for Midwifery Education*. ICM, The Hague, The Netherlands. Available from: http://www.internationalmidwives. org/Whatwedo/Policyandpractice/ICMGlobalStandardsCompetenciesandTools/ GlobalStandardsEnglish/ [last accessed 24.05.2012]

Islam MT, Hossain MM, Islam MA, Haque YA (2005) Improvement of coverage and utilization of EmOC services in south western Bangladesh. *International Journal of Gynecology and Obstetrics* **91**: 298–305

Kak N, Burkhalter B, Cooper M-A (2001) *Measuring the competence of healthcare providers*. The Quality Assurance Project: Bethesda, MD

Knowles MS (1978) *The adult learner: A neglected species*. Gulf Publishing Co, Houston

Knowles MS (1989) *The making of an adult educator*. Jossey-Bass, San Francisco

Kolb DA (1984) *Experiential learning: Experience as the source of learning and development*. Prentice-Hall, New Jersey

Kolb DA, Boyatzis R, Mainemelis C (2001) Experiential learning theory: Previous research and new directions. In R Sternberg, L Zhang (eds) *Perspectives on cognitive learning and thinking styles* (pp. 228–47). Erlbaum, Mahwah, NJ

Kristof ND (2009) His maternal instinct. *The New York Times* 18 July. Available from: http://www.nytimes.com/2009/07/19/opinion/19kristof.html [last accessed 31.05.2012]

Lawrence G (1982) *People types and tiger stripes: A practical guide to learning styles* (2nd edn). Center for Applications of Psychological Type, Gainesville, Florida

Mesko N, Osrin D, Tamang S et al (2003) Care for perinatal illness in rural Nepal: a descriptive study with cross-sectional and qualitative components. *BMC International Health and Human Rights*. Available from: http://www.biomedcentral.com/content/pdf/1472-698X-3-3.pdf [last accessed 08.10.2012]

Mezirow J (1971) *Transformative dimensions of adult learning.* Jossey-Bass, San Francisco

Mezirow J (2000) *Learning as transformation: Critical perspectives on a theory in practice.* Jossey-Bass, San Francisco

Mrisho M, Schellenberg JA, Mushi AK, Obrist B, Mshinda H, Tanner M, Schellenberg D (2007) Factors affecting home delivery in rural Tanzania. *Tropical Medicine and International Health* **12**: 862–72

Mumtaz Z, Salway S (2005) I never go anywhere: extricating the links between women's mobility and uptake of reproductive health services in Pakistan. *Social Sciences and Medicine* **60**(8): 1751–65

Myers IB, Myers PB (1980) *Gifts differing.* Consulting Psychologists Press, Palo Alto, CA

Naidu PM (2005) Vesico-vaginal fistulae: An experience with 208 cases. *British Journal of Obstetrics and Gynaecology* **69**(2): 311–16

Okonofua F (2005) Reducing the scourge of obstetric fistulae in Sub-Saharan Africa: A call for a global repair initiative. *African Journal of Reproductive Health* **9**(2): 7–13

Pattinson R (2006) *Saving mothers: Third report on Confidential Enquiry into Maternal Deaths in South Africa 2002–2004.* Department of Health, Pretoria

Revans R (2011) *Abc of action learning.* Gower Publishing, Farnham, Surrey

Rottach E, Schular SR, Hardee K (2009) *Gender perspectives improve reproductive health outcomes: New evidence.* IGWG/USAID, Washington DC

Save the Children (2012) *State of the World's mothers 2012, The 2012 Mothers' Index.* Available from: http://www.savethechildren.org/ [last accessed 13/07/2012]

Schön D (1983) *The reflective practitioner.* Basic Books, New York

Senarath U, Gunawardena NS (2009) Women's autonomy in decision making for health care in South Asia. *Asia Pacific Journal of Public Health* **21**(2): 137–43

Siddiqui GK, Hussein R, Dornan JC (2011) Dying to give birth: The Pakistan Liaison Committee's strategies to improve maternal health in Pakistan. *British Journal of Obstetrics and Gynaecology* **182**(s2): 96–9

Söderbäck M, Wilhelmsson E, Häggström-Nordin (2012) Absence and reliance: Liberian women's experience of vaginal fistula. *African Journal of Midwifery and Women's Health* **6**(1): 28–34

Stock R (1983) Distance and the utilisation of health services in rural Nigeria. *Social Sciences and Medicine* **17**(9): 563–670

Syed S with Ishtiaq H (2012) *Vision...not just a dream.* Scherzade Publications, Karachi

Thaddeus S, Maine D (1994) Too far to walk: Maternal mortality in context. *Social Sciences and Medicine* **38**(8): 1091–110

UNFPA (2001) *Report on the meeting for the prevention and treatment of obstetric fistulae.* London July 2001. UNFPA/AMDD/FIGO. UNFPA New York

UNFPA (2011) *The state of the World's midwifery: Delivering health, saving lives.* UNFPA, New York

UNICEF (2011) *State of the World's children 2011.* UNICEF, New York

UNICEF (2012) *State of the World's children 2012.* UNICEF, New York

van den Broek N, Hofman J (2010) Increasing the capacity for essential obstetric and newborn care. In: Kehoe S, Neilson J, Norman J (eds) *Maternal and infant deaths: Chasing Development Goals 4 and 5* (pp. 229–40). RCOG Press, London

Wall LL (2006) Obstetric vesico-vaginal fistulae as an international public health problem. *The Lancet* **368**(9542): 1201–9

WHO (2004) *Making pregnancy safer: The critical role of the skilled attendant.* A Joint Statement by WHO, ICM and FIGO. WHO, Geneva

WHO (2006) *Midwifery education modules. Education for safe motherhood. Educational material for teachers of midwifery* (2nd edn) WHO, Geneva

WHO (2010) *10 facts on obstetric fistulae.* Fact file, World Health Organization, Geneva. Available from: http://www.who.int/features/factfiles/obstetric_fistula/en/ [last accessed 28.05.2012]

WHO (2011a) *Strengthening midwifery toolkit. Module 4: Competencies for midwifery practice.* WHO, Geneva

WHO (2011b) *Strengthening midwifery toolkit. Module 8: Monitoring and assessment for continued competency for midwifery practice.* WHO, Geneva

WHO (2011c) *Sexual and reproductive health core competencies in primary care.* WHO, Geneva.

WHO (2011d) *Strengthening midwifery toolkit.* WHO, Geneva. Available from: http://www. who.int/maternal_child_adolescent/documents/strenthening_midwifery_toolkit/en/ index.html [last accessed 23.05.2012]

WHO (2012) *Trends in maternal mortality 1990 to 2010.* WHO, UNICEF, UNFPA and World Bank. WHO, Geneva

World Facts and Figures (2012) *World facts and figures.* Available from: http://www. worldfactsandfigures.com/ [last accessed 21.05.12]

Ying C, Li Y, Hui H (2011) The impact of husbands' gender equity awareness on wives' reproductive health in rural areas of China. *Obstetrics and Gynaecology Survey* **66**(2): 103–8

Chapter 10

A task unfinished

You can only enter half way into the dark forest before you begin to come out the other side.

(Chinese Proverb)

Having avoided selective abortion, been protected from female infanticide, recovered from preventable childhood infections, survived partner violence and other abuses, a woman lies naked, alone and…

…desperate on a labour ward bed. Is it any wonder that she considers the life and lot of an animal more privileged than her own? Insult will be added to injury if her husband has, through no fault of his either, contributed his X chromosome to their imminent offspring

Hospitals and those for whom they provide a service in diverse parts of the world differ dramatically. Standards and expectations are poles apart and the chances of survival are weighed heavily in favour of those already privileged

Subject strands introduced

- The nature of consultancy
- Contracting
- Terms of reference
- Report writing
- The art of evaluation

- Bride prices and dowries
- Son preference
- Discrimination against daughters
- Reverse culture shock
- Beyond 2015

Practice points

- Administrative skills
- The art of listening
- Increasing awareness

- Developing evaluation skills
- Preparing to return home

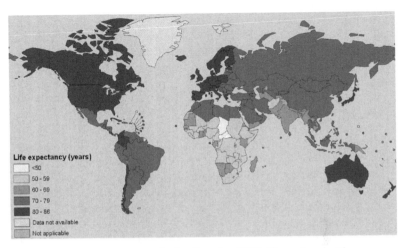

Figure 10.1. Life expectancy at birth - Females 2009 (Reproduced with permission from the World Health Organization).

Exploring experience

All in a day's work

Every job has its excitements and its exasperations, its satisfaction and sometimes its elements of suffering. Whichever way it is viewed there are some aspects that challenge more than others and some tasks that demand attention when one would rather be giving it elsewhere. For me, some essential administrative duties fall into the latter category, but unless one tackles them efficiently the quality of the whole assignment is likely to be affected. Administrative responsibilities associated with consultancy work include clarifying terms of reference, contracting, report writing and keeping accounts. Students also need to clarify the terms of their elective period, identifying and agreeing expected learning outcomes and establishing their responsibilities and accountability. They need to maintain accurate records that relate to their travel, experience and finances as well as completing any pre-arranged assignments and obligations to report back on completion.

In my experience as a consultant, it is sometimes necessary to clarify and sometimes to modify terms of reference before agreeing a contract, and the importance of this issue was raised in *Chapter 4*. It is also essential to recognise one's own limitations and decline a contract that is not realistic or within one's professional capability. I have been asked to undertake assignments in which the timescale was just not realistic for the expected outcomes. Understandably, stakeholders want to achieve the optimum outcome at a minimal cost, and time is costly in any business, not least when international travel is involved. Consultants are normally expected to have their own travel and health insurance and students and lecturers being released for assignments need to establish whether or not they are personally responsible for this.

Listening and learning

Administrative skills are necessary, but I am convinced that among the greatest attributes a cross-cultural visitor can acquire are a sense of awareness and an ability to demonstrate empathic listening skills. These perhaps comprise the 'essentials of international effectiveness'. Certainly without them there is potential for disaster. I recall one situation where a worker confided in me about an expatriate who was acting in a supervisory capacity, 'She doesn't understand us!' she complained. I sensed that the grievance extended beyond the obvious linguistic barriers into a deeper realm where there was confusion and hurt at a palpable impatience and intolerance. Such a situation is liable to cause damage which might prove to be irreparable in the cross-cultural context.

Developing a heightened sense of awareness in a new environment is an important stage of development and every sense needs to be finely tuned to meet the challenge. In some parts of the developing world where sanitation leaves much to be desired, a good sense of humour needs to be balanced with a poor sense of smell. One can develop the former, but with the latter the need is rather to attempt to minimise the impact – and I have found no easy approach to that!

Reading local newspapers and, where accessible, following national radio and TV news programmes provides some insights into what is important in a society, what is acceptable, and what is not acceptable and possibly even punishable. I find it helpful to read national news when alone at mealtimes or while waiting. There is usually no shortage of time spent waiting in countries that work to a totally different time schedule, as discussed in *Chapter 4*. In the airport of one African country only flights that had already departed were displayed. No-one seemed to have any confidence in advance that the scheduled flights would depart, certainly not at a predicted time. Learning to utilise time that would otherwise seem wasted can indeed be a valuable skill.

Listening is a dying art in many modern societies. Shop assistants who carry on conversations over the heads of customers in a store swamped by decibel-rich music may engender annoyance. However, healthcare workers who adopt the same strategy over the heads of their patients devalue them, creating discrimination and disrespect that is totally unacceptable. Standing back and checking that you have really heard what is being said is vital.

Listening to the silences too, and taking time to reflect at the end of each day helps to gain perspective. Hearing and seeing not only what is in front of you, but also looking for other clues in any new environment are all part of the adaptation process in a new country.

I recall an African anthropologist advising young people about to set off on a cross-cultural mission that a very useful place to study was the city rubbish dump. 'Notice what they throw away!', he had urged, 'What comprises rubbish to these people.' Experience later taught me to note too what happened to that rubbish. The scavengers who came and claimed what they could from the rotting heaps were neither vermin nor vultures. They were the pitifully poor and destitute; children and professional rubbish pickers salvaging what they could to sell to supplement their begging. Such sights, sounds and smells are intensely painful and can be a shock for the unprepared Westerner. These salutary experiences should not be avoided but noted with concern and filed in the cultural memory as part of the reality of life in such a land. Aristotle warned that we cannot learn without pain, and certainly a painful experience can be a steep learning curve.

A Chinese proverb cautions that 'distant water won't help to put out a fire close at hand' and such is the truth associated with grasping the reality of the dilemmas that face our colleagues in developing countries. Dwight Eisenhower is credited with saying, 'Farming looks mighty easy when your plough is a pencil and you're a thousand miles from the corn field.' How true. We cannot learn about reality at a distance, we need to get our hands dirty, to get involved.

Inequity and injustice

Culture shock was discussed in *Chapter 4*. However, it is prudent to consider that this can be intensified by some of the inequities and injustices that are experienced in different cultures, and culture shock tends to be further accentuated when one is working in isolation. When working alone it is helpful to try to establish networks that provide support during an assignment, and the opportunity to debrief afterwards can be valuable.

Concepts such as dowries, bride prices and son preference are alien to modern Western thinking. I had the experience of being consulted by an African student in the UK whose family were negotiating a bride price for her. It appeared that they were offering 30 walking cattle for her and that had seemed a fair price. I did not feel qualified to judge on the matter, but did what I could in putting her in touch with others who might be of more help to her. When working overseas I had witnessed some terrible tragedies associated with women, often little more than children, who had not proved worthwhile wives. There were those who had reportedly taken rat poison 'inadvertently', and others who had had an 'unfortunate accident', such as their clothes catching fire when they were cooking. National colleagues could sometimes read the situation well but did not dare to suggest foul play for fear of reprisal. Such crimes are not, nor should they be, easily tolerated, and some humanitarian and religious organisations seek to address such injustices.

I saw evidence of son preference in an African village. National colleagues debated with parents and elders why one twin should be healthy and well-nourished while the other was failing to thrive. The reason came as no surprise to them that the little boy had received all the immunisations and priority in feeding while his sister struggled to survive. The family was unable to afford healthcare and adequate food for them both. In an Asian village son preference was evident in another form. Colleagues shared how they had discovered grandmothers justifying feeding newborn girls with indigestible food which rapidly choked them. The women reasoned that it was more merciful for them to end their lives than allow them to grow up in a society where they would suffer as they had themselves, where there was no justice, no compassion and only cost incurred to families to rear them and arrange their marriages. In one Asian hospital I was informed of the practice of avoiding informing the mother as to whether she had given birth to a boy or girl until after the placenta was expelled for fear that her distress at the birth of a daughter would cause third stage complications. In a large Asian city a female doctor had told me that it was better to be an animal in her country than a woman. If this was true for an educated and employed professional woman, I painfully reflected on the fate of her poorer compatriots.

It is distressing too to observe women suffering not only the pains of labour but also the indignity of lying naked on a bed. This is unacceptable in any country and most certainly in countries where women are always expected to dress modestly. Elsewhere, women lie on unsanitary floors; the demand for beds far exceeding availability. Low staff numbers add to the improbability of these women receiving adequate, leave alone skilled, care at this most critical time in their lives.

Coming home

Given the harsh realities of life on an overseas placement, it is no wonder that returning home can stretch one's powers of adaptability to the limit. Resuming a job or studies in a Western setting, or merely preparing for the next overseas assignment, may not be easy. I remember meeting a midwife at a refresher course in England who was experiencing the stresses of reverse culture shock and struggling to re-establish practice in an NHS hospital. After working overseas for a few years she looked at me in despair, confiding that she had been home for six months and was still finding life very difficult. She was heartened by the fact that I was able to assure her from my own experience, as well as that of others, that this was very normal. When we travel we are changed for ever. The world to which we return has changed too. What was once perfectly normal and expected can cause irritation; and it is not unusual to become intolerant with colleagues who appear to fuss about things that have long since ceased to cause us concern. I met with disbelief a commotion about having more than two visitors at the bedside; I had become accustomed to the whole family setting up camp around their sick relative. Students moaning about poor pay seemed selfish after one had witnessed the sacrifices that people make to obtain an education and professional training elsewhere. Patients and relatives complaining and making demands seem unreasonable in a world where they appear to have everything and a health service free of charge.

I recall an incident where a five-year-old girl had been admitted to a referral hospital in Nepal late one evening. In the absence of medical and nursing staff, ancillary workers had set up an intravenous infusion and given antibiotics. When we arrived late at night there was no blanket to comfort her tiny form as she gradually lost her grip on life; such possessions were locked safely away lest they should be stolen, and the family was too poor to provide blankets. There are of course many stresses in Western society and in a national health system, but they are generally very different from those across the world. Neither can be demeaned or ignored. The differences just appear heightened after exposure to such contrasting circumstances. Being prepared for the need to readjust is half the battle and appreciating that there will be relatively few people who can truly understand our experiences is also essential. However, there will be people who can listen with understanding and facilitate guided reflection, particularly through the most distressing issues.

Conferences provide opportunities to share overseas experiences. Consultants may be approached to contribute to study days and undergraduate programmes, students may be required to lead seminars. Some ill-advised approaches to sharing one's experiences were revealed in *Chapter 2,* and using such events to debrief is unacceptable when it is at the expense of our hosts. Denigration or derision, especially relating to culture, religion or tradition is never acceptable. A patronising attitude can prove equally irritating or offensive. There are also issues of a confidential nature that must be kept so, and criticisms, which may be overt or oblique, cannot be justified in a public domain. If action needs to be taken on particular concerns, then appropriate channels need to be sought. This could help another student or professional confronting a similar situation or enable them to prepare for the inevitable.

Examining the evidence

The spirit of consultancy

The evolving nature of international consultancy emanates to some extent from the roots of management consultancy. Consultants function within numerous specialties and it has been claimed that there are as many definitions of consultancy as there are consultants. However, the best definitions share three important concepts. These comprise identifying a problem, recommending a solution and helping with implementation (Rassam, 1998). As indicated in *Chapter 8* discussing draft recommendations with the implementers contributes to good practice, and in some situations a further contract may be instigated if a consultant is required to assist with implementing recommended changes. Beyond management consultancy, there are increasing links too between consultants and professional evaluators and this topic is discussed below.

Care needs to be taken if the consultant is not to be viewed with cynicism and mistrust. Consultants have been likened to someone who turns up without being invited, answering questions that were not being asked – and to which the local population already knows the answers – and seeking payment for the privilege. Insult is added to injury if the consultant is perceived not to be skilled in the particular area of practice. The titles describing a consultant are sometimes interchangeable with adviser, authority, counsellor or specialist (Collins, 2012). Those most often used in the context of international development, along with the various roles of the consultant, were outlined in *Chapter 1*. Clark (1995: 110) maintains that the characteristics of consultancy differentiate services from goods, explaining:

> *Consultancy is one of the most intangible parts of the service sector, until the service is produced it only has potential, indeed it remains just a promise.*

Since a promise and its fulfilment depend on a trust that is common to both parties, it is essential that such trust is established early in a consultancy arrangement. If there is to be progress in a mutually agreeable direction and dimension, a shared vision needs to exist. This is dependent upon both client and consultant acquiring reciprocal insight into the situation and developing mutual respect and meaningful communication strategies (Maclean, 1998, 2011a).

Consultant contracting

Terms of reference include the background to the project, the aim of the exercise, the composition and skill requirements of the consultant or team

---

Box 10.1. Terms of reference checklist

- Is the overall purpose of the assignment described unambiguously?
- Are the evaluation or research questions stated clearly? Are they relevant and feasible?
- Is the assignment achievable given the available resources and in the stated timeframe?
- Are the terms of the agreement and employment clear?
- Is the line of accountability clear?
- Are budget issues clearly defined and is it apparent how costs and expenses will be met?
- Do the terms of reference give the consultant(s) freedom to design their own approach and adapt to the clients' expectations?
- Do the terms of reference limit the number of pages in the final report and if so is this realistic?
- Is there a plan in place for disengagement and follow up?

Derived from: Cockman et al, 1992; Forss et al, 2008

---

and the timescale. The expected input and outcomes of the consultancy will be specified. There should also be an indication of the remuneration and expenses to be included. This is the critical time to consider whether it is an appropriate assignment to accept at all or whether some negotiations are called for to modify the expectations. Phillips and Shaw (1989) maintain that in the experience of most consultants problems that are identified late in an assignment usually derive from poor initial contract arrangements or else a failure to renegotiate a contract in the light of changed circumstances. Forss et al (2008), in appraising 34 evaluation reports of development consultancies for the Swedish Government, identify several problems with the terms of reference in that they are frequently not clearly formulated and focused. They estimate that many were unrealistic in their expectations given the limited time and resources available. It behoves the consultant therefore to check rigorously the terms of reference before entering into a contractual agreement (*Box 10.1*).

Cockman et al (1992) specify that contracting involves a process enabling both parties to clarify what the other wants. They perceive contracting as identifying expectations of the consulting relationship and any boundaries that may exist. Contracting leads to a commitment to action and most certainly involves the establishment of a relationship. Berger et al (1993), considering the issue from a nursing administrative viewpoint, perceive the consultant–client relationship as the single most important factor contributing to success of the consultation. It is as well to remember from the outset that:

All relationships between people are based on expectations in one form or another.

(Cockman et al, 1992: 96)

Box 10.2. The symptomatology of a weak contract

- The consultant has uneasy feelings and is unsure why
- The client's extent of commitment is unclear
- The activity has a low priority for the client
- There is inadequate planning time before the event
- The timescale for the assignment is unrealistic
- There remain ambiguities in the terms of reference or contract

Derived from: Cockman et al, 1992; Maclean, 1998
Reproduced courtesy of the *British Journal of Midwifery* (Maclean, 2011b)

Both the consultant and the client have expectations and the contract serves to crystallise these and search for common ground in the emerging partnership. Bellman (1990: 238) states that a partnership has been formed when:

...the client's investment in the consultant's unique combination of abilities equals the consultant's investment in the client's unique combination of opportunities.

Box 10.2 offers some guidance to assist the consultant in the principles of contracting and in seeking to avoid unsatisfactory arrangements.

Writing reports

Reports need to be accurate, clear, succinct and submitted within the agreed timescale. The ability to present information in clear English was stressed in *Chapter 1*. Reports need to be user friendly and contain recommendations not only that the writer believes is going to make a difference, but also that are highly likely to be acceptable to the implementers. In my own research, a respondent lamented that:

We once had a consultant and after six months she sent her report and we cannot use it. She was critical and rude and not even accurate in what she was criticising.

(Maclean, 1998: 286)

Box 10. 3. Quality check on report recommendations

- Do the recommendations follow from the analysis and conclusions?
- Are the recommendations practical: can they be translated into decisions?
- Are the recommendations for clearly specified groups of actors?
- Are the value judgements from which the recommendations follow clearly stated?

Source: Forss et al, 2008: 62
Reproduced courtesy of the *British Journal of Midwifery* (Maclean, 2011c)

I also discovered evidence of sending organisations identifying suitable consultants by studying reports that they had written, and conversely deciding not to re-employ a consultant whose reports had proved critical and unacceptable to the client (Maclean, 1998). Forss et al (2008) offer a quality check in respect of report recommendations and this is summarised in *Box 10.3*.

Some organisations require reports at various stages of an assignment. These may include an inception report, followed by a draft report and ultimately a final report. The early information that is required has been defined thus:

An inception report should be prepared by the evaluators before going into the full-fledged evaluation exercise. It should detail the evaluators' understanding of what is being evaluated and why, showing how each evaluation question will be answered by way of: proposed methods; proposed sources of data; and data collection procedures.

Furthermore:

The inception report should include a proposed schedule of tasks, activities and deliverables, designating a team member with the lead responsibility for each task or product.

It is reasoned that an inception report

...provides the programme unit and the evaluators with an opportunity to verify that they share the same understanding about the evaluation and clarify any misunderstanding at the outset.

(UNDP, 2012: 197)

Forss et al (2008) perceive an inception report as a useful step enabling evaluators to make an informed judgement about the feasibility

---

of an assignment, especially where the questions to be addressed are complex, difficult or wide ranging. They warn that in smaller straightforward projects they may only add to the time and the cost. Most organisations have a house-style for the required reports and that style needs to be heeded.

Insights into evaluation

Rebien (1996) acknowledges that the subject of evaluation is hard to define and the process a complicated endeavour. Scriven (1991: 1) regards evaluation as

...a key analytical process in all disciplined intellectual and practical endeavors

and defines the practice as that used to determine

the merit, worth and value of things.

Vedung (2009: 2) claims that 'evaluation implies looking backward in order to better steer forward', maintaining that interventions made by governments now are so considerable and complex and the implications so far reaching that science and social research are needed to assess impact. Evaluations are increasingly required by donors to assess the value of their investments in projects in developing countries. Currently, efforts to accelerate progress towards MDG5 have attracted much attention and demands for funds which sooner or later need to be justified. In the context of international development aid, Forss et al (2008: 5) state that:

Evaluations are 'reality tests' of aid efforts and strategies intended to be used in support of accountability, decision-making and learning.

They proceed to stress that currently there is an increased demand in development co-operation, for information based on evidence-based results, along with a greater emphasis on results-based management.

Like all honest professionals, on reflection I have to confess in the context of this emerging and complex skill, that some of my approaches to evaluation may well have left much to be desired, especially in the early days. Evaluation, whether deemed an art or a science, relates to an evolving profession that has long since been established in the USA, admired in Scandinavia and more recently introduced in the UK (Cracknell, 2005). Yet, in an assessment of the evaluation system used by the Swedish

International Development Cooperation Agency (Sida), although it was acknowledged as being well established, its quality assurance mechanism was perceived as embryonic. Further it was recognised that very little had been done to find effective ways of assuring quality and making improvement in evaluations (Forss et al, 2008). The art of evaluation may be considered as a learning exercise as well as a subjective process. Since international health consultancy tends to be a hybrid derived from management consultancy and evaluation, the professional who crosses borders in these pursuits would do well to keep abreast with current developments in these fields. Some useful resources are offered to assist in this purpose at the end of the chapter.

In the realm of monitoring and evaluation of development aid programmes, getting it right and making a difference have been hailed as important ideals. While it has been acknowledged that neither a 'methodological monoculture' nor a single solution actually exists, there are recommended approaches and attitudes. Among these, Cracknell (2005) lists inventiveness, learning from errors as well as successes, self-critical awareness, welcoming and managing change, and freely sharing information. He also stresses that

No aid evaluation can be satisfactory if it does not take sustainability into account.

(Cracknell, 2005: 31)

Different subject areas may exist, but Cracknell points out that there are similar methodologies in use and that among evaluators of various disciplines there is a growing and greater willingness to learn from one another. In considering some of the issues that contribute to consultant effectiveness, and drawing from numerous sources, I have identified priorities that assist international midwifery consultants reflect on their practice and evaluate it. These include asking critical questions relating to technical, interpersonal and cross-cultural skills (Maclean, 2011c). Not unexpectedly, problems have been encountered in the various approaches to development aid evaluation. Rebien (1996) associates rigidity with the use of logical frameworks and identifies issues that have arisen during the transition from project aid towards programme and sector support.

Cracknell (2005) hails feedback as the Achilles heel of evaluation, but stresses that how, where and with whom it takes place is crucial. In consideration of who is empowered and who stands to gain, he advocates participatory monitoring and evaluation. He warns that evaluation is essentially a subjective exercise with the cultural background of the evaluator being hugely influential in the results.

Prices and preferences

Cultural backgrounds are likely to dictate how we will react to certain phenomena. While the cost of a wedding currently tends to be extortionate in the West, in other cultures it is the cost to or for the bride that can prove crippling and sometimes fatal. Although there is historical evidence of the customs of paying dowry or bride price across the world, the practices have long since disappeared from European marriage arrangements (Anderson, 2007).

Dowries expect women to bring money, goods or estate to her husband or his family in patrilineal societies. By contrast, in some cultures a bride price is paid to the woman's parents by the husband or his family. Dowry is more usual in monogamous societies, where women have little personal wealth and there is a relative scarcity of men who can afford to choose from numerous women (Mace, 2007). The dowry system has a long history in Asian societies (Lee, 1982) and despite two-thirds of women in India disapproving of the practice it is considered likely to be resistant to change in an increasingly materialistic culture (Srinivasan and Lee, 2004). Financial transfers between families have been reported to exceed the annual household income by as much as six times in South Asia and four times in Sub-Saharan Africa (Anderson, 2007). It is interesting to note that these are the regions displaying the highest maternal mortality ratios in the world (WHO, 2012a) (see *Figure 1.1* in *Chapter 1*). Evidence cited below relating to the suffering and injustices to which women may be subjected could indicate that the maternal mortality ratio statistics are not entirely coincidental with these factors.

In theory, bride price may be expected to express the value of a woman and protect her, but in practice it is reported to limit a woman's control over her body and has been linked to domestic violence (Ansell, 2001). Women's rights campaigners in Africa have associated bride price with a greater exposure to HIV/AIDS and a loss of their rights (Wendo, 2004). Dowry payment in South Asia is believed to impoverish the bride's family. It has a drastic effect on the other unmarried women in the family and can lead to female infanticide. Bride-burning and dowry-deaths have been reported as a means of extracting outstanding dowry payments (Bloch and Rao, 2002). The National Crime Bureau of India has reported an annual dowry-related death toll of 6000 but Menski (1998) implies that this is under-rated and estimates that there are 25 000 incidents of dowry-related violence each year that are never reported across that country.

It is not surprising therefore that in some societies a marked preference for the birth of a son is expressed. This bias is believed to be rooted in cultural, religious, economic and political attitudes and expectations (Dil, 1985; Bélanger, 2002; Bandyopadhyay and Singh, 2003). Anthropologists explain that son preference tends to be evident in patriarchal societies (Miller, 2001). Hudson and Den Boer (2002) maintain that no greater discrimination against women exists than that evident in prenatal offspring sex selection. Further they contend that violence against women and violence between societies is inter-related, so that:

...the long-term security trajectory of a region is affected by this relationship.

(Hudson and Den Boer, 2002: 5)

Son preference can have serious effects on the health of girls and influence their chances of survival (Sudha and Rajan, 1999; Croll, 2000; Bandyopadhyay, 2003; Das Gupta, 2006). Owing to this and other reasons evident throughout this book, the life expectancy of women in some countries is severely jeopardised if global comparisons are made *(Figure 10.1)*. It can result in high fertility rates where contraception is declined and women continue childbearing attempting to achieve the birth of a son. In a statistical analysis to determine gender bias and sex preference in Nepal, Leone et al (2003) demonstrated a decrease in contraceptive use by 24% and a total fertility rate increase of 6% relating to these predispositions. High 'wastage' of unwanted offspring can also occur as a result of infanticide or fatal neglect. Since the late 1980s selective abortion in some countries has led to a large number of female fetuses being destroyed and a resultant imbalance of sex ratios in the population (Miller, 2001).

Disadvantage has been shown to persist beyond infancy. Song and Burgard (2008), comparing growth in the height of children in China and the Philippines, found that boys in China, where there is a relatively strong son preference, demonstrated a height advantage by comparison with girls. This was not apparent among Filipino boys where son preference is relatively low. It is acknowledged that height and growth are affected by long-term nutritional status and exposure to infectious diseases, both being influenced by household decision making which is likely to be prejudiced by son preference. Beyond the immediate and the obvious it has been argued that son preference leads to discrimination against daughters (Das Gupta, 1987; Pebley and Amin, 1991; Li, 2004). This is an issue that has been highlighted in attempts to promote safe motherhood. Numerous factors can place a woman's health at higher risk and these are only accentuated during childbearing. There can be devastating outcomes for mother and baby and examples of these are presented in *Table 10.1*.

It is held that in many cultures sons have traditionally been desired as they usually provide the only form of social security for parents in their old age (Dil, 1985). Mixed evidence exists as to whether son preference

Table 10.1. Some dangers during childbearing associated with discrimination against daughters

Basic deprivation resulting in	Health problem	Potentially higher risk	
		to mother	to baby
Inadequate nutrition	• Anaemia (the main indirect cause of maternal mortality) • Stunted growth	• Postpartum haemorrhage • Infection • Contracted pelvis leading to obstructed labour, ruptured uterus, obstetric fistulae	• Prematurity • Low birth weight • Infection • Increased risk of perinatal death • Impairment of mental and physical capacity
Lack of childhood immunisations	Preventable infectious diseases • Poliomyelitis • Tetanus • Tuberculosis (TB)	• Contracted pelvis leading to prolonged and obstructed labour, ruptured uterus, obstetric fistulae • Postpartum tetanus especially if exposed to some traditional practices or unhygienic conditions • General debility associated with systemic illness	• Hypoxia, intrauterine death • Neonatal tetanus • Prematurity, early exposure to TB if mother infected
No control over own body	• Sexually transmitted diseases including HIV/AIDS • Intimate partner violence	• AIDS predisposing to anaemia, malnutrition, opportunistic infections • Physical and psychological trauma	• Abortion, premature birth, low birth weight, acquired disease through mother to child transmission, child mortality • Miscarriage, premature birth, physical and psychological trauma
Gender inequity and son preference	• High fertility • High parity	• Increasing anaemia with associated sequelae (see above), exhaustion	• Increasing risks associated with poverty and inadequate resources

Table 10.1. /cont			
Gender inequity and son preference (cont)	• Selective abortion of female fetuses	• Infection and haemorrhage if performed inexpertly, secondary infertility, psychological trauma	• Death
Additionally, illiteracy, poverty and residence in a rural location are associated with higher maternal and perinatal mortality rates			
Sources: Sudha and Rajan, 1999; Croll, 2000; Bandyopadhyay, 2003; Leone et al, 2003; Das Gupta, 2006; Health Protection Agency, 2006; WHO, 2006; Song and Burgard, 2008; UNICEF, 2011; Save the Children, 2012			

declines in the face of modernisation and development (Croll, 2000). Some observers have noted that in a changing economic climate, employed women no longer need to be dependent on their husbands or adult sons. This has been noted in areas of Bangladesh where the attitudes of women factory workers have challenged the patriarchal system and where daughters are assuming a different value (Ahmed and Bould, 2004). South Korea notably has experienced a marked decline in son preference since the mid-1990s. Urbanisation, the process of industrialisation, increasing women's education, political and social change along with the rise of women's organisations are all reported to have influenced attitudes towards gender inequality and noticeably reduced son preference among Korean families (Chung and Das Gupta, 2007). Efforts are being made in other societies. For example, in promoting child rights, the Filipino government has sought to draw attention to girls' rights and counteract a prevailing opinion that gender equality already exists (Croll, 2006). In 2003, China launched a government initiative attempting to enhance the value of the girl child and redress the striking imbalance of the sexes in the country (Care for Girl Campaign, 2006). These issues were discussed in *Chapters 7 and 9* and the advantages of introducing women to schemes of micro-finance that can elevate their position in the family and in society were explored in *Chapter 8*.

Cross-cultural experience: Awareness and empathic listening

Awareness and empathic listening have been highlighted as critical skills in effective international encounters. They are the building blocks of human interaction. In the purely etymological sense, these words can be defined, although their acquisition is inevitably more elusive, especially when cultures are crossed. Awareness has been defined as 'knowledge or perception of a situation or fact' and listening as 'giving one's attention to a sound'. Understanding can be depicted as being 'sympathetically or knowledgeably aware of the character or nature of something' and empathy encompasses 'the ability to understand and share the feelings of another' (Oxford English Dictionary, 2012). While these human communication skills cannot be assumed basic in any modern society, crossing international frontiers calls for a heightened ability in bridging intercultural gaps. Adair and Brett (2005) contrast communication norms from Western and Eastern perspectives. They describe the former approach as being low context and direct, while the latter is high context and indirect. They explain that whereas in a low context meaning tends to be explicit from the spoken words and surface messages, in a high context, second level inferential skills are needed to interpret the message which is likely to be more implicit. They claim that there is likely to be:

> *...subtle meaning embedded behind and around the spoken or written words.*
> *(Adair and Brett, 2005: 37)*

In common parlance, what you hear or what you see ain't always what you get! Adair and Brett (2005), writing from a management and organisational point of view, conclude that high context negotiators are less likely to engage in priority information sharing than their Western counterparts. They emphasise that cross-cultural negotiations demand an understanding of the other's communication and interaction norms and it is time consuming. They illustrate the matter thus:

> *Just as it will take time for a Cuban, who is accustomed to the rapid, staircase movements of Latin social dancing, and an American accustomed to smooth walking dances like the waltz to get in sync, it will take time for cross-cultural negotiators to synchronize their movements.*
> *(Adair and Brett, 2005:46)*

The injunction of Fox (2004) to the ethnographic researcher could well be reassigned to the international consultant or elective student seeking to acquire essential information, in that there is a need to:

> *...find ways to observe, participate in, and come to understand the social world she is studying from the vantage points of as many persons who belong to it as possible.*
> *(Fox, 2004: 325)*

Learning to reverse

When I was learning to drive, I found reversing somewhat easier than other manoeuvres, although reversing around corners called for rather more concentration. Returning home after an overseas assignment or elective can place considerable demands on an individual. It perhaps equates to reversing around a corner blindfolded, especially if one is unprepared for what awaits around that once familiar spot. Arising from my doctoral research (Maclean 1998, 2011b), I have discussed the likely lags, gaps and shocks confronting the international traveller in earlier chapters. The returnee now faces jet lag, an epoch gap, a quality gap and culture shock – in reverse. These issues were examined in *Chapter 6*. For the health professional or student, the quality gap serves to heighten the experiences of reverse culture shock, sometimes to a distressing level.

Reverse culture shock is now a recognised phenomenon affecting students, business people, professionals, aid workers and others. Jordan (1992), in considering the experiences of young short-term Christian volunteers, likens their return home to the process of re-entry experienced by an astronaut. He points out that while orbiting 135 miles above the earth in a space shuttle might appear a dangerous pursuit, the riskiest time is in re-entering the earth's atmosphere. This is the process that calls for all the skills the astronaut can muster and his very survival depends on it. Similarly, reverse culture shock can be particularly challenging and returnees have reported symptoms of irritability, an inability to concentrate, fatigue, depression and decreased productivity. Some experience feelings of loneliness and yet a need to be alone, a shift in their own values and attitudes and a sense that they are unappreciated professionally. Owing to the unfamiliar and unexpected feelings, Knell (2006) likens re-entry to be more akin to an alien arriving from another planet rather an astronaut returning to earth.

Pascoe (2000), a clinical psychologist writing from her own experience, identifies several words that are associated with coming home from an overseas assignment. She lists re-entry, returning, repatriation, and resettlement, adding that one more 'R', reality, is often omitted. This describes the very real world of home which seems incredibly distant from what some returnees wistfully describe as their almost fairytale-like existence before leaving for the assignment. She explains that the risk factors to self-esteem and identity are considerable since we do not see what we thought we saw in our own culture, we have changed and our foray into another culture seems to have been a one-way ticket. It then appears that there is no such thing as going home, since 'home' has become just a nostalgic memory. Strong words, but very real to many who have walked that path. Re-entering one's own culture can therefore be a very lonely experience. Schuetz (1945), in a classic essay, muses that home is the place where:

Things in substance will continue to be what they have been so far.
(Schuetz, 1945: 371)

But that is just what they no longer are for the returnee. A New Zealand aid worker describes her experience on returning home as no longer feeling like a round peg in a round hole, but rather 'a square peg in a hole that didn't seem to be there at all' (Storti, 2001: xvii)

Thogersen (2000), commenting on the struggles of attempting to reintegrate into the home situation, avers that a realisation of what she terms the 'destiny of loneliness' can be the turning point for many returnees. This is the time when they grasp new ideas about how they can get on with the rest of their lives, realising that they can only share some of their experiences while others must remain secret. She explains:

In order to grow, however, repatriates have to find a way to contain their past without hurting themselves trying to integrate what cannot be integrated.
(Thogersen in Pascoe, 2000:185)

In a small study of returned elective students Raschio (1987) reports that reverse culture shock usually arises from comparisons made between societies and lifestyles. Personal conflict was found to stem from the recognition of changes perceived in the students themselves as well as in others. They reported that they had experienced adjustments in their friendships and peer interactions. Personal growth had resulted for students in respect of greater independence, a changing global perspective and increased language skills. The respondents considered themselves to be more patient and objective after their period overseas. Traditionally, students had sought support from family and friends to moderate the effect during the readjustment period, but the researcher advocates further consideration of institutional support systems.

Storti (2001) contends that the negative emotions of loneliness, unpleasantness and frustration can often be the precursors of personal growth and insight. He admits that:

...re-entry is an experience to be reckoned with, but when the reckoning is done and the accounts are cleared you are likely to find that the price you paid for your overseas sojourn was the bargain of a lifetime.
(Storti, 2001: xxi)

Box 10.4. Softening the touchdown experience of re-entry

- Talk to someone familiar with the culture you have left and the experience of re-entry
- Seek opportunities to debrief with an organisation, skilled individual or with other students who have undertaken electives
- Associate with people from overseas, especially those from the country you have left
- Reflect on your experiences. List the new skills that you have acquired and how your attitudes may have changed
- Acknowledge that you have changed and moved on – and so have others
- Accept that readjustment will take time and that your reactions are normal
- Be aware that there are some issues that you may never be able to share and some experiences which you relate that cannot be appreciated by others
- Remember you are now viewing your own culture from a different frame of reference
- Identify your goals, specifying what you will do with what you have learned
- Make an action plan for achieving your goals including strategies for overcoming any perceived obstacles
- When the experience is most painful, recall that you are experiencing personal growth and developing insight and critical awareness
- Value the home comforts and conveniences that you had to manage without
- Appreciate the beauty around you that you longed for when you were away
- Value the freedom and privacy of home that you may have missed

Sources: Jordan, 1992; Pascoe, 2000; Storti, 2001; Knell, 2006

The writer admits that the negative experiences of re-entry are recorded more frequently than the positive, but only because repatriates are often totally unprepared for the former. Highlights of the process beyond reunion with family and the familiar are cited to include the experience of managing to persuade a boss or an organisation to change practice or strategy. Then there is the reaction of a friend, more wide-eyed than ever before, to a story you relate, or when your experience inspires others to go abroad. A new critical awareness is born as the returnee views his or her own culture from a different frame of reference. These are surely the diamonds in the dust generated during re-entry. In all the trials of re-entry, Knell (2006: 4) offers a reassuring word:

> *You can make it into whichever part of the earth's atmosphere you're destined for. There are people around you who speak your language, who have survived the impact. But you need to have the heat shields in place, the life support systems working and a good reception committee on the other end steering you back.*

Box 10.4 summarises approaches that might help in the re-entry process.

Table 10.2. Some signs of success and the challenges that remain		
Progress	*Challenge*	*Source*
Globally maternal deaths almost halved between 1990 and 2010	Disparities persist across and between regions	WHO, 2012a
By 2010, 10 countries had reached the target for MDG5 of reducing maternal deaths by 75%	In 2010, there were 10 countries that still accounted for 60% of the global maternal deaths	WHO, 2012a
It has been established that inexpensive treatments could save the lives of 75% of the million preterm babies that die each year, these include: kangaroo care, use of antibiotics and antiseptic cream and antenatal steroid injections	Eleven countries have preterm birth rates >15%, nine of these are in sub-Saharan Africa	WHO, 2012b
Risk factors for preterm birth have been identified and a baby born at >39 weeks gestation is more likely to survive	The problem of preterm birth is not confined to low income countries. Brazil and USA are among those with the highest numbers of preterm births	WHO, 2012b
Article 7 of the Convention of the Rights of the Child states that a child has the right to a legally registered name and a nationality	Worldwide, more than one third of children born in urban areas are not registered, making them vulnerable to exploitation in many forms	UNICEF, 2012a, b
Millions of lives have been saved as a result of improvements in maternal and child healthcare, expansion of HIV treatment and targeted interventions to prevent and treat malaria. Under-5 mortality decreased by 35% between 1990 and 2010	Poorly functioning health infrastructure, inadequate quantities of skilled health workers and slow adoption of evidence-based health policies all contribute to the 2 million lives still lost every year as a result of complications of childbirth. Abject poverty persists	UN, 2012; WHO/ UNICEF, 2010

Moving forward

While it has been acknowledged that much progress has been made in the latter part of the 20th and the early 21st century, much remains to be done (*Table 10.2*). Efforts are set to continue beyond 2015 and will no doubt extend far into the future (UN, 2012).

As a post-2015 development agenda evolves, technical experts will undoubtedly be needed in various parts of the globe. Travel theoretically should become easier and communication more accessible and less complicated. However, reality often defies the best of predictions. What is certain is that the world needs those of every nation who are prepared to give of themselves in expertise and effort to make the needless tragedies of today the history of tomorrow. Only then can the tears shed and shared through this book become tears of joy rather than of grief or exasperation (*Figure 10.2*).

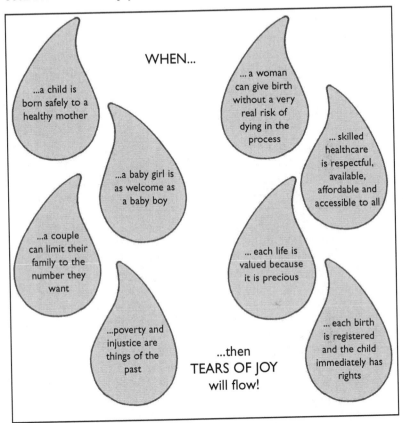

WHEN...

...a child is born safely to a healthy mother

...a woman can give birth without a very real risk of dying in the process

... skilled healthcare is respectful, available, affordable and accessible to all

...a baby girl is as welcome as a baby boy

...a couple can limit their family to the number they want

... each life is valued because it is precious

...poverty and injustice are things of the past

...then **TEARS OF JOY** will flow!

... each birth is registered and the child immediately has rights

Figure 10.2. When... then tears of joy will flow.

Personal reflections on practice

- The terms of reference will dictate my activities, refining them can make all the difference.
- Things are not always what they seem. Inequity and injustice lie beneath the surface of so many tragedies I witness.
- Reverse culture shock can strike hard – and can exceed any culture shock on entering another country.

Some lessons learned and shared

- Terms of reference are the signposts in an assignment. Renegotiating them may be necessary and the courage is sometimes needed to decline an assignment not suited to our skills or experience.
- Evaluation is an evolving art as well as a science, opportunities to update on current trends need to be taken.
- Recommendations are often the first and most widely read section of any report. It is critical that they follow on logically from the analysis and above all are achievable.
- Be prepared to encounter reverse culture shock on return, before leaving home take steps to address it.

Reflective exercises

- Access an evaluation report or consider one you have written previously. Using *Boxes 10.1 and 10.3* assess the quality of the terms of reference and recommendations.
- Consider the circumstances of a woman such as the one described in the 'tear' that heads this chapter. What social, health, educational, legislative and ethical issues are implicated in such a situation? What protects women in your society from such tragedies?
- Rachel Kass, a psychologist with short-term overseas experience, suggests that, following a debriefing exercise, returnees write a letter to themselves containing reflections on their insights, goals, and plans for overcoming obstacles as well as feedback from other participants. She suggests that this is placed in a sealed, self-addressed envelope and given to a trusted friend or facilitator to post five months later (Jordan, 1992).

Resources

Some useful websites and resources concerned with monitoring and evaluation
- International Development Evaluation Society (IDEAS) has a particular focus on developing and transitional economies.
  www.ideas-int.org/
- European Evaluation Society focuses mainly but not exclusively within Europe:
  www.europeanevaluation.org/
- WHO (2010) Packages of interventions for family planning, safe abortion care, maternal, newborn and child health. Includes lists of key supplies and commodities needed:

http://www.who.int/reproductivehealth/publications/maternal_perinatal_
health/fch_10_06/en/index.html
*   WHO/UNICEF/UNFPA/AMDD (2009) Monitoring emergency
    obstetric care. A handbook. Provides emergency obstetric care
    indicators to assist programme planners in identifying priorities and
    interventions:
    http://whqlibdoc.who.int/publications/2009/9789241547734_eng.pdf
*   WHO (2006) Essential medicines for reproductive health:
    http://whqlibdoc.who.int/hq/2006/a91388.pdf

References

Adair WL, Brett JM (2005) The negotiation dance: time, culture and behavioral sequences
in negotiation. *Organic Science* **16**(1): 33–51

Ahmed SS, Bould S (2004) One able daughter is worth 10 iliterate sons: Reframing the
patriarchal family. *Journal of Marriage and Family* **66**(5): 1332–41

Anderson S (2007) The economics of dowry and bride price. *Journal of Economic
Perspectives* **21**(4): 151–74

Ansell N (2001) Because it's our culture! (Re)negotiating the meaning of 'Lobola' in
Southern Africa secondary schools. *Journal of Southern African Studies* **27**(4): 697–716

Bandyopadhyay M (2003) Missing girls and son preference in rural India: looking beyond
popular myth. *Health Care for Women International* **24**(10): 910–26

Bandyopadhyay S, Singh A (2003) History of son preference and sex selection in India and the
West. *Bulletin of the Indian Institute of the History of Medicine, Hyderabad* **33**(2): 149–67

Bélanger D (2002) Son preference in a rural village in North Vietnam. *Studies in Family
Planning* **33**(4): 321–34

Bellman GM (1990) *The consultant's calling.* Jossey Bass, San Francisco

Berger MC, Ray LN, Togno-Armanasco VD (1993) The effective use of consultants.
Journal of Nursing Administration **23**: 7–8

Bloch F, Rao F (2002) Terror as a bargaining instrument: A case study of dowry violence in
rural India. *American Economic Review* **92**(4): 1029–43

Care for Girl Campaign (2006) A resource of knowledge. The Office of the Leading Group of
the National Care for Girls Campaign, China Population House. Cited in Eklund L (2011)
Rethinking son preference: Gender, population dynamics and social change in the People's
Republic of China. *Lund Dissertations in Sociology* **96**, Lund University, Sweden

Chung WJ, Das Gupta M (2007) The decline of son preference in South Korea: The roles of
development and public policy. *Population and Development Review* **33**(4): 757–83

Clark T (1995) *Managing consultants. Consultancy as the management of impressions.*
OUP, Bucks, England

Cockman P, Evans B, Reynolds P (1992) *Client-centred consulting. A practical guide for internal advisers and trainers.* McGraw-Hill Book Company, London

Collins (2012) *English Thesaurus on line.* Available from: http://www.collinsdictionary.com/english-thesaurus [last accessed 11.08.2012]

Cracknell BE (2005) *Evaluating development aid: Issues, problems and solutions.* Sage Publications, London

Croll E (2000) *Endangered daughters: Discrimination and development in Asia.* Routledge, London

Croll EJ (2006) From the girl child to girls' rights. *Third World Quarterly* **77**(7): 1285–97

Das Gupta M (1987) Selective discrimination against female children in rural Punjab, India, *Population and Development Review* **13**(1): 77–100

Das Gupta M (2006) Cultural versus biological factors in explaining Asia's missing women: Response to Oster. *Population and Development Review* **32**(2): 328–32

Dil SF (1985) Women in Bangladesh: Changing roles and sociopolitical realities. *Women and Politics* **5**: 51–67

Forss K, Vedung E, Kruse SE, Mwaiselage A, Nilsdotter A (2008) *Are Sida evaluations good enough? An assessment of 34 evaluation reports.* Sida Studies in Evaluation 2008: 1. Available from: http://www.oecd.org/dataoecd/23/36/41390724. pdf [last accessed 10.09.2012]

Fox R (2004) Observations and reflections of a perpetual fieldworker. *Annals of the American Academy of Political and Social Science* **595**: 309–26

Health Protection Agency (2006) *Pregnancy and tuberculosis: Guidance for clinicians.* NHS Health Protection Agency, London

Hudson VM, Den Boer A (2002) A surplus of men, a deficit of peace: Security and sex ratios in Asia's largest States. *International Security* **26**(4): 5–13

Jordan P (1992) *Re-entry: Making the transition from missions to life at home.* YWAM Publishing, Seattle

Knell M (2006) *Burn up or splash down: Surviving the culture shock of re-entry.* Authentic Publishing, Milton Keynes

Lee GR (1982) *Family structure and interaction: A comparative analysis* (2nd edn). University of Minnesota Press, Minneapolis

Leone T, Matthews Z, Zuanna GD (2003) Impact and determinants of sex preference in Nepal. *International Family Planning Perspectives* **29**(2): 69–75

Li J (2004) Gender inequality, family planning, and maternal and child care in a rural Chinese county. *Social Science and Medicine* **59**(4): 695–708

Mace R (2007) The evolutionary ecology of family size. In: Dunbar R, Barret L (eds) *The Oxford handbook of evolutionary psychology.* Oxford University Press, Oxford

Maclean GD (1998) *An examination of the characteristics of short term international midwifery consultants.* Thesis submitted for the degree of Doctor of Philosophy. University of Surrey, Guildford, England

Maclean GD (2011a) Short term international consultancy: Discussing the need. *British Journal of Midwifery* **19**(6): 315–19

Maclean GD (2011b) Short term international consultancy: Preparing and promising. *British Journal of Midwifery* **19**(9): 594–9

Maclean GD (2011c) Short term international consultancy: Evaluating and enhancing practice. *British Journal of Midwifery* **19**(12): 814–19

Menski W (1998) *South Asians and the dowry problem.* Vistaar Publications, New Delhi

Miller BD (2001) Female-selective abortion in Asia: Patterns, policies and debates. *American Anthropology* **103**(4): 1083–95

OED (2012) *Oxford English Dictionary.* Available from: http://oxforddictionaries.com/definition/english/ [last accessed 24.08.2012]

Pascoe R (2000) *Homeward bound.* Expatriates' Press, Vancouver

Pebley AR, Amin S (1991) The impact of a public-health intervention on sex differentials in childhood mortality in rural Punjab, India. *Health Transition Review* **1**(2): 143–70

Phillips K, Shaw P (1989) *A consultancy approach for trainers.* Gower Publishing, Aldershot

Raschio RA (1987) College students perceptions of reverse culture shock and re-entry adjustments. *Journal of College Student Personnel* **28**(2): 156–62

Rassam C (1998) The management consultancy industry. In Sadler P (ed) *Management consultancy: A handbook for best practice* (pp. 3–30). Kogan Page, London

Rebien CC (1996) *Evaluating development assistance in theory and in practice.* Avebury Ashcroft Publishing, Aldershot, Hants

Save the Children (2012) *State of the World's mothers 2012.* Save the Children: Westport, USA and London. Available from: http://www.savethechildren.org/ [last accessed 28.07.2012]

Schuetz A (1945) The homecomer. *American Journal of Society* **50**: 369–76

Scriven M (1991) *Evaluation thesaurus* (4th edn). Sage Publications, London

Song S, Burgard SA (2008) Does son preference influence children's growth in height? A comparative study of Chinese and Filipino children. *Population Studies* **62**(3): 305–20

Srinivasan P, Lee G R (2004) The dowry system in Northern India: Women's attitudes and social change. *Journal of Marriage and Family* **66**(5) 1108–17

Storti C (2001) *The art of coming home.* Intercultural Press, Maine, USA

Sudha S, Rajan SI (1999) Female demographic disadvantage in India 1981–1991: Sex selective abortions and female infanticide. *Development and Change* **30**(3): 585–618

Thogersen K (2000) Afterword. In Pascoe R (ed) *Homeward bound* (pp. 181–85). Expatriates' Press, Vancouver

UN (2012) *Accelerating progress towards the Millennium Development Goals: options for sustained and inclusive growth and issues for advancing the United Nations development agenda beyond 2015.* Annual report of the Secretary General. UN General Assembly 6 August 2012, A/67/257

UNDP (2012) *Handbook on planning, monitoring and evaluation for development results.* UNDP. Available from: http://web.undp.org/evaluation/handbook/documents/english/pme-handbook.pdf [last accessed 08.10.2012]

UNICEF (2011) *State of the World's children 2011.* UNICEF, New York

UNICEF (2012a) *State of the World's children 2012.* UNICEF, New York

UNICEF (2012b) *A summary of the rights under the Convention of the Rights of the Child. Fact sheet.* Available from: http://www.unicef.org/crc/files/Rights_overview.pdf [last accessed 13.09.2012]

Vedung E (2009) *Public policy and program evaluation.* Transaction Publishers, New Jersey

Wendo C (2004) African women denounce brideprice. *Lancet* **363**(9410): 716

WHO (2006) *Foundation module: The midwife in the community. Session 10: HIV/AIDS and safe motherhood. Midwifery education modules. Education for Safe Motherhood, Educational material for teachers of midwifery* (2nd edn). WHO, Geneva

WHO (2012a) *Trends in maternal mortality 1990 to 2010.* WHO, UNICEF, UNFPA and World Bank. WHO, Geneva

WHO (2012b) *Born too soon: the global action report on preterm birth.* WHO, Geneva. Available from: http://www.who.int/maternal_child_adolescent/documents/born_too_soon/en/index.html [last accessed 13.09.2012]

WHO/UNICEF (2010) *Countdown to 2015 decade report (2000–2010): taking stock of maternal newborn and child survival.* WHO, Geneva

Index